THE CHANKA:

ARCHAEOLOGICAL RESEARCH IN ANDAHUAYLAS (APURIMAC), PERU

UCLA COTSEN INSTITUTE OF ARCHAEOLOGY PRESS
MONOGRAPHS
CONTRIBUTIONS IN FIELD RESEARCH AND CURRENT ISSUES IN ARCHAEOLOGICAL METHOD AND THEORY

Monograph 67   *Inca Rituals and Sacred Mountains: A Study of the World's Highest Archaeological Site*, Johan Reinhard and Maria Constanza Ceruti

Monograph 66   *Gallinazo: An Early Cultural Tradition on the Peruvian North Coast,* Jean-François Millaire (ed.), with Magali Morlion

Monograph 65   *Settlement and Subsistence in Early Formative Soconusco: El Varal and the Problem of Inter-Site Assemblage Variation*, Richard Lesure (ed.)

Monograph 64   *The South American Camelids*, Duccio Bonavia

Monograph 63   *Andean Civilization: A Tribute to Michael E. Moseley,* Joyce Marcus and Patrick Ryan Williams (eds.)

Monograph 62   *Excavations at Cerro Azul, Peru: The Architecture and Pottery,* Joyce Marcus

Monograph 61   *Chavín: Art, Architecture and Culture,* William J Conklin and Jeffrey Quilter (eds.)

Monograph 60   *Rethinking Mycenaean Palaces II: Revised and Expanded Second Edition*, Michael L. Galaty and William A. Parkinson (eds.)

Monograph 59   *Moche Tombs at Dos Cabezas*, Christopher B. Donnan

Monograph 58   *Moche Fineline Painting From San José de Moro*, Donna McClelland, Donald McClelland, and Christopher B. Donnan

Monograph 57   *Kasapata and the Archaic Period of the Cuzco Valley*, Brian S. Bauer (ed.)

Monograph 56   *Berenike 1999/2000*, Steven E. Sidebotham and Willeke Wendrich (eds.)

Monograph 55   *Roman Footprints at Berenike: Archaeobotanical Evidence of Subsistence and Trade in the Eastern Desert of Egypt*, René T. J. Cappers

Monograph 54   *Advances in Titicaca Basin Archaeology 1*, Charles Stanish, Amanda B. Cohen, and Mark S. Aldenderfer

Monograph 53   *Us and Them: Archaeology and Ethnicity in the Andes*, Richard Martin Reycraft

Monograph 52   *Archaeological Research on the Islands of the Sun and Moon, Lake Titicaca, Bolivia: Final Results from the Proyecto Tiksi Kjarka*, Charles Stanish and Brian S. Bauer (eds.)

Monograph 51   *Maya Zooarchaeology: New Directions in Theory and Method*, Kitty F. Emery (ed.)

Monograph 50   *Settlement Archaeology and Political Economy at Tres Zapotes, Veracruz, Mexico*, Christopher A. Pool (ed.)

Monograph 49   *Perspectives on Ancient Maya Rural Complexity*, Gyles Iannone and Samuel V. Connell (eds.)

Monograph 48   *Yeki bud, yeki nabud: Essays on the Archaeology of Iran in Honor of William M. Sumner*, Naomi F. Miller and Kamyar Abdi (eds.)

Monograph 47   *Archaeology in the Borderlands: Investigation in Caucasia and Beyond*, Adam T. Smith and Karen S. Rubinson (eds.)

Monograph 46   *Domestic Ritual in Ancient Mesoamerica,* Patricia Plunket (ed.)

Monograph 45   *Pathways to Prismatic Blades*, Kenneth Hirth and Bradford Andrews (eds.)

Monograph 44   *Ceramic Production and Circulation in the Greater Southwest*, Donna M. Glowacki and Hector Neff (eds.)

Monograph 43   *Pottery of Postclassic Cholula, Mexico*, Geoffrey McCafferty

Monograph 42   *Pompeian Households: An Analysis of the Material Culture*, Penelope M. Allison

Monograph 41   *Rethinking Mycenaean Palaces: New Interpretations of an Old Idea*, Michael L. Galaty and William A. Parkinson (eds.)

Monograph 40   *Prehistory of Agriculture: New Experimental and Ethnographic Approaches*, Patricia C. Anderson (ed.)

Monograph 39   *Recent Advances in the Archaeology of the Northern Andes: In Memory of Gerardo Reichel-Dolmatoff*, Augusto Oyuela-Caycedo and J. Scott Raymond (eds.)

Monograph 38   *Approaches to the Historical Archaeology of Mexico, Central and South America*, Janine Gasco, Greg Charles Smith, and Patricia Fournier-Garcia

Monograph 37   *Hawaiian Adze Production and Distribution: Implications for the Development of Chiefdoms*, Barbara Lass

Monograph 36   *New Light on Old Art: Recent Advances in Hunter-Gatherer Rock Art Research*, D. W. Whitley and L. L. Loendorf (eds.)

Monograph 35   *Pottery of Prehistoric Honduras: Regional Classification and Analysis*, J. S. Henderson and M. Beaudry-Corbett

Monograph 34   *Settlement Archaeology of Cerro de las Mesas, Veracruz, Mexico*, Barbara Stark (ed.)

Monograph 33   *Girikihaciyan: A Halafian Site in Southeastern Turkey*, P. J. Watson and S. LeBlanc

Monograph 32   *Western Pomo Prehistory: Excavations at Albion Head, Nightbirds' Retreat and Three Chop Village, Mendocino County, California*, Thomas N. Layton

Monograph 31   *Investigaciones Arqueológicos de la Costa Sur de Guatemala*, David S. Whitley and Marilyn P. Beaudry (eds.)

Monograph 30   *Archaeology of the Three Springs Valley, California: A Study in Functional Cultural History*, Brian D. Dillon and Matthew A. Boxt

Monograph 29   *Obsidian Dates IV: A Compendium of Obsidian Hydration Readings from the UCLA Obsidian Hydration Laboratory*, Clement W. Meighan and Janet L. Scalise (eds.)

Monograph 28   *Archaeological Field Research in the Upper Mantaro, Peru, 1982–1983: Investigations of Inka Expansion and Exchange*, Timothy Earle et al. (eds.)

Monograph 27   *Andean Archaeology: Papers in Memory of Clifford Evans*, Ramiro Matos M., Solveig Turpin, and Herbert Eling, Jr. (eds.)

Monograph 26   *Excavations at Mission San Antonio 1976–1978*, Robert L. Hoover and Julio J. Costello (eds.)

Monograph 25   *Prehistoric Production and Exchange in the Aegean and Eastern Mediterranean*, A. Bernard Knapp and Tamara Stech (eds.)

Monograph 24   *Pots and Potters: Current Approaches in Ceramic Archaeology*, Prudence Rice

Monograph 23   *Pictographs and Petroglyphs of the Oregon Country, Part 2*, J. Malcolm Loring and Louise Loring

Monograph 22   *The Archaeology of Two Northern California Sites*, Delmer E. Sanburg, F. K. Mulligan, Joseph Chartkoff, and Kerry Chartkoff

Monograph 21   *Pictographs and Petroglyphs of the Oregon Country, Part 1*, J. Malcolm Loring and Louise Loring

Monograph 20   *Messages from the Past: Studies in California Rock Art*, Clement W. Meighan (ed.)

Monograph 19   *Prehistoric Indian Rock Art: Issues and Concerns*, JoAnne Van Tilburg and Clement W. Meighan (eds.)

Monograph 18   *Studies in Cypriote Archaeology*, Jane C. Biers and David Soren

Monograph 17   *Excavations in Northern Belize, Central America*, Raymond Sidrys

Monograph 16   *Obsidian Dates III: A Compendium of Obsidian Hydration Determinations Made at the UCLA Obsidian Hydration Laboratory*, Clement Meighan and Glenn Russell

Monograph 15   *Inland Chumash Archaeological Investigations*, David S. Whitley, E. L. McCann, and C. W. Clewlow, Jr. (eds.)

Monograph 14   *Papers in Cycladic Prehistory*, Jack L. Davis and John F. Cherry (eds.)

Monograph 13   *Archaeological Investigations at the Ring Brothers Site Complex, Thousand Oaks, California*, C. W. Clewlow, Jr., David S. Whitley and Ellen L. McCann (eds.)

Monograph 12   *The Running Springs Ranch Site: Archaeological Investigations at VEN-65 and VEN-261*, Jack Prichett and Allen McIntyre

Monograph 11   *The Archaeology of Oak Park, Ventura County, California*, C. William Clewlow, Jr. and David S. Whitley (eds.)

Monograph 10   *Rock Art of East Mexico and Central America: An Annotated Bibliography*, Matthias Strecker

Monograph 9   *The Late Minoan I Destruction of Crete: Metal Groups and Stratigraphic Considerations*, Hara Georgiou

Monograph 8   *Papers on the Economy and Architecture of the Ancient Maya*, Raymond Sidrys (ed.)

Monograph 7   *History and Prehistory at Grass Valley, Nevada*, C. W. Clewlow, Jr., Helen F. Wells, and Richard Ambro (eds.)

Monograph 6   *Obsidian Dates II: A Compendium of Obsidian Hydration Determinations Made at the UCLA Obsidian Hydration Laboratory*, C. W. Meighan and P. I. Vanderhoeven (eds.)

Monograph 5   *The Archaeology of Oak Park, Ventura County, California*, C. W. Clewlow, Jr., Allen Pastron, and Helen F. Wells (eds.)

THE CHANKA:

ARCHAEOLOGICAL RESEARCH IN ANDAHUAYLAS (APURIMAC), PERU

BY

BRIAN S. BAUER, LUCAS C. KELLETT, AND
MIRIAM ARÁOZ SILVA

WITH CONTRIBUTIONS BY
SABINE HYLAND AND
CARLO SOCUALAYA DÁVILA

Monography 68
Cotsen Institute of Archaeology Press
University of California, Los Angeles

THE COTSEN INSTITUTE OF ARCHAEOLOGY PRESS is the publishing unit of the Cotsen Institute of Archaeology at UCLA. The Cotsen Institute is a premier research organization dedicated to the creation, dissemination, and conservation of archaeological knowledge and heritage. It is home to both the Interdepartmental Archaeology Graduate Program and the UCLA/Getty Master's Program in the Conservation of Archaeological and Ethnographic Materials. The Cotsen Institute provides a forum for innovative faculty research, graduate education, and public programs at UCLA in an effort to positively impact the academic, local and global communities. Established in 1973, the Cotsen Institute is at the forefront of archaeological research, education, conservation and publication and is an active contributor to interdisciplinary research at UCLA.

The Cotsen Institute Press specializes in producing high-quality academic volumes in several different series, including Monographs, World Heritage and Monuments, Cotsen Advanced Seminars, and Ideas, Debates and Perspectives. The Press is committed to making the fruits of archaeological research accessible to professionals, scholars, students, and the general public. We are able to do this through the generosity of Lloyd E. Cotsen, longtime Institute volunteer and benefactor, who has provided an endowment that allows us to subsidize our publishing program and produce superb volumes at an affordable price. Publishing in nine different series, our award-winning archaeological publications receive critical acclaim in both the academic and popular communities.

This book is set in Janson Text
Editing, production, and cover design by Leyba Associates, Santa Fe, New Mexico
Index by

Library of Congress Cataloging-in-Publication Data
Bauer, Brian S.
 The Chanka : archaeological research in Andahuaylas (Apurimac), Peru / by Brian S. Bauer, Lucas C. Kellett, and Miriam Aráoz Silva ; with contributions by Sabine Hyland and and Carlo Socualaya Dávila.
  p. cm. — (Monograph / Cotsen Institute of Archaeology ; 68)
 Includes bibliographical references and index.
 ISBN 978-1-931745-60-4 (trade paper) — ISBN 978-1-931745-59-8 (trade cloth)
1. Chanca Indians—Peru—Andahuaylas (Province)—Antiquities. 2. Chanca Indians—Peru—Andahuaylas (Province)—Social conditions. 3. Andahuaylas (Peru : Province)—Antiquities. 4. Archaeological surveying—Peru—Andahuaylas (Province) 5. Social change—Peru—Andahuaylas (Province)—History. 6. Land settlement patterns—Peru—Andahuaylas (Province)—History. 7. Social archaeology—Peru—Andahuaylas (Province) 8. Incas—Peru—Andahuaylas (Province)—Antiquities. I. Kellett, Lucas C. II. Aráoz Silva, Miriam. III. Hyland, Sabine, 1964- IV. Socualaya Dávila, Carlo. V. Title. VI. Series.

F3430.1.C4B38 2010
985'.38—dc22

201001460

In past times the [the Chanka] were so brave, so it is said, that they not only won lands and domains, but were so strong that they besieged the city of Cuzco and great battles were fought between them and those of the city, until in the end the bravery of [Pachacuti] Inca Yupanqui defeated them.

Pedro de Cieza de León 1553

[T]he body of Pachacuti Inca Yupanqui, …was embalmed and well preserved as were all [the mummies] that I saw. I found with him the principal idol of the province of Andahuaylas, because he conquered it and placed it under the domination of the Incas when he defeated and killed Valcuvilca, their principal lord…

Polo de Ondegardo 1571

CONTENTS

ILLUSTRATIONS

TABLES

PREFACE

Today the people of Andahuaylas (Apurimac, Peru) take great pride in the fact that the Chanka once dominated this area of the Andean highlands, and stories of Chanka warriors are deeply embedded in local lore (Figure P.1). In the town of Andahuaylas itself, numerous commercial ventures have incorporated the term "Chanka" into their names, including a book shop, an automobile parts supplier, the local bus line, various hotels, many restaurants, and a host of general stores. Most fittingly, the locally produced cable television news program is called *Chanka Vision*. References to the Chanka are also publicly displayed and endorsed by the local authorities of Andahuaylas through the naming of streets, parks, and other public facilities, such as the Ministry of Public Health and the soccer stadium. Even the local military barracks, which holds members of the national army, is named after this legendary group.

Perhaps the most overt display of local pride in Chanka heritage has been the development of an annual festival called Sondor Raymi. This celebration, held each year on the 19th of June, was developed in 1997 by local authorities with hopes of attracting additional tourists to the Andahuaylas region. Some funds are provided by the national government, and the festival's coordination is overseen by the National Institute of Culture's representative in Andahuaylas. In a massive feat of organization, the celebration includes thousands of actor-participants, many from high schools across the region, and involves "reenactments" of the Chanka origin myth, the development of the Chanka confederation, and the war with the Inca. Attended by as many as 6,000 people, the celebration begins on the shore of Lake Pacucha and reaches a climactic finish with a battle between the Inca and the Chanka in the ruins of Sondor. Throughout the day, a narration of the unfolding reenactments is broadcasted over loudspeakers to the audience in both Quechua and Spanish. Dramatic events include the burning of staged villages, mock battles, the release of condors, and plenty of singing and dancing.

Despite the great pride that the citizens of Andahuaylas have in their ancestors, it is widely recognized that very little is known about the

FIGURE P.1. An election sign in 2002 in the town of Pacucha, stating
"We are Chankas" (Somos Chankas).

Chanka themselves. From 2002 to 2004 we had the privilege to live and work in the Andahuaylas region, while conducting a regional archaeological survey and extensive archival research on the Chanka. Since the Chanka are popularly known in the region, yet poorly documented archaeologically, a major goal of the project was to have the results of our research widely available to the broader public in Andahuaylas. The public education phase of the research program is ongoing, but we have already made some important local contributions (Kellett 2006). For example, we reorganized the Municipal Museum of Andahuaylas so that it offers a more complete overview of the history of the region. We have also written local newspaper and journal articles and have been interviewed on numerous local radio programs. Broad dissemination of the project's results will continue, in both English and Spanish, through various academic and popular publications.

We owe a great deal of thanks to the many individuals and organizations that have supported the project at different stages of its development.

We would first like to thank Peru's National Institute of Culture (INC) for their support of the project and for the survey permits provided in 2002 (Credential C/DQPA 065 2002) and 2004 (Credential C/062-INC-2004/DREPH-DA-D). Preliminary field reports were submitted to the INC in 2002 (Bauer, Araóz Silva, and Kellett 2002) and 2004 (Bauer, Araóz Silva, and Kellett 2004). We would like to thank the staff at the INC headquarters in Lima and in their regional offices in Abancay, Cuzco, and Ayacucho, for their help during the project. Also we thank the staff at the Municipal Museum of Andahuaylas, specifically Mariano Luna Rozas and Carlos Pandal, for their support and for providing us the opportunity to present the preliminary results of the project (Figure P.2).

We are also indebted to the people of Andahuaylas who accepted us into their communities and helped us in innumerable ways during the project. The municipalities of Andahuaylas, Talavera, San Jerónimo, and Pacucha were especially supportive, as were the numerous small

FIGURE P.2. Project members and supporters at the opening of the new Municipal Museum of Andahuaylas (2004) The project was awarded the Gold Medal of the City of Andahuaylas for its work on the museum. (*From left to right*: Carlos Pandal, Brian S. Bauer, Carlo Socualaya Dávila, Miriam Aráoz Silva, Jorge Flores Sanchez, Lucas C. Kellett, Mariano Luna Rozas.)

communities which we had the pleasure of visiting during fieldwork. We are especially thankful for the aid of several individuals, including Arturo Gutiérrez Velasco, Hiliana Montoya Molero, and Martha Salcedo de Luna. Project members included Henry Gamonal Quillilli, Máximo López Quispe, Kimberly Kloke, Axel Aráoz Silva, and Jorge Flores Sánchez. Nicole Coffey Kellett and Ismael Pérez Calderón also helped in many aspects of the fieldwork. Sabine Hyland and Donato Amado González were responsible for the archival research and thus played critically important roles in the project. We also acknowledge Carlo Socualaya Dávila's fine work in the Uranmarca region and thank him for allowing us to include it within this study. Preparation of the final manuscript was aided by critical readings from several individuals, including Elizabeth Arkush, R. Alan Covey, Carol Leyba, and Katharina Schreiber. Gabriel E. Cantarutti helped produce various maps.

Major funding for the project was provided by the Curtiss T. Brennan and Mary G. Brennan Foundation, the John Heinz III Charitable Trust, the National Science Foundation (NSF 0107074), and the National Endowment for the Humanities (FA 53142), as well as the University of Illinois at Chicago (the Institute for the Humanities, the Office of Social Science Research, and the Department of Anthropology).

CHAPTER 1

UNDERSTANDING THE CHANKA

According to Inca legends, a battle took place outside the city of Cuzco that forever changed the trajectory of South American history. The Chanka, a powerful ethnic group from the Andahuaylas region some 160 km west of Cuzco, had begun an aggressive program of expansion. Conquering a host of smaller polities, their army is said to have advanced well inside the territory of their traditional rival, the Inca. While much of Cuzco's leadership abandoned the besieged city, a young prince named Inca Yupanqui assumed power from his father and led a counterattack. Bolstered with divine aid—as the stones of the Cuzco region came to life—the young prince defeated the invading Chanka, and the Inca emerged as the most powerful people of the central Andes. In the words of Brundage (1963: 95), "The Chanka victory is presented to us . . . as the most striking event in all Inca history, the year one, as it were."

Much of the information we have on the Chanka is contained within general histories of the Inca, which were written long after their own defeat by the Spaniards in AD 1532.[1] Although several of these histories offer detailed accounts of the legendary Chanka-Inca War, they provide very little information on the developmental history of the Chanka themselves. For example, the accounts of Garcilaso de la Vega (1966 [1609]) suggest that the last battle of the war may have involved thousands of warriors on each side. It is also suggested that the Chanka made a series of

1

mistakes while approaching Cuzco, which led to catastrophic losses (Betanzos 1996 [1557]; Sarmiento de Gamboa 2007 [1572]), and that the Inca skinned the fallen Chanka warriors and put them on public display (Cieza de León 1998 [1554]). We are told, however, almost nothing about how and why the Chanka expanded from the Andahuaylas region or what their homeland was like. By the time the Europeans arrived, the history of the Chanka had been reduced by the Inca to a few accolades that were heaped upon the Inca kings in heroic songs. As so often happens in the aftermath of war, the history of the vanquished is only recorded as it pertains to the triumphs of the victors.

Most historical research on the Chanka has focused on readings of the Spanish chronicles, as investigators compare and synthesize information presented in various accounts (Markham 1871, 1923; Arca Parró 1923; Navarro del Águila 1937, 1939; Guillén 1946; Rowe 1946; Rostworowski 1953, 1978, 1988; Pardo 1969; Schaedel 1978; Niles 1999). Besides striving to reconstruct the major events of the Chanka-Inca War, much of the historical research has concentrated on reports that the Chanka allied themselves with several other Central Andean ethnic groups during the later periods of their development. This alliance is generally referred to as the "Chanka Confederation." Since the 1960s, most archaeological work on the "Chanka" has been conducted at sites of confederation members, rather than at known Chanka sites in the Andahuaylas region. Following Lumbreras's (1959, 1974a, 1974b, 1978) influential works, the term "Chanka" has been loosely applied to various late prehistoric sites found throughout the departments of Ayacucho, Huancavelica, and Apurimac, areas in which members of the Chanka Confederation are believed to have lived. For example, research at what have been called Pocras-Chanka sites near the modern city of Ayacucho has been particularly strong (Benavides 1976; Degregori and Balutansky 1980; González Carré 1982; González Carré and Gálvez Pérez 1987; Valdez, Vivanco, and Chávez 1990; Vivanco Pomacanchari 1999; Valdez 2002). Unfortunately, the area believed to

have contained members of the Chanka Confederation covers an immense region of the central Andes and is known to have been populated by many different and distinct ethnic groups. The generalized use of the term "Chanka" to describe all of the populations and ethnic groups who inhabited this vast territory in late prehistoric times has caused considerable confusion in the literature. Most importantly, the use of this term has suggested to many researchers and readers that the Chanka Confederation was immense and that the social and political organization of this vast region of the central highlands was highly stratified, perhaps even state-like. It has also deflected archaeological investigations from the Andahuaylas region, by suggesting that the research results from projects that have been conducted within the territories of other contemporary highland groups can be used as a proxy to understand the late prehistoric social development of the Chanka themselves.

Furthermore, although there has been increased scholarship on the rise of the Inca in the Cuzco region, and new archaeological findings have helped to reshape much of what was once believed about the development of the Inca state (Bauer 2004; Covey 2006), the history of the Chanka has gone unexamined. As Inca scholarship begins to overhaul its 60-year-old interpretive models using new archaeological and historical information, the prehistory of the Chanka comes into focus as a compelling research issue.

In sum, despite the crucial position that the Chanka may have held in South American prehistory, their homeland, the Andahuaylas region, has remained largely unexplored, and the cultural processes that led to the development of this particular ethnic group and their subsequent defeat by the Inca have not been investigated (Figure 1.1). Furthermore, what little is "known" about the Chanka has been filtered through Inca, and subsequently Spanish, eyes. In other words, although the most powerful native civilization to develop in the Americas claimed that its imperial campaign was set in motion by Chanka invaders, no research project has systematically investigated the Chanka region to determine whether a

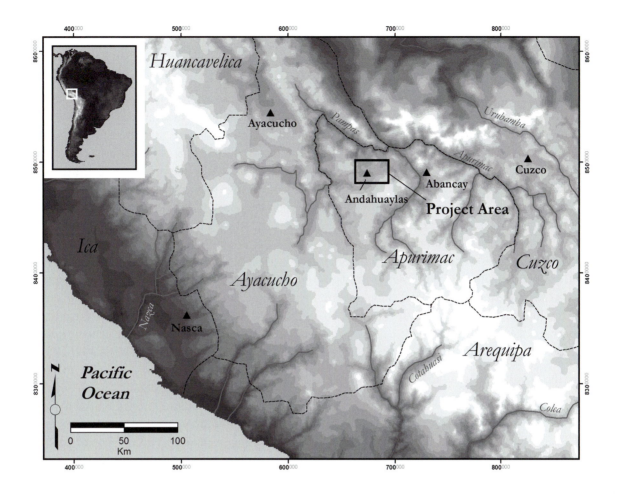

FIGURE 1.1. Andahuaylas and the central Andes of the Peru.

local polity capable of such aggression even existed. Accepting this challenge, the goal of this study is to begin to explore, through local documents and archaeological research, the complex history of the Andahuaylas region, and in doing so initiate a new history of the Chanka.

THE CHANKA-INCA WAR

An introduction to the Chanka would not be complete without at least a brief discussion of the Chanka-Inca War. A definitive analysis of the war is difficult, of course, since no two chronicles present identical accounts, and some authors offer what appears to be contradictory information. We also know that most of the accounts of the Chanka-Inca War were written in Cuzco with information pro-

vided by Inca elites, and thus, the Chanka seem to have had little say in the recording of their own history. Instead, what is preserved are overtly Cuzco-centric and pro-Inca versions of the events.[2]

Retellings of the Chanka-Inca War

Although some writers provide only brief accounts of the Chanka-Inca War, for many it was seen as a crucial turning point of Inca history and was thus worthy of extensive descriptions. For example, Betanzos, who was fluent in Quechua and was married to a noble Inca woman, devotes five chapters to describing the events of the war. Likewise, Sarmiento de Gamboa, whose account was read aloud to the leaders of all the major kin groups of Cuzco, includes eight chapters on the war and its immediate aftermath. In these accounts, the encounter between the two groups is hailed as the most important event in the development of the Inca as a pan-Andean power.

While the surviving accounts of the Chanka-Inca War vary in details, many share similar event sequences. This shared narrative structure suggests that the accounts were based on public retellings of the Chanka-Inca War. Much of the historic information contained in the chronicles appears to have been based on stories provided in the epic songs sung by the Inca elite during festivals in the imperial capital. Betanzos specifically describes the singing of such a song in honor of Pachacuti Inca Yupanqui. In doing so, he provides a concise abstract of the major events included in most retellings of the Chanka-Inca War. He writes:

> While the drums were played in the middle [of the plaza], they began to sing all together. The ladies, who were behind the men, started the singing. In this song they told of the coming of Uscovilca [i.e., the Chanka] against them, the departure of Viracocha Inca, and how Inca Yupanque, saying that the Sun had favored him as its son, had captured and killed Uscovilca. They also told how he defeated, captured and killed the captains who had brought the last [Chanka] forces together.[3] (Betanzos 1996: 56 [1557: Pt. 1, Ch. 13])

As outlined in the above quote, the story of the Chanka-Inca War frequently unfolds within the following scenes: (1) The Chanka arrive on the outskirts of Cuzco, and the reigning Inca king, Viracocha Inca, flees the city. (2) The king's youngest son, Pachacuti Inca Yupanqui, remains in Cuzco to defend the city and has a vision during which he is promised success. (3) The first battle takes place on the edge of Cuzco, during which several important Chanka are killed and their idols are captured.[4] (4) A second and final battle takes place during which the Chanka are defeated.[5] (5) After Pachacuti Inca Yupanqui's triumph over the Chanka, he assumes the kingship, and the captured Chanka warriors are paraded through Cuzco before being killed.

The Cuzco Landscape and Remembrances of the Chanka-Inca War

While we may never be able to judge the actual veracity of the different accounts of the Chanka-Inca War, it appears that most retellings included within their narrative structure the basic five events listed above. Remembrances of the Chanka-Inca War were kept alive not only through songs sung by the Inca, but through the public and ritual display of objects related to the war and through visits to locations where important events were believed to have taken place.[6] Many of the locations were considered to be so special that they were included within a complex system of shrines that surrounded the city of Cuzco, frequently referred to as the Cuzco *ceque* system, and offerings were made at them on specific days during the year (Cobo 1990 [1653]; Bauer 1998: 24–25).

Among the most important of the shrines in the Cuzco region related to the Chanka-Inca War were a series of large standing stones believed to have been supernaturally transformed into warriors to help the young prince in his victory over the Chanka. These stones were specifically called *pururaucas*. We learn about them through the writings of Polo de Ondegardo (1990: 41 [1571]) and Cobo (1990 [1653]).[7] Cobo explains the origin of the shrines in the following passage:

> The Inca had himself carried on a litter along with his retinue out through the countryside. He said that he knew the stones that had been converted into the *pururaucas*; so he went around pointing out the ones that struck his fancy, which were at some distance apart, and he named each one. Then he had them brought to Cuzco with great dignity, where some of them were placed in the Temple of the Sun, while others were placed in other places designated by the Inca. He gave all of the stones people to serve them and oversee their sacrifices. From then on these stones were worshiped as idols. Whenever strangers came to Cuzco, they would be shown these stones and told about their exploits. . . . The

stones were offered a great number of sacrifices, especially when the Inca went to war or returned from one, during the coronations of the kings, and for other major festivals that they celebrated. Although this name pururaucas was applied to all of these idols together, each one had its own special name, and many of their names will appear ahead in the account of the guacas and shrines of the city of Cuzco.[8] (Cobo 1990: 36 [1653: Bk. 13, Ch. 8])

Additional information on the pururaucas and the Chanka-Inca War can be found within Cobo's detailed listing of the shrines of Cuzco. At least 12 standing stones within the shrine system were believed to be pururaucas, and there were most likely many more.[9] Other shrines related to the Chanka-Inca War include a storage house in which Pachacuti Inca Yupanqui's weapons were kept,[10] the spring of Susumarca where the Inca had his vision,[11] and three locations within the battlefields of the war.[12]

While the pururaucas stood in silent testimony to the supernatural powers involved in the Inca victory over the Chanka, the remains of various Chanka soldiers offered a more gruesome display of Inca might.[13] Betanzos provides a detailed retelling of the end of the Chanka-Inca War and the killing of Chanka prisoners:

> Thus Inca Yupanque ordered them [Chanka prisoners] to be brought before him at the site where the battle took place. As a reminder of it, in the presence of all his people, he had set in the ground many posts from which they would be hanged. And after being hanged, their heads would be cut off and placed on top of the posts. The bodies would be burned, turned into dust, and from the highest hills cast to the winds so that this would be remembered. Thus Inca Yupanque ordered that nobody dare bury any of the bodies of the enemies who had died in the battle so that they would be eaten by foxes and birds and their bones would be seen all the time. All of this was done in the way that you have heard.[14] (Betanzos 1996: 41 [1557: Pt. 1, Ch. 10])

Three generations later, the skins of the Chanka prisoners were still on display in the capital city. Cieza de León (1998: 317 [1554: Pt. 3, Ch. 69]) states that when Pizarro's forces entered the city of Cuzco for the first time in 1534, "They saw two large houses with human [trophy] skin, which were the Chancas, killed in the time of Viracocha Inca."[15] Elsewhere in his chronicle, Cieza de León includes an even more detailed description of these human war trophies:

> And for all those who had died in battle defending his cause, the new Inca ordered a new burial, with the customary obsequies. As for the Chancas, he ordered a large house to serve as a tomb on the site of the battle, where, as a warning, the skin was flayed from the bodies of the dead and stuffed with ashes or straw so that they retained their human shape; they were left in a thousand different ways: some, with a drum protruding from their stomachs, and their hands in praying position; others with a flute in their mouth. In this guise and others they remained until the Spaniards entered Cuzco. Pero Alonso Carrasco and Juan de Pancorvo, of the old conquistadors, told me of seeing these ash-stuffed skins, as did many others of those who entered Cuzco with Pizarro and Almagro.[16] (Cieza de León 1976: 227–228 [1554: Pt. 2, Ch. 46])

The skinned remains of the Chanka warriors after the war served as grim reminders to all of the fate that awaited enemies of the empire, and would become even more potent through time, with the growing success of Inca expansionism outside the Cuzco region. Perhaps the most remarkable reminder of Pachacuti Inca Yupanqui's triumph over the Chanka was recovered by Polo de Ondegardo in 1559, as he searched for the mummified remains of Inca kings. When Polo de Ondegardo finally discovered the body of Pachacuti Inca Yupanqui hidden in a temple on the edge of Cuzco, he found the principal idol of the Chanka with it. Polo de Ondegardo writes:

> [T]he body of Pachacuti Inca Yupanqui Inca . . . was embalmed and well preserved as

were all those that I saw. I found with him the principal idol of the province of Andahuaylas, because he conquered it and placed it under the domination of the Incas when he defeated and killed Valcuvilca, their principal lord.[17] (Polo de Ondegardo 1990: 86 [1571]; translation by the authors)

Thus, it seems that the central idol of the Chanka was treasured by Pachacuti Inca Yupanqui as a reminder of the growth of Inca regional power under his rule. Clearly, by being kept with the principal idol of Andahuaylas, it was Pachacuti Inca Yupanqui's intention to continue to dominate the Chanka, even after his own death.

THE ORIGIN MYTH OF THE CHANKA

Rather than attempting to "reconstruct" the details of the legendary Chanka-Inca War and the final events said to have played out on the edge of Cuzco, we have concentrated our research efforts on understanding the cultural developments of the Chanka homeland. Accordingly, we begin this study with a discussion of the Chankas' own origin myth.

Many Andean ethnic groups believed that they had descended from distinct mythical ancestors who emerged from specific locations in the landscape. The places from which these ancestral kin were believed to have emerged were classified as sacred objects or *huacas* (shrines).[18] Among Quechua speakers, the origin places were called *pacarinas* or *pacariscas* (origin shrines), and these took various forms, including caves, lakes, boulders, and ravines. Members of different ethnic groups made offerings at their own origin places on specific days. Cristóbal de Albornoz, a major figure in the early anti-idolatry campaigns of the Spaniards, recognized the pan-Andean presence of these ritual places and wrote the following:

[T]he principal class of huacas which [the natives of the region] had before being conquered by the Inca, are called *pacariscas*, which means the founders of their nation. They take different forms and names depending on the province: some were out-

crops, others springs, rivers, caves, animals, birds and other types of trees and plants. They believed that they were created by and descended from these things, like the Incas say they are from [the area of] Pacari[q]tambo, [having emerged] from a cave called Tambotoco.[19] (Albornoz 1984: 197 [ca. 1582]; translation by the authors)

The Inca traced their descent to the first mythical Inca king, Manco Capac, who emerged from a cave called Tambotoco, which was located immediately south of Cuzco in the region of Pacariqtambo (Bauer 1991). Manco Capac is then said to have traveled northward from his origin place to the Cuzco Valley. A second, most certainly later, origin myth of the Inca tells of the first Inca and his sister/wife emerging from two islands in Lake Titicaca, far to the southeast of Cuzco, and their journey to the imperial valley (Bauer and Stanish 2001: 48–51). Following a similar oral tradition, the Chanka of Andahuaylas traced their origins back to a mythical ancestor named Hanco Huallu,[20] who emerged from Lake Choclococha in the modern Province of Castrovirreyna, Department of Ica.[21]

Located at an altitude of 4,700 masl, Lake Choclococha is in a remote and desolate region known for its mineral wealth and camelid production (Figure 1.2). The lake is of regional importance, as it forms the headwaters of the Pampas River, which separates the departments of Ayacucho and Apurimac. The indigenous writer Felipe Guaman Poma de Ayala provides one version of the Chankas' origin myth and tells of the emergence of the Chanka culture hero, Hanco Huallu, from Lake Choclococha:

They say that Anca Uallo Chanka left from the Lake Choclococha with five hundred thousand Indians, but with no women, elders, or children. And their king, Anca Uallo, wanted to be Inca, in the time of the first Manco Capac. That Inca presented his sister to Topa Uaco. But (the sister) Uarmi Auca tricked him and killed the lord, king and captain Anca Uallo.[22] (Guaman Poma de Ayala 1980: 66 [1615: 85]; translation by the authors)

FIGURE 1.2. Lake Choclococha (4,700 masl), the mythical origin place of the Chanka,
is located in the Province of Castrovirreyna.

Guaman Poma de Ayala (1980: 964 [1615: 1045 (1053)]) also provides a drawing of the town of Castrovirreyna and the two largest lakes above it: Urcococha and Choclococha (Figure 1.3). In the drawing, he shows the continental divide with Urcococha[23] flowing toward the Peruvian coast and Choclococha draining in the opposite direction toward the Amazon.[24] The zealot priest Albornoz also notes the importance of Choclococha as a regional shrine, although he does not specifically mention the Chanka:

> Choclococha, a large lake in the puna of Guaytara, is widely worshiped for the rivers that start there, and they offered many sacrifices to it. In the area around the lake there are many silver mines, according to the old people. (Albornoz 1984: 208 [ca. 1582]; translation by the authors)[25]

It is, however, the early colonial writer Pedro de Cieza de León who provides the most detailed retelling of the Chanka origin myth. His account is especially interesting, since Cieza de León lived in Andahuaylas for several months between 1548 and 1549 as a member of Pedro de la Gasca's army, and he spoke with various locals concerning the history of the Chanka.[26] He writes:

> When I asked these Chankas what ideas they had about themselves, and where they came from, they told another fairy story or fable like those of Jauja, saying that their forefathers appeared and emerged from a little lake called Choclococha, from which they went forth conquering until they came to a place they named Chuquibamba, where they settled. And after some years had passed, they fought with the Quechuas, an ancient tribe that ruled this province of Andahuaylas, which they conquered and where they have remained as rulers to the present day. The lake from which they

FIGURE 1.3. The town of Castrovirreina as depicted by Guaman Poma de Ayala (1980: 964 [1615: 1045 (1053)]). The lake of Choclococha, the mythical origin place of the Chanka, can be seen in the lower right. The lake of Urcococha is shown in the upper right. *Courtesy of Det Kongelige Bibliotek.*

emerged was sacred to them, and their principal shrine where they worshiped and made sacrifices.[27] (Cieza de León 1976: 132 [1553: Pt. 1, Ch. 90])

Therefore, in mythical terms the Chanka are portrayed as outsiders, or foreigners, to the very region that would become their homeland. Hanco Huallu is said to have emerged from Lake

Choclococha and to have fought with and conquered the indigenous people of Andahuaylas. As such, the Chanka origin myth is similar to those of many other large ethnic groups of the central Andes, including the Inca (Bauer 1991). The mythical journey of an ancestor, from the periphery of an area to its center, and an imaginary battle for control of a heartland are both important aspects of many chiefly and state-level societies' origin myths across the world (Sahlins 1983, 1985). The emergence of a mythical ancestral king outside of a soon-to-be conquered region defines him, and his descendants, as powerful foreigners who won the right to rule the homeland in the distant past. In late prehistoric times, the leaders of the Chanka would have claimed direct descent from Hanco Huallu, just as the rulers of Cuzco claimed direct descent from the first mythical Inca, Manco Capac. The legitimacy of their rule would have been supported through offerings made at their mythical origin places as well as through ritual reenactments of the mythical events that brought the founding ancestors to the region (Bauer 1996).

The Chanka also appear to have closely associated their mythical origins with the great mountain lions, or pumas, of the Andes. This is illustrated by the fact that the people of Andahuaylas sent groups of dancers dressed in puma skins to Cuzco during the time of the Inca, a tradition that continued even after the conquest of the Andes by the Spaniards. In describing the Corpus Christi celebrations of Cuzco in the 1550s, the well-known author Garcilaso de la Vega specifically describes the puma-skin costumes of the Chanka.[28] He writes:

> [The Chanka] boast of their descent from a lion, which they worshiped and held as god, and in their great festivities both before and after their conquest by the Inca kings, two dozen Indians used to appear in the same guise as Hercules, covered with a lionskin with the Indian's head inside the lion's. I have seen this at the celebration of Corpus Christi in Cuzco. (Garcilaso de la Vega 1966: 218 [1609: Pt. 1, Bk. 4, Ch. 15])[29]

The image of Chanka warriors dressed in puma skins has ignited the imagination of the modern inhabitants of Andahuaylas, and they frequently portray their ancestors dressed in puma skins. For example, during the first phase of the local celebration of Sondor Raymi (held annually near the time of the June solstice), the mythical hero Hanco Huallu emerges from the local lake of Pacucha (used to represent Lake Choclococha) dressed in a puma skin (Figure 1.4). Clearly, the sight of warriors dressed in puma skins helps to galvanize the modern mystique of the Chanka as having been a bellicose society that challenged the Inca for control of the Andes.

Anthropologists have long understood that myths are religious narratives that help cultures explain the genesis of basic social relationships. Myths, in other words, offer explanations for how the current world came to be as the result of actions that occurred in the primordial past. Unfortunately, some scholars have read the Choclococha origin myth as having some historical truth and have proposed that the Chanka were originally from the Castrovirreyna or Ayacucho region and that the Chanka slowly expanded their control westward toward Andahuaylas (for example, González Carré 1992a: 78). It has even been proposed that the Chanka represented the Wari state, which occupied parts of the Cuzco Valley (ca. AD 700–1000) and whose Ayacucho-based capital declined near the end of the first millennium AD (Barreda Murillo 1991: 31; 1995: 68). Following the logic of these researchers, the historical records and the archaeological remains of the Andahuaylas region should not be privileged above those of other regions in the departments of Ayacucho, Huancavelica, and Apurimac in understanding the Chanka, since the Chanka arrived in Andahuaylas relatively late in prehistory. We do not support these mytho-historical models, but instead believe that the Chanka were indigenous to Andahuaylas. In short, we propose that only systematic archaeological research within the Andahuaylas region can lend insights into the autochthonous development of the Chanka.

FIGURE 1.4. The inhabitants of the Andahuaylas region take great pride in their Chanka heritage. Here, Hanco Huallu dressed in a puma skin, leaves Lake Pacucha, near Andahuaylas, during the Sondor Raymi celebration of 2003.

AN INTRODUCTION TO ANDAHUAYLAS

The province of Andahuaylas is located within the Department of Apurimac, one of the smallest and poorest departments of modern Peru (Figure 1.5). Situated between Ayacucho and Cuzco, Apurimac has long been overshadowed by these larger and more populated departments.[30] The Andahuaylas Valley itself is approximately 25 km long and contains one of the largest areas of maize production in the department (Figure 1.6). The valley is drained by the east-west-running Chumbao River. The headwaters of this river are located to the east, and it ultimately drains into the Pampas River. There are three principal communities in the valley: Talavera, Andahuaylas, and San Jerónimo. Talavera (2,820 masl) is the lowest and is located near the western end of the valley,

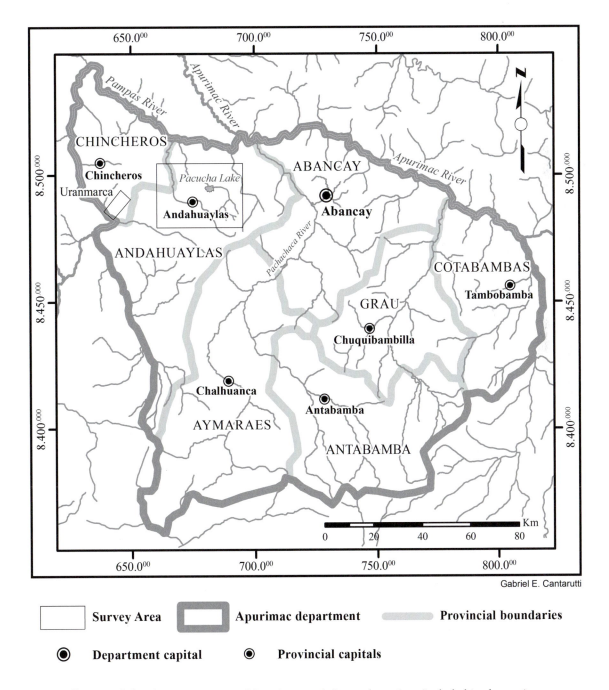

Gabriel E. Cantarutti

FIGURE 1.5. The Department of Apurimac and the study regions included in the project.

FIGURE 1.6. The town of San Jerónimo and the Andahuaylas Valley looking west. With a mild climate and gentle slopes, the valley is exceptionally productive and contains some of the best maize lands in the department.

where the Chumbao River makes a sharp turn northward. Andahuaylas (2,920 masl), which is by far the largest of the settlements, is located at approximately mid-valley. It is the capital of the province and plays a dominant role in the economics and local politics of the region. San Jerónimo (2,950 masl), the smallest of the three communities, is located farther upstream, toward the eastern end of the valley. Each of these three communities dates back to early colonial times and is organized around a traditional Spanish plan that includes a central plaza and gridded streets.

The climate of this intermontane valley is mild, with a rainy season that spans from November to March. The lush valley floor and lower slopes are currently used for maize cultivation, while farther up, wheat, beans, quinoa, and potatoes predominate. With its mild climate and gentle slopes, Andahuaylas is an area of exceptionally good agri-cultural production and is among Peru's largest producers of potatoes. Each week the community hosts an enormous regional agricultural market, which is currently one of the largest in Peru.

A prominent feature of the region is Lake Pacucha (3,125 masl), located 12 km northeast of the city of Andahuaylas (Figure 1.7). Measuring about 8 km² in size, Pacucha is not only the largest lake in the Department of Apurimac, but it is the only sizable lake situated within the maize-producing elevations. The lake is relatively deep at its center (30 m), although stands of lake reeds (*totora*)[31] can be found growing in the shallower areas along its shores. The fields surrounding the lake, especially those on the northern side, support excellent maize production. The lake drains to the northwest, through a narrow valley that also holds a much smaller reservoir several kilometers downstream called Lake Pucullo. Some 24

FIGURE 1.7. Lake Pacucha looking south.
The drainage for the lake can be seen in the lower right of the photograph.

km farther downstream, to the north, this stream joins with the Pampas River. With its expansive, dark blue waters, Lake Pacucha is a stunningly beautiful feature of Andahuaylas and a well-known landmark in the region.

Late Nineteenth-Century Accounts of the Andahuaylas Region

Andahuaylas is on the major road of the central highlands which links Ayacucho with Cuzco, and as such, innumerable travelers passed through the town during the nineteenth and early twentieth centuries. A few of these travelers left accounts of their trips, including the well-known writers Léonce Angrand (1972 [1847]), Lardner Gibbon (1854), Antonio Raimondi (1876), and Ernst F. Middendorf (1895, 1974). Most travelers spent only a short time in the valley. For example, E. George Squier (1877: 557) rested in Andahuaylas for a day, but only for the want of new mules. However, for many, even a short visit was enough to see the great agricultural potential and rural beauty of the region. Clements Markham, who was briefly in the area in 1852, writes the following:

The vale of Andahuaylas is the most beautiful I have yet seen in the sierra. Running nearly east and west, it contains three small towns about a league distant from each other, called Talavera, Andahuaylas, and San Gerónimo. Through its centre runs the little river, lined on either side by very tall poplars. . . . Every part of the valley is carefully cultivated, with maize, potatoes and all kinds of vegetables, and the sides of the hills are covered with maize crops. Andahuaylas, one hundred miles from Ayacucho by the road, consists of a plaza, with a handsome stone church and a fountain, and with a few streets leading from it. (Markham in Blanchard 1991: 79 [1852])

A few travelers, such as Charles Wiener (1993 [1880]), were so favorably impressed with Andahuaylas that they spent several days in the town (Figure 1.8). Wiener's visit is of particular importance to our study, because, as will be discussed later, he provides the earliest known description of Sondor, the largest and most important Inca site in the region.

FIGURE 1.8. The central plaza of Andahuaylas by Wiener (1993: 294 [1880]). Although the plaza is now resurfaced for automobiles, the buildings surrounding it remain largely unchanged. The former Inca settlement was most likely located on the hill in the center of this drawing and historic information indicates that the Inca *tambo* (way station) was located near to where the church was later built.

Previous Archaeological Work in the Andahuaylas Region

Throughout the twentieth century, there have been a relatively small number of archaeological studies conducted within the Department of Apurimac and fewer still in the Andahuaylas area.[32] The first formal inventory of ancient remains near Andahuaylas is provided by Hugo Pesce (1942). Pesce, who later emerged as a well-known medical researcher in Peru, spent some six years in the region practicing medicine and published a brief catalog of 17 archaeological sites found in the province. He includes the names, approximate locations, and the state of preservation for some of the largest, and what are now the best known, ruins of the province.[33]

A little more than ten years after Pesce's publication, in 1954, researchers John H. Rowe and Oscar Núñez del Prado spent two weeks visiting archaeological sites in the Department of Apurimac. Rowe (1944) had completed his doctoral research on the archaeology of Cuzco and was eager to document sites in the surrounding departments. He was especially impressed with the density of sites in the Andahuaylas region. Describing his brief trip into Apurimac, Rowe (1956: 143) writes, "The valley of Andahuaylas, in contrast, is thickly sprinkled with sites, and we visited several as large and as rich in decorated pottery as any we saw in the Peruvian highlands. We explored the south side of the valley rather thoroughly and made side trips to Huancabamba and Lake Pakucha." Rowe and Núñez del Prado visited some 15 sites, and they offered the first initial descriptions of local pottery styles.

In the early 1970s Joel Grossman, a student of Rowe's, conducted his dissertation fieldwork in the Andahuaylas region (1972a, 1972b, 1983), which largely focused on the Formative Period occupations. Grossman was drawn to the region because of its traditional association with the Chanka and because Rowe had identified what appeared to be one of the earliest pottery styles in the area. During his time in Andahuaylas, Grossman visited some 70 sites in the valley and developed a basic ceramic sequence for the region. Wanting to understand more about the early vil-

lages of the area, Grossman concentrated most of his research efforts on excavating the site of Waywaka, situated on a low ridge just above the city of Andahuaylas. Both Grossman and Rowe had found various ceramic styles at this site, and through his excavations Grossman was able to demonstrate that Waywaka was one of the largest and earliest villages of the area. He also published the first radiocarbon dates for the department. Our work, although conducted some three decades later, builds directly on Grossman's research and examines the distribution patterns of many of the ceramic styles he helped to define.

Like much of the central highlands of Peru, Andahuaylas fell into a state of political and economic chaos during the 1980s and early 1990s. Formed in the crucible of desperate rural poverty, rising expectations, and decades of failed governmental reforms, the guerrilla organization the "Shining Path" (Sendero Luminoso) emerged in the Ayacucho region in 1980. This violent, neo-Maoist, revolutionary group soon established strongholds in the neighboring departments, including Apurimac. In December of 1981, the Shining Path attacked and partially destroyed the relatively isolated agricultural cooperative of Toxsama, north of Andahuaylas. Three months later, the department was placed under a state of emergency, and most civil liberties were suspended (Berg 1987, 1992). Conditions continued to deteriorate, and by the end of 1982 the departments of Ayacucho, Huancavelica, and Apurimac were declared Emergency Military Zones; national troops were sent in from Lima. A dark decade followed, when tens of thousands of urban dwellers and rural villagers died, trapped between the fanatic revolutionaries and a vengeful national military. The economy and the infrastructure of the region collapsed and were slow to recover even after the capture of Abimael Guzmán, the leader of the Shining Path, in 1992. Little archaeological work could be conducted in the region during those difficult times.[34]

In the mid-1990s, archaeological investigations began again in the Andahuaylas region, with researchers focusing their efforts on the site of Sondor, one of the most impressive ruins in the area (Truyenque Caceres 1995).[35] The site contains several clusters of Inca buildings as well as a magnificently terraced conical hill (Figure 1.9). A large outcrop at the summit of the hill was most certainly a major prehistoric shrine. Ismael Pérez (Pérez, Vivanco, and Amorín 2003) and José Amorín Garibay (1998) from the Universidad Nacional de San Cristóbal de Huamanga (Ayacucho), initiated a large-scale excavation and restoration project at Sondor in 1997. Although this research at Sondor marked the first time that a site with Inca remains had been examined in the Andahuaylas region, the distribution of Inca sites across the region and the processes through which the Chanka became incorporated into the Inca Empire were not investigated in detail.

The Andahuaylas Archaeological Project

Starting in 2002, the authors of this book began working in the Andahuaylas region. From its very

conception, our work was to encompass an interdisciplinary research program involving both archaeological fieldwork within the Chanka homeland and historic research in various archives of Peru and Spain. The overall goal of the project was to examine issues of cultural development through time in the Andahuaylas region as well as indigenous responses to the three imperial conquests that had engulfed the area during the past two millennia (the Wari [AD 600–1000], the Inca [AD 1400–1532] and the Spanish [AD 1532–1821]). Ultimately, we were interested in examining issues of political power: how it develops over time, and what shifts occur as local polities are incorporated into larger, expansionistic states. We were also keen to understand how the Chanka people adapted to state incorporation and to fluctuating imperial demands over time, whether or not a secondary state formed within the relatively unexplored

FIGURE 1.9. The archaeological site of Sondor is one of the most impressive ruins in the Andahuaylas region.

region of Andahuaylas, and how the prehistoric developments of this region compared with those of other, better-studied areas of the Andes.

Over the course of several years of fieldwork, we established a large database of archaeological and historical information on the Chanka. From 2002 to 2004, Brian S. Bauer directed a systematic archaeological survey of the Chanka homeland. The purpose of the survey was to document the location, size, and distribution of all archaeological sites in the Andahuaylas region. During this same period, Sabine Hyland oversaw extensive archival research in the cities of Andahuaylas, Cuzco, Lima, and Seville. The rationale for the historic research was to recover information on the social organization of the Andahuaylas region at the time of Spanish contact and to document the long-term impact that resulted from the European occupation of this part of the Andes. We were also especially interested in recovering archival documents, since they generally provide more locally focused information than that presented by the classic chroniclers.

The Archival Research

Previous historical research on the Chanka has been extremely narrow, as scholars have generally limited themselves to reading the classic chronicles of Peru. With the exception of Stern's (1982) outstanding work on the indigenous reactions to Spanish rule in the Ayacucho region during the Colonial Period, which briefly touches upon the Chanka, and the publication of Diego Maldonado's 1539 *encomienda* grant (Julien 2002), little detailed archival research has been conducted on the inhabitants of the Andahuaylas region.[36] Recognizing this limitation, our project included a large-scale archival research component to collect additional historical information on the Chanka. Archival research on the Chanka was begun in 2001 in the Archivo Departamental del Cuzco under the direction of Bauer, Hyland, and Donato Amado González. Cuzco was the logical place to begin, since many public records from Andahuaylas were moved to the Archivo Departamental del Cuzco in the late 1980s because of the political problems that were

occurring at that time in Ayacucho and Apurimac. During the course of the project, historical research was also conducted in the Archivo del Ministerio de Agricultura del Cuzco, the Archivo General de la Nación (Lima), the Biblioteca Nacional del Perú (Lima), the Archivo del Ministerio de Agricultura (Andahuaylas), the Archivo Municipal de Uranmarca, and the Archivo General de los Indias (Seville, Spain) as well as in the Latin American Manuscript Collection at Yale University (New Haven, USA).

By the close of the research phase of the project, we had produced summaries, transcriptions, and copies of approximately 430 previously unknown documents related to the Chanka, dating from AD 1550 to 1700. This archival work resulted in the recovery of new information concerning the social, political, and economic organization of the Chanka under both Inca and Spanish rule. For example, we found a unique manuscript in the archives of Uranmarca, a rural village in the Andahuaylas area, which offers a brief description of Inca rule in the region and outlines the work of various individual Inca governors (*Acta de Uranmarca*; see Appendix 4). Several documents provide information on the colonists (*mitimaes*) that the Inca brought from the Chachapoya area into the Andahuaylas region. Others describe the 64 communities inhabited by the Chanka at the time of the Spanish conquest, along with the names of the village leaders (Julien 2002; AGI, Patronato 93, No. 11, Ramo 2, ff. 186v–188v). A series of other important manuscripts describe the tribute obligations of the Chanka to the Spanish Crown throughout the sixteenth century. We also found the wills of various important individuals of the region, including Diego Maldonado and his son Juan Arias de Maldonado, as well as various local lords such as Diego Condorguacho. Additional documents record both the good works and abuses of local political and religious leaders and landowners. Such documents provide crucial data on the Colonial Period kinship and political structures of the Chanka homeland. A detailed summary of the historical findings of the project is currently being prepared (Hyland and Amado González n.d.).

The Archaeological Research

Archaeological surveys were conducted in the Andahuaylas region in 2002 (approximately six months) and in 2004 (approximately three months). Laboratory analysis and petroglyph studies occurred during 2003 (two months) and at the end of the 2004 survey work. The fieldwork was conducted under the direction of Bauer, Lucas C. Kellett, and Miriam Aráoz Silva. Field assistance was provided by a number of individuals from the archaeology departments of the Universidad San Antonio Abad del Cuzco and the Universidad Nacional San Cristóbal de Huamanga. During the course of the project, the locations of more than 600 archaeological sites, dating from the pre-ceramic period (9500–2100 BC) to imperial Inca times (ca. AD 1400–1532), were documented.

The Archaeological Survey. The archaeological survey concentrated on documenting the prehistoric settlement patterns of the greater Andahuaylas region, which included the Andahuaylas Valley as well as a significant amount of territory surrounding it (Figure 1.10). In all, the archaeological survey covered approximately 300 km² and included the core area of the Chanka ethnic group. The two sides of the east-west-running Andahuaylas Valley differ greatly and have held different population densities through time. The northern valley slopes rise relatively quickly from the valley floor (ca. 2,900 masl) to reach heights of about 4,200 masl along a series of massive ridges, before descending into the remote, lower Pampas River area. In contrast, the southern valley slopes are relatively gentle, and the horizon is much farther from the valley floor. Beyond the southern hori-

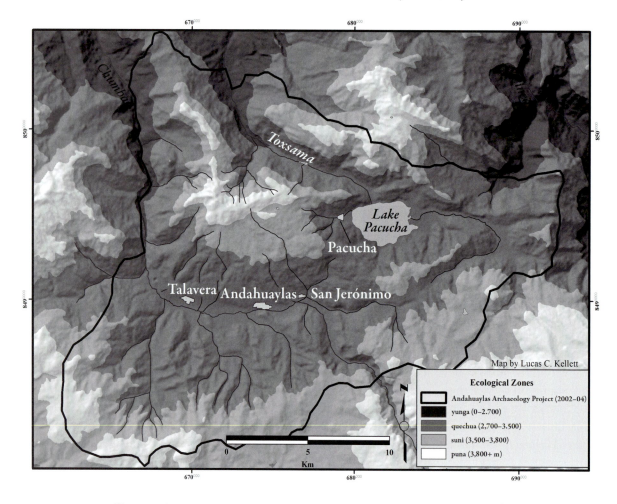

FIGURE 1.10. The archaeological survey covered approximately 300 km² and included the homeland of the Chanka.

zon is an expansive, relatively flat area of high-altitude potato cultivation and camelid grazing (*puna*, 3,900–4,200 masl), and still farther up is an immense and largely barren region of glacial lakes and mountain summits (4,200+ masl). Some colonial documents refer to this desolate and cold region as the "wilds above Andahuaylas."

The southern edge of the survey region was established in the Huancabamba puna, and the northern limits were set by the impressive Achanchi and Utupata ridges. The eastern limits of the survey were set at the edge of the Pincos River Valley, and the western boundary was established where the Chumbao River makes its sharp turn to the north and begins a deep descent toward the Pampas River. While this study region does not take in all of the territory known to have been occupied by the Chanka, it does cover a large portion of it and includes what we believe represents the center of the Chanka homeland (see Chapter 2). During the course of the project, Carlo Socualaya Dávila also conducted a survey in the Uranmarca area (see Appendix 3), between the towns of Vilcashuamán and Andahuaylas. We also undertook various reconnaissance trips to the Pampas River, as well as to the communities of Andarapa, Chincheros, Cocharcas, Huancarama, Huancaray, Ongoy, Pampachiri, Pincos, Uripa, and Vilcashuamán, to better understand the local geography, its ancient occupations, and the early colonial history of the region.

The Survey Methodology. The Andahuaylas region, like many areas of the central Andes, provides excellent conditions for archaeological surveys and surface collections. The terrain is relatively free of trees and ground-covering plants, such as grasses,[37] and most fields are still cultivated with scratch plows, which bring artifacts to the surface without causing serious damage to archaeological sites. The modern population level of the region is relatively low, although the city of Andahuaylas is quickly encroaching on several important prehistoric occupations. Unfortunately, there has also been accelerated road construction and urban growth along the valley floor, between the communities of Talavera, Andahuaylas, and San Jerón-

imo, over the past decade, which is threatening many additional sites.

The archaeological survey of the Chanka homeland was designed as a full coverage survey. The analysis of the data took place within the confines of a cultural evolutionary model that anticipates that with strong population growth, there will be a greater dependence on domesticated foods, larger settlements, and increased specialization over time (Marcus 2008). Through the use of a cultural evolutionary model, the survey results can be compared with those of other regional archaeological studies completed in Peru, and the project can provide comparative information on the emergence and development of sociopolitical complexity elsewhere in the ancient Americas.

The survey work followed guidelines introduced by Parsons, Hastings, and Matos Mendieta (2000a, 2000b) and further developed by many other Andean archaeologists (for example, Schreiber 1987, 1999; Earle et al. 1988; Bauer 1992, 2004; Billman 1999; Stanish 1997, 2003). These studies, and many others worldwide, are built on the realization that broad changes in the settlement patterns (including the size of archaeological sites and their locations in the countryside) can be identified through surface survey (Kowalewski 2008). Assuming that the settlement pattern in a region reflects indigenous patterns of resource use, subsistence procurement, and social organization, archaeological surveys are perhaps the most cost-effective way to gain a general understanding of previously unexplored regions. To conduct the survey in Andahuaylas, teams of three to four persons, spaced at approximately 50-m intervals, walked assigned areas identifying the locations of prehistoric sites. When a site was found, its coordinates were recorded with a global positioning system (GPS), and its location was marked on 1:25,000 topographic maps and on aerial photographs of the region. Standardized survey forms were used to record such information as the size of the site, its location relative to natural and cultural features, the presence or absence of architecture, the presence or absence of burials, and the density of ceramics and lithics visible on the surface.

Diagnostic surface pottery and lithic artifacts were collected at each site and then analyzed in the laboratory to determine the periods during which the site was occupied. During the surface collections, a team of surveyors walked in lines, set approximately 5 m apart, over the surface of the site, systematically collecting the artifacts. If architectural units or field boundaries were present at the site, separate collections were made in each. At the end of the fieldwork, using information from both survey and laboratory analysis, all sites were assigned to one of several generalized site types (Table 1.1). These generalized site types were then used to develop the settlement pattern maps presented in this study.

After the surface materials were collected from the sites, they were brought to Andahuaylas to be processed. In the laboratory, the ceramics were washed and the decorated sherds were separated into homogeneous groups based on wares, design elements, pigment colors, and surface treatment. These groups were then further subdivided according to vessel form. Both photographs

TABLE 1.1
Generalized site types

TYPE	DESCRIPTION
Type 1A (Household)	Extremely light to light scatters of ceramics that are less than 0.25 ha. Generally these sites contain no architectural remains and their surface materials are highly eroded. They most likely represent the remains of single households.
Type 1B (Households)	Extremely light to light scatters of ceramics that are greater than 0.25 ha but less than 1 ha. Generally these sites contain no architectural remains and their surface materials are highly eroded. Many of these sites most likely represent a series of single households that have been rebuilt over time or a few scattered households.
Type 2 (Hamlets)	Medium scatters of ceramics (5–15 fragments per 2 × 2 m) that are greater than 0.25 ha but less than 1 ha. These sites most likely represent several clustered households or hamlets. In the Andahuaylas region, these sites tend not to contain any architectural remains.
Type 3 (Small Villages)	Medium to dense scatters of ceramics (15+ fragments per 2 × 2 m) that are larger than 1 ha but less than 5 ha. These sites most likely represent small villages. In the Andahuaylas region, some of these sites contain poorly preserved structures, although many do not.
Type 4 (Medium Villages)	Medium to dense scatters of ceramics (15+ fragments per 2 × 2 m) that are larger than 5 ha but smaller than 10 ha. These sites most likely represent villages and, depending on the time period, may represent regional centers. Most of these sites contain intact architecture.
Type 5 (Large Villages)	Medium to dense scatter of ceramics (15+ fragments per 2 × 2 m) that are greater than 10 ha. These sites most likely represent large villages and, depending on the time period, may represent regional centers. All of these sites contain intact architecture.
Type 6	Burial towers, cliff tombs, or cemeteries
Type 7	Corrals
Type 8	Lithic scatters
Type 9	Petroglyphs
Type 10	Other

Note: The generalized site typology used during the Andahuaylas Archaeological Project is largely base on site sizes, although the density of surface materials at the site is also given some consideration.

and drawings were made of numerous diagnostic sherds. At the close of the project, the artifacts were deposited in the National Institute of Culture, Cuzco, in specially constructed, wooden containers for permanent storage.

Carbon samples were also collected at some sites. These samples were taken from archaeological contexts that had been exposed through road cuts, canal construction, or other activities. (Many of the samples included pottery fragments that contained carbonized residue encrusted on the exterior or interior of the vessel. These were preferred samples, since their radiocarbon results can be used to directly date when the vessel, and its related style, were in use.) At the end of the survey, 25 carbon samples were submitted for radiocarbon dating (Appendix 1). While we recognize the limitations of carbon samples collected during the course of survey work, especially as compared with samples collected from better-understood contexts revealed during the course of excavations, it was important for our project to begin to build a regional ceramic and site chronology based on absolute dates. Our regional chronology has been further strengthened through additional data and carbon samples collected during Kellett's (2010) excavations at several of the late prehistoric sites in the region as well as through six radiocarbon dates provided by Grossman (1983) from the early ceramic site of Waywaka.

Because this study addresses cultural changes that occurred within the Andahuaylas region, we have elected to use an Andahuaylas-based chronology to organize the archaeological materials, although for comparative purposes we also refer to the widely used Horizon system developed by Rowe and Menzel (1967). The temporal periods used to organize most of the chapters in this work are largely defined by the appearance of specific ceramic and architectural styles in the Andahuaylas region (Figure 1.11). The calendar years assigned to each period are based on the relatively few carbon dates that are currently available for the region and are open to reassessment as more data become available. The use of a broadly defined ceramic typology and the subdivision of the regional chronology into time periods that run

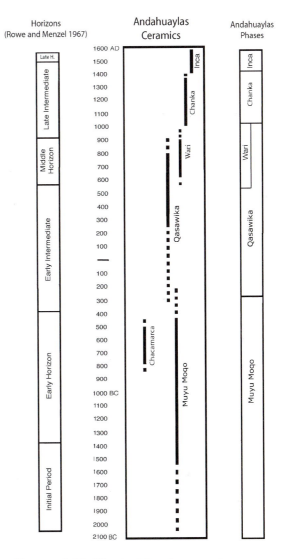

FIGURE 1.11. The Andahuaylas ceramic sequence.

many hundreds of years represent a weakness in the project's database. That is to say, our current reliance on general chronological markers and broad subdivisions of the past limit our abilities to define and discuss subtleties that may have occurred in the regional settlement patterns through time. Yet, this coarse-grained chronology has also provided us with critical new information and has allowed us to outline the long-term history of the Andahuaylas region, from the arrival of hunter-gatherers to the coming of the Spaniards and the end of indigenous rule in the Andes.

NOTES

1 Songs of the Inca's victory over the Chanka continued to be sung at public festivals in Cuzco well into the seventeenth century (Romero 1940: 20–21, cited in Dean 1999).

2 It is also important to note that the accounts we have concerning the Chanka-Inca War are not even the direct products of the Inca. While there is evidence that the Inca recorded some of the deeds of their kings on painted boards, retold past actions in epic songs, and recalled specific events with the aid of knotted strings (*quipo*), small stones, and other mnemonic devices, none of these original histories survived the European conquest. Instead, what remains for us to study are post-conquest accounts. These accounts are largely written by Spaniards, many of whom needed translators to understand their native informants. These writers, like their informants and translators, were heavily influenced by the politics of their era and by their own personal biases.

3 "... e tocando los atambores que ansi en medio [de la plaza] estaban empezaron a cantar todos juntos comenzando este cantar las señoras mujeres que detrás de ellos estaban en el cual cantar decían e declaraban la venida que Uscovilca [ie. los Chankas] había venido sobre ellos e la salida de Viracocha Inga e como Inga Yupangue le había preso e muerto diciendo que el sol le había dado favor para ello como a su hijo e como después ansi mismo había desbaratado y preso e muerto a los capitanes que ansi habían hecho la junta postrera [de los Chankas] ..." (Betanzos 1987: 61 [1557: Pt. 1, Ch. 13]).

4 There are considerable disagreements and confusion over the names of the Chanka leaders and the names of the idols that were carried into the war. We find the accounts written by Sarmiento (2007 [1572]) and Albornoz (1984 [1582]) to be especially helpful in sorting out some of the confusion.

5 In some retellings, there is only one battle between the Chanka and the Inca.

6 For additional information on the mnemonics of the Chanka-Inca War, see Niles (1999: 56–61).

7 Cobo's information on the pururaucas most certainly comes from a now lost manuscript of Polo de Ondegardo. Acosta (2002: 363–364 [1590: Bk. 4, Ch. 21]) also used Polo de Ondegardo's information on the pururaucas in his chronicle.

8 "... el cual se hizo llevar en andas por los campos y despoblados, diciendo que él conocía las piedras en que se habían convertido los pururáucas, y así iba señalando las que le parecía, lejos unas de otras, y poniendo nombre a cada una. Las cuales hizo traer con gran solemnidad al Cuzco y poner algunas en el templo del sol y otras en otros lugares que les señaló, y a todas dió quien las sirviese y tuviese cuidado de sus sacrificios; y desde entonces fueron las dichas piedras tenidas por ídolos y muy veneradas. Las cuales mostraban a los forasteros que venían al Cuzco. ... Ofrecíanles grande suma de sacrificios, especialmente cuando iban a la guerra y volvían della, en las coronaciones de los reyes y en las demás fiestas universales que hacían. Aunque daban nombre de Pururáucas a todos estos ídolos juntos, cada uno por sí tenía su nombre particular, como de muchos parecerá adelante en la relación de las guacas y adoratorios de las ciudad del Cuzco" (Cobo 1964: 162 [1653: Bk. 13, Ch. 8]).

9 These include shrines Ch. 2:2, Ch. 4:1, Ch. 5:3, Ch. 6:1, Ch. 7:1, Co. 1:1, Co. 7:2, Co. 9:2, Co. 9:12, Cu. 1:1, Cu. 4:1, and Cu. 5:2 (Bauer 1999).

10 Shrine Ch. 8:1 (Bauer 1999).

11 Shrine An. 5:8 (Bauer 1999).

12 Shrines Ch. 9:7, Ch. 9:8, and Ch. 9:9 (Bauer 1999).

13 Regardless of the historical accuracy of the *Quito Manuscript*, the author does provide a vivid account of the grim fate of those who resisted Inca expansionism. At one point in the work, the author describes the triumphal return of an Inca to Cuzco following his victory over the Chanka:

[The Inca officers] were elaborately adorned; on their heads they wore very elaborate head-dresses and medals, with many plumes of various colours, and with great plates of gold upon their breasts and shoulders; the men wore silver ones which they got as spoils from the conquered. In the midst, at intervals, they bore six drums in human form, made of the skins of the [hostile] caciques and captains who had distinguished themselves in the battle. Their skins were peeled off while they were yet alive, and, filled with air, they represented their owners in a very lifelike fashion [and the victors] played upon their bellies with sticks out of contempt. Last of these, came the drum made from the Lord of Andaguáilas whom they took prisoner in battle. To the sound of these drums marched four thousand more soldiers. Behind them were many captive caciques and captains. They were followed by still more soldiers, and then came six more drums like the first, and in the rear of the captives, came [the other] Lord of Andaguáilas, whom they took prisoner in battle. He came naked, with his hands tied behind him, like the other captives, but he was placed on an unadorned litter, so that he might be ignominiously seen by all. Around his litter were six drums made of his relatives, with which sound was made. Next, came a troop of criers who ceaselessly told how the king treated those who rebelled against him, and others told of the actions of the people of Andaguáilas; and then the trumpets and drums made a great noise and clamour, which caused horror and fear (in the hearers). Following this spectacle, came three thousand orejones, richly dressed, and adorned with a diversity of plumes.

These kept singing the huali (huaylli), a song of victory relating the events of the battle, the spirit and valour of the conquering king. (Montesinos 1920: 93–94 [1644: Ch. 22])

. . . yban [los capitanes incaicos] muy adornados; en las caveças leuauan muy rricos tocados y medallas, con muchas plumas de diuersos colores, y en los pechos y espaldas grandes patenas de oro; los soldados trayan de plata que ubieron en los despoxos de los rrendidos. Lleuauan en medio, a trechos, seis atambores en la forma de hombre, echos de los pellexos de los caçiques y capitanes que se hauían señalado en la vatalla; quitarónles viuos los pellexos, y llenos de aire, venían representando muy al viuo a sus dueños y tañendo con los palillos en las varrigas por vilipendio. En último lugar venía echo atambor el Señor de Antaguailas que mataron en la vatalla. Al son déstos yban marchando quatro mill soldados; detrás de ellos yban muchos caçiques y capitanes cautiuos. A ellos seguían otros soldados, y luego yban otros seis atambores como los primeros, y a la postre de los cautiuos el Señor de Andaguailas que tomaron viuo en la vatalla. Yba desnudo y las manos atadas atrás, como los demás cautibos, en unas andas altas y mal adereçadas, para que ignominiosamente fuese de todos visto. Iban alrededor de las andas seis tambores de los pellejos de parientes suyos, con que le ivan haçiendo son. Yban aquí una tropa de pregoneros que no zesauan de dezir, que de aquella manera trataua el rey a los que se le rrevelauan, y otros deçían las naziones que habian cometido los de Andaguailas; y luego las voçines y atavales haçían grande rruido y estruendo, que caussa orror y espanto. Seguían a este espetáculo tres mil indios orexones, ricamente vestidos, adornados con diuersidad de plumas; éstos iban cantando el huali, canto de la victorio y suçesos de la vatalla, ánimo y valor del rey vençedor. (*The Quito Manuscript* 2007: 142 [1644: Ch. 22])

14 ". . . e ansi los mandó llevar de delante de sí y que en el sitio do la batalla se diera y para que della hubiese memoria en presencia de todos los de su campo mandasen hincar muchos palos de los cuales fuesen ahorcados y después de ahorcados les fuesen cortadas las cabezas y puestas en lo alto de los palos e que sus cuerpos fuesen allí quemados y hechos polvos y desde los cerros más altos fuesen aventados por el aire para que desto hubiesen memoria y ansi mismo mandó que ninguno fuese osado de enterrar ningún cuerpo de los enemigos que ansi habían muerto en la batalla porque fuesen comidos de zorros e aves y los huesos de los tales fuesen allí vistos todo el tiempo todo lo cual fue hecho en la manera que habeis oído . . ." (Betanzos 1987: 45 [1557: Pt. 1, Ch. 10]).

15 "Vieron dos galpones grandes de cueros de hombres que heran los chancas que allí fueron muertos en tiempo de Viracoche Ynga" (Cieza de León 1997: 233 [1554: Pt. 3, Ch. 69]).

16 "Y a todos los que murieron de la parte suya en la vatalla los mandó el nuevo Ynga enterrar, mandando hazerles las oçequias a su usança; y a los chancas mandó que se hiziese una casa larga a manera de tanbo en la parte que se dio la vatalla, adonde para memoria fuesen desollados todos los cuerpos de los muertos y que hinchesen los cueros de çeniza o de paja de tal manera que la forma umana pareçiese en ellos, haziéndolos de mill maneras, porque a unos, pareçiendo honbre, de su mismo vientre salía un atambor y con sus manos hazía[n] muestra de le tocar, otros ponían con flautas en las bocas. Desta suerte y de otras estuvieron hasta que los españoles entraron al Cuzco. Pero Alonso Carrazco y Juan de Pancorbo, conquistadores antiguos, me contaron a mí de la manera que vieron estos cuerpos de çeniza y otros muchos de los que entraron con Piçarro y Almagro en el Cuzco" (Cieza de León 1996: 135–136 [1554: Pt. 2, Ch. 46]).

17 ". . . el cuerpo Pachacutec Inca Yupanqui Inca, . . . estaba embalsamado y tan bien curado como todos vieron, que hallé con él el ídolo principal de la provincia de Andahuaylas, porque la conquistó éste y la metió debajo del dominio de los incas cuando venció a Valcuvilca el señor principal de ella, y le mató . . ." (Polo de Ondegardo 1990: 86 [1571]).

18 The Quechua terms, toponyms, and personal names contained in this work are written according to their Hispanicized spellings as found in the Spanish chronicles and on modern maps. The English and Spanish plural form *s* is used in this text rather than the Quechua form (*kuna* or *cuna*).

19 ". . . el prencipal género de guacas que antes que fuesen subjetos al ynga tenían, que llaman pacariscas, que quieren dezir criadoras de sus naturalezas. Son en diferentes formas y nombres conforme a las provincias: unos tenían piedras, otros fuentes y ríos, otros cuebas, otros animales y aves e otros géneros de árboles y de yervas y desta diferencia tratavan ser criados y descender de las dichas cosas, como los yngas dezia[n] ser salidos de Pacaritambo, ques de una cueba que se dize Tambo Toco . . ." (Albornoz 1984: 197 [ca. 1582]).

20 The name of this mythical ancestor is spelled a number of different ways, including Anca Uallo and Anco Allo.

21 Murúa (1946: 389 [1590: Bk. 4, Ch. 8]) suggests that the name of the lake, which translates as Corn Cob Lake, is derived from the aftermath of a battle when corn was cast into the lake by a retreating army. The corn later sprouted and grew to reproduce. At 4,700 masl this is impossible, and the account should be read as a mythical explanation for the origins of corn,

rather than a historical event. This interpretation is also consistent with the belief that the nearby lake of Urcococha was the origin place of llamas. In this respect, it is worth noting that several other, south central Andean highland ethnic groups also traced their ancestral origins to Choclococha. These include the Soras and the Angaraes (Albornoz 1984: 197 [ca. 1582]), and perhaps the Jauja (Cieza de León 1976: 132 [1553: Pt. 1, Ch. 90]). Also see Vázquez de Espinosa (1948: 509 [1629]).

22 "Dizen que *Anca Uallo* Changa, que salieron de la laguna de Chocllo Cocha cincuenta mil millones de yndios, cin las mujeres ni biejos, niños. Y el rrey de ellos, *Anca Uallo*, quizo ser *Ynga* en tienpo de *Mango Capac Ynga* primero. Y se la presentó a su ermana, a *Topa Uaco*, el dicho *Ynga*. Y le engañó y le mató al señor rrey y capitán *Anca Uallo Uarmi Auca*" (Guaman Poma de Ayala 1980: 66 [1615: 85]).

23 Arriaga (1968: 70 [1621]) notes that camelids were sacrificed to Choclococha and to the nearby lake of Urcococha, since they were believed to be the origin place of llamas.

24 Elsewhere in his work, Guaman Poma de Ayala (1980: 326 [1615: 354 (356)]) shows the road to Choclococha in relation with the town of Vilcashuamán. Also see the Anonymous Description of Peru (1972: 110 [ca 1610]) for a description of colonial mining operations near Choclococha.

25 "Choclo cacha, laguna grande en la puna de Guaytara, de grande beneración, que nacen della ríos, y le hazían muchos sacrificios. Hay alrededor della muchos minerales de plata, según dicen los antiguos" (Albornoz 1984: 208 [ca. 1582]).

26 Also see Cieza de León (1976: 207 [1554: Pt. 2, Bk. 37]).

27 "Preguntándole yo a estos Chancas, que sentían de sí propios, y donde tuuo principio su origen: quentan otra niñería o nouela como los de Xauxa: y es, que dicen que sus padres remanescieron y salieron por vn palude pequeño llamado Soclococha: desde donde conquistaron, hasta llegar a vna parte que nombran Chuquibamba: adonde luego hizieron su assiento. Y passados algunos años, contendieron con los Quichuas nasción muy antigua, y señores que eran desta provincia de Andabaylas la qual ganaron: y quedaron por señores della hasta oy. Al lago de donde salieron tenían por sagrado, y era su principal templo donde adorauan y sacrificauan" (Cieza de León 1995: 254 [1553: Pt. 1, Ch. 90]).

28 See Garcilaso de la Vega (1966: 557 and 1416 [1609: Pt. 1, Bk. 6, Ch. 20, and Pt. 2, Bk. 8, Ch. 1]) for other brief descriptions of the Chanka in puma skins. See Betanzos (1996: 63 [1557: Bk. 8]) and Cristóbal de Molina (1989: 108 [ca. 1575]) for the use of puma skins in other Cuzco ceremonies.

29 "[Los Chankas] jáctanse descender de un león, y así lo tenían y adoraban por dios, y en sus grandes fiestas, antes y después de ser conquistados por los reyes Incas, sacaban dos docenas de indios de la misma manera que pintan a Hércules, cubierto con el pellejo del león, y la cabeza del indio metida en la cabeza del león. Yo las vi así en las fiestas del Santísimo Sacramento en el Cozco" (Garcilaso de la Vega 1960: 135 [1609: Pt. 1, Bk. 4, Ch. 15]).

30 Because Andahuaylas is located midway between Cuzco and Ayacucho, its jurisdiction has oscillated between these two powerful cities.

31 *Schoenoplectus Californicus*, Cyperaceae.

32 Research conducted within the Department of Apurimac, but outside of the Andahuaylas region, includes Frank Medden's (1985, 1991, 2001, 2006) work in the Pampachiri region, Gladys Lagos Aedo's work near Abancay (1999), Maarten Van de Guchte's (1990) study of the Saywite region, and Italo Oberti's (1997) description of Usno-Moq'o near Abancay. It is also worth noting that Burger, Fajardo Ríos, and Glascock (2006) have recently documented that there are two important sources of obsidian in the Department of Apurimac.

33 Three of the sites reported by Pesce (Sondor, Curamba, and Achanchi) were especially important sites during the Chanka and Inca periods and are described in this book.

34 In an event unrelated to the Shining Path, Andahuaylas was the scene of a brief, four-day revolt led by a major of the Peruvian army, Antauro Igor Humala Tasso, in January of 2005.

35 Other recent archaeological work in the Andahuaylas region includes Hostnig's (1988, 1990, 2003) documentation of some of the petroglyphs, and brief listings of various sites in González Carré et al.'s (1988) ambitious site catalog for the departments of Ayacucho, Huancavelica, and Apurimac.

36 Exceptions to this statement include Busto Duthurburu's (1963) biography of Diego Maldonado and Arturo Gutiérrez Velasco's (1999) chronology of historical events in Andahuaylas.

37 An exception to this statement is the puna, which is covered in ichu grass (*Stipa ichu*).

CHAPTER 2

WHO WERE THE CHANKA?

Determining the exact area that was occupied by a prehistoric, or protohistoric, group is a difficult task. This is particularly true in Peru, where few documents have survived from the contact period and where tragic, large-scale demographic collapses occurred during early colonial times. Nevertheless, it has been long understood that there were a host of different groups in the Andean highlands at the time of European contact, and their territories are gradually being defined, frequently through a combination of archival research and archaeological fieldwork (for example, Bauer 1992; Schreiber 1993; Covey 2006; Wernke 2006, 2007; Arkush 2006, 2008). In this chapter, we will discuss what is currently known concerning the traditional territory of the

Chanka and trace how those holdings were subsequently divided by the Spaniards. In doing so, the chapter provides a historical introduction to the Chanka and briefly explores their changing relationships with the Spaniards during the early Colonial Period.

NOTES ON THE CHANKA CONFEDERATION

Although it is well documented that the homeland of the Chanka was in the Andahuaylas region (AGI, Patronato 93, No. 11, Ramo 2, ff. 186v–188v), it is important to note that since at least colonial times, the term "Chanka" has also been used to refer to a broader group of people. The term has been, and continues to be, used indiscriminately to refer to the people who lived in the central Peruvian departments of Huancavelica, Ayacucho, and Apurimac at the time of the Inca expansion. This tradition may have begun with Garcilaso de la Vega (1966 [1609]), as he places several distinct and differently named groups under the general rubric of "Chanka" (Figure 2.1). For example, in his account of the legendary campaigns of Inca Roca, Garcilaso de la Vega (1966: 218 [1609: Pt. 1, Bk. 4, Ch. 15]) states that after defeating the Chanka of Andahuaylas, Inca Roca continued his westward expansion, entering into the territories of several other groups who were also considered as Chanka, including the Uranmarca, Hancohuallu, Sulla, Utunsulla, and the Vilcashuamán. Garcilaso de la Vega provides

additional information about these ethnic groups as he details the legendary westward conquests of Inca Roca:

Leaving the necessary officials [in Andahuaylas], the Inca went on to conquer another province called Ura[n]marca, also peopled by Chancas. . . . The Inca then passed to the province and tribe called Hancohuallu and Villca, which the Spaniards called Vilcas . . . These tribes, also Chancas, were masters of other provinces which they had conquered by force of arms. . . . From Villca, the Inca bore to the left, or westwards towards the seacoast, reaching one of two very large provinces, both bearing the same name, Sulla, though they are distinguished [from each other] by one of

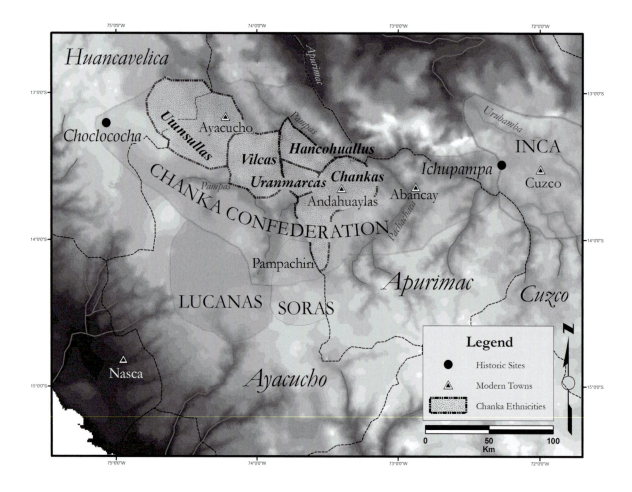

FIGURE 2.1. The area associated with the Chanka Confederation as described by Garcilaso de la Vega (1966: 218–220 [1609: Pt. 1, Bk. 4, Ch. 15]).

them being called Utunsulla. These two provinces include many tribes of various names, some numerous, others scanty, which, to avoid prolixity, I shall not enumerate. . . . In the last two provinces conquered by the Inca, Sulla and Utunsulla, mines of silver and quicksilver were discovered some thirty-two years ago. They are very rich and the latter are of great value in founding the silver.[1] (Garcilaso de la Vega 1966: 219–220 [1609: Pt. 1, Bk. 5, Ch. 15])

The locations of some of these groups are well known, others are not. Uranmarca is situated immediately west of Andahuaylas near the Pampas River, while Vilcashuamán is located farther west in the Department of Ayacucho (Garcilaso de la Vega 1966: 220 [1609: Pt. 1, Bk. 4, Ch. 15]). The Sulla and the Utunsulla were situated between modern-day Ayacucho and Huancavelica, a region long associated with both silver and mercury mines. The area of the Hancohuallu has not been clearly identified; however, we currently believe that they may have been located in the agriculturally rich region of Chincheros, immediately north of Uranmarca and to the northwest of Andahuaylas.

Garcilaso de la Vega (1966: 282 [1609: Pt. 1, Bk. 5, Ch. 15]) also suggests that generations after Inca Roca's rule, these same groups (Chanka, Uranmarca, Hancohuallu, Villca, Sulla, and Utunsulla) joined together to stage an attack on Cuzco. While this combined force is frequently referred to by modern scholars as the "Chanka Confederation," the information contained in the classic chronicles concerning the social composition of this confederation is so ambiguous that no one clearly understands how it was organized, or whether it even existed. Lumbreras (1974a: 198) aptly sums up the general state of uncertainty: "It is not known whether these warriors belonged to a single political organization or whether they represented a confederation of small groups that joined forces for warfare, nor is there concrete information on the territory they inhabited or whether all or a major portion of the 'province' of the Central highlands belonged the 'Chanka alliance'." It should also be noted that there is no

clear understanding of how long this confederation might have lasted. Some archaeologists suggest that it endured at least several generations and formed the basis for a broad regional "culture group" (González Carré (1979, 1982, 1992a; González Carré et al. 1987; González Carré, Pozzi-Escot, and Vivanco 1988). Alternatively, it could have lasted very briefly, perhaps only a few years. Or more intriguing, it may have never really existed: the historic portrayal of a Chanka menace may have been largely an invention of the Incas used to justify their own imperial expansion.

The Current Use of the Term "Chanka"

Despite the ambiguity of the colonial documents concerning the composition and longevity of the Chanka Confederation, there is a long history of scholars trying to define its territorial area and to identify its archaeological remains. Among the first modern attempts to explicitly define the territory of the Chanka and their allies were those made by Clements R. Markham (1871, 1923) and Alberto Arco Parró (1923). Both of these authors focused on the Ayacucho region as the original homeland of the Chanka and suggested that this ethnic group was somehow related to the immense site of Wari. Soon afterward, Navarro del Águila (1939) reached a similar conclusion and helped to promote the idea that several ethnic groups of the greater Ayacucho region banded together to form a Chanka Confederation (also see Barreda Murillo 1991, 1995). The most influential work defining the area of the Chanka Confederation was, however, written by Luis Lumbreras. In his seminal article "Sobre los Chancas," Lumbreras (1959) attempted to address the growing misconceptions, suggesting that the Chanka were related to the Wari culture (AD 600–1000) of the Ayacucho region and correctly concluded that the Chanka were instead a post-Wari culture that thrived during what is now generally called the Late Intermediate Period (AD 1000–1400). He also correctly associated several archaeological features of the central highlands, including large hilltop settlements, clusters of circular structures, and above-ground burial chambers (*chullpas*), with the Late Intermediate Period. In later studies, Lumbreras (1974a, 1974b, 1978, 1999) expanded on these observations. Although he recognizes that the chroniclers firmly place the Chanka themselves within the Andahuaylas region, Lumbreras continues, like various authors both before and after him, to propose that a large area of the central Andes should be considered as having been within their cultural influence. He writes:

> The modern province of Andahuaylas is traditionally identified as Chanka territory, but historical references tend to define their area to include the extensive valley of the Río Pampas and the region west of the Apurímac. . . . Archaeological investigations undertaken by the universities of San Marcos in Lima and San Cristóbal de Huamanga in Ayacucho have made it possible to recognize a more or less homogenous culture over the Río Pampas Basin. (Lumbreras 1974a: 198)

Lumbreras's model was quickly accepted, and many archaeologists have taken the generalized term "Chanka" to refer to any archaeological remains in the departments of Apurimac, Ayacucho, or Huancavelica that date to the Late Intermediate Period. In other words, the term "Chanka" is now widely used to classify *all* Late Intermediate Period remains in the above-mentioned departments, even those found in territories known to have been occupied by other ethnic groups. This is why, for example, the Late Intermediate Period sites in the Province of Vilcashuamán are recorded as being "Chanka" even though that area is known to have been inhabited by the Vilcas ethnic group (Lumbreras 1959; González Carré and Pozzi-Escot 2002).

One of the most prolific researchers of the central highlands, who has concentrated on studying the archaeological remains of the Late Intermediate Period, is Enrique González Carré (1979, 1982, 1992a). Working with various colleagues, González Carré has identified hundreds of different Late Intermediate Period sites across the central highlands (González Carré, Pozzi-Escot, and Vivanco 1988) and defined the various ceramic styles, stone tools, and architectural fea-

tures associated with them (González Carré et al. 1987). This research has done much to help promote the central highlands as an archaeologically and historically defined culture area. González Carré writes:

> The information provided by the documents, as well as by the archaeological evidence, leads us to conclude that when we talk about the Chanka nation and who it included, we are dealing with various groups which had similar material cultures, and who shared the control and occupation of a particular territory; [they also] probably shared a common language and a series of culturally particular features and characteristics.[2] (González Carré 1992a: 87) (translation by the authors)

It is important to note, however, that many of the archaeological features used to define the Chanka culture area (hilltop occupations, groups of circular buildings, and chullpas) are now known to extend well beyond the central highlands, and can be found across much of the Andes (see Parsons and Hastings 1988; Arkush 2006; Covey 2008). Our research in the Andahuaylas region indicates that the overuse of a single ethnic group's name to classify all archaeological remains dating to the Late Intermediate Period in three vast departments has served to perpetuate an inaccurate image of the Chanka as an emergent power of the central highlands of Peru prior to the Inca. More specifically, the widespread and generalized use of the term "Chanka" to include various groups that lived outside of the Andahuaylas region lends the impression that the central highlands was more politically unified during late prehistoric times than it actually was. Our brief reconnaissance work in both the Soras and Vilcashuamán regions, and our intensive research in the Andahuaylas region, indicate that each of these ethnic groups developed unique aspects of material culture, including different ceramic styles, and we found no archaeological evidence of political unification between them. The generalized use of the term also belies the numerous hilltop fortifications that were constructed across the region, as well as documents suggesting that active raiding occurred between different groups (Monzón 1965: 222 [1586]). Some researchers have gone so far as to imply that the Chanka were a unified political entity—almost state-like—which controlled a vast territorial area, even though there is no archaeological evidence to support such claims.

The use of "Chanka" as an umbrella term for Late Intermediate Period archaeological remains in the central Andes is distracting. More specifically, it impedes researchers from developing detailed local chronologies and it provides a homogenizing lens through which the past of the central highlands is being reconstructed. It also ignores the simple fact that we know that the various groups living across the region saw themselves in many, if not most, contexts as distinct entities, with their own names, boundaries, leaders, traditions, shrines, and mythologies.

In short, clearer definitions and a more regionally specific use of terms are critical not just for a more complete understanding of the Chanka, but for more accurate reconstructions of the many other ethnic groups that occupied the highlands during late prehistoric times. Furthermore, there are substantial questions that cannot be addressed until we carefully define the Late Intermediate Period archaeological remains within the central Andes. For example, how socially and ethnically distinct were the people of the central highlands from one another? How politically unified or fragmented were the groups of the region? Was there a Chanka Confederation, and if so, how was it organized?

In this work, when we discuss the Chanka, we are referring to a select group of people who lived within what is now the Province of Andahuaylas during late prehistoric and early historic times. While the nature and composition (and even the existence) of the Chanka Confederation can be debated, the fact that the Chanka occupied the Andahuaylas region is indisputable, since it is independently recorded in over a dozen major chronicles and in hundreds of other colonial documents (Stern 1982; Julien 2002; Hyland and Amado González n.d.). These archival records not only establish beyond a doubt that the Andahuaylas region formed a socially and cultur-

ally distinct unit, but the documents also, as shown below, provide details on the distribution of Chanka settlements and on the internal social organization of this important ethnic group.

The Establishment of Encomiendas

To reconstruct the region that was once occupied by the Chanka, we must turn to a particular tool of Spanish colonization. Beginning in the time of Columbus, the Spanish crown gave the leaders of expeditions in the Americas control over a limited number of labor-service grants, called *encomiendas* (Lockhart 1968; Stern 1982; Puente Brunke 1992). These grants were used to reward service to the crown, usually in military affairs, and to encourage members of expeditions to settle in newly conquered regions. Through this system, different native groups were assigned to specific Spaniards, and in theory, a formal set of rights and obligations was established between the holder of the encomienda and the natives included within it. The Spaniard was to provide protection and religious instruction to the natives under his care, while the natives were to provide their newly assigned overseer with specific goods and tribute labor. From its very conception, however, the encomienda system was ripe for exploitation. Under the original tenets of the system, the land itself remained in the possession of the natives; however, the holders of the encomiendas were soon able to establish large estates in their natives' territories, and the Spaniards gradually became de facto controllers of both the people and the land. The earliest encomiendas helped to establish a feudal-like system in the Andes, and some encomienda holders grew so powerful that they began to question the crown's authority to govern the region.

Diego Maldonado and the Andahuaylas Encomienda

Soon after establishing his control over Cuzco (1534), Francisco Pizarro began to divide the Inca Empire into a series of encomiendas.[3] Even the smaller encomiendas generally consisted of whole villages and their associated lands, while the larger ones included the territories of entire ethnic groups. On April 15, 1539, the region of the Chanka of Andahuaylas, along with a nearby village called Vilcaparo[4] and a number of other smaller holdings, were granted as an encomienda to Diego Maldonado.[5] Around this same time, Pizarro also granted the territories of various other ethnic groups to other members of his army. For example, the Soras, who occupied the region south of Andahuaylas near the modern towns of Soras and Pampachiri, were given to Melcher Palomino, who, like Maldonado, had been with Pizarro in Cajamarca (Toledo 1975: 260–261 [1570–1575]; Lockhart 1972: 339–341). Sometime later, the remote area of Ongoy, located to the north of Andahuaylas, was granted to Garci Núñez de Castañeda (Toledo 1975: 281 [1570–1575]).[6] However, it is widely noted that the Andahuaylas encomienda was one of the most important of the early grants.

Through extraordinary luck, the original 1539 *Andahuaylas Encomienda Document* has been preserved within the General Archive of the Indies in Seville (Julien 2002; AGI, Patronato 93, No. 11, Ramo 2, ff. 186v–188v). The document is especially important for our study since it includes a list of 63 villages that were included within Maldonado's Andahuaylas encomienda, as well as the names of each of the community leaders. In a few cases, cryptic information on the ethnic identity (for example, Chachapoya, Inca, Quichuas, Yauyo) or political status (for example, Orejon, Tucuyrico) of the local leader is also noted in the document. This unprecedentedly detailed list of Chanka towns can be used to establish the geographical area that was associated with the Chanka at the time of the Spanish invasion.

The first attempt to define the territorial limits of the Chanka using the 1539 *Andahuaylas Encomienda Document* was conducted by Catherine Julien (2002). By examining toponyms provided on modern maps of the region, she was able to suggest locations for some 15 (24%) of the 63 villages that were included in the territory in 1539. Through our archaeological survey work in the Andahuaylas region and our readings of additional archival documents and maps, we are able to expand this list and to suggest some 30 (48%) former village locations.[7] We have also been able to find archival references to 10 (16%) additional

villages; however, their precise locations in the countryside have yet to be determined (Table 2.1). Several of the villages listed in the 1539 *Andahuaylas Encomienda Document* fell within our research region, and their locations have been confirmed through our archaeological survey. However, many of the suggested village locations are situated outside of our research area and remain to be visited. Nevertheless, a plotting of the proposed settlement locations indicates that the original Chanka encomienda granted to Maldonado included most of the area currently found within the modern provinces of Andahuaylas and Chincheros (Figure 2.2). Most importantly, the plotting of these villages provides us with a clear idea of the region that the Inca, and most likely the Chanka themselves, considered to fall within the territory of the Chanka.

Pedro de la Gasca and the Establishment of Additional Encomiendas in the Andahuaylas Region (1547–1548)

The power and wealth of certain encomienda holders dramatically increased over time, as they relentlessly pressed labor demands on their indigenous populations (Lockhart 1968; Stern 1982; Puente Brunke 1992). In 1542, worried about retaining political control over his newly conquered territories in the Americas and inspired by Bartolomé de Las Casas's pleas to reform the abusive encomienda system, King Charles V of Spain instituted what are generally called the New Laws. This stunning set of regulations required a detailed reassessment of the tributary demands placed on natives by the *encomenderos* and for the holdings to be given to the crown on the death of the present owner. Angered by these new regulations, many Spaniards in Peru revolted against the king, and Gonzalo Pizarro, the half-brother of Francisco Pizarro, emerged as the leader of the rebel forces. The ensuing civil war resulted in the death of the newly appointed viceroy, Blasco Núñez Vela (1546), the very individual that the king had sent to the Andes to implement the New Laws.

Shocked and politically weakened by the largely unforeseen consequences of his encomienda reform legislation, King Charles V suspended

Table 2.1. Possible identifications of Chanka communities listed in the 1539 *Andahuaylas Encomienda Document* [*]

NAME OF TOWN IN 1539	POSSIBLE MODERN IDENTIFICATION	NAME OF TOWN IN 1539	POSSIBLE MODERN IDENTIFICATION
Alcaracay		Lachi	Cachi
Andaquechua	Anda Quechua (near Talavera)[1]	Laracalla	
Andasco	Antasgo	Layoguacho	Cataguacho[5]
Aychica		Llamay	Lamaypampa
Aymaras	Aymara (near San Jerónimo)[2]	Loroya	
Aymayba		Magusycamalca	
Banbamalca	Pampamarca	Mayomarca	Mayomarca[6]
Bilcabanba	Vilcabamba[3]	Ococho	Ojocha
Capacalla	Capac Calla	Omamarca	Umamarca
Capaçalla	Capaccalla	Ongoro	Ongoy
Caquesamarca		Opabacho	Oponguanche[7]
Chabibanba		Orcomalca	Urconmarca
Chacana		Pacocha	Pacucha
Chiara	Chiara	Paracaya	Parocay[8]
Chilaçeni		Pocollo	Pucuyo
Chua		Pomachaca	Pumachaca
Chuayapo		Pomaguacho	
Chuchunbe		Pupuca	Pupusa (near Cayara)
Chunbihallanga		Queca	Quecapata[9]
Chuquibanba		Quenoabilca	
Chuquisguayo	Chuspiguacho (near Talavera)[4]	Quevilla	
Cocas	Cocas	Sillusque	Silcahue
Cochabamba	Jochapampa	Suya	
Cocpalla	Japllac	Tiquillo	Tecllo
Cola	Cula	Tolpo	Turpo
Gualguayo	Huallhuayoc	Tororo	Toruro[10]
Guamanilla	Huamanilla	Vilcaporo	Vilcaporo (near Andarapa)[11]
Guarillane		Yanama	Yanama
Guataray	Huancaray	Yanapasco	
Guayaconi		Yatubi	
Guayana	Huayana	Yslana	Isjaña
Lacacha	Ccaccacha		

Continued on next page

[*] AGI, Patronato 93, No. 11, Ramo 2.

Table 2.1, Notes

[1] The modern location is unknown. Anda Quechua is listed as an *ayllu* of Talavera in 1684 (ADC, Corregimiento de Andahuaylas, Leg. 2 [1680–1699]).

[2] The modern location is unknown. There was an Aymara Orcco (Aymara Hill) near Talavera (ADC, Corregimiento de Andahuaylas, Leg. 6 [1750–1763]) and a field called Aymarapata near San Jerónimo (ADC, Notariales de Andahaaylas del siglo XVIII, Leg. 3 [1700–1820], Escritura publica de José Gabriel Pacheco [1786–1796]).

[3] The modern location is unknown. A place called Vilcabamba in the region of Huancarama is mentioned in a 1713 document (ADC, Corregimiento de Andaguaylas, Leg. 3 [1701–1729]). The vast area to the north of Andahuaylas is also known as Vilcabamba.

[4] The modern location is unknown. A place called Chuspiguacho is mentioned in various documents (e.g., ADC, Notarial de Andahuaylas del siglo XVIII, Protocolo 1, Cuaderno de escrituras publicas de Joseph Antonio Castro [1742–1744]; ADC, Corregimiento Andahuaylas, Leg. 5 [1745–1749]).

[5] There are two possible locations for this village. Toledo (1975: 207 [1572]) indicates that Curamba was also known as Cataguacho, and the Inca site of Sondor was also known as Cotahuacho.

[6] The modern location is unknown. An area called Mayomarca is mentioned several times as an area of coca production in an early document of the region (AGN, Derecho Indígena, Leg. 3, Cuaderno 17 [1568–1573]). Also see Stern (1982: 31).

[7] The modern location is unknown. A town call Oponguanche is mentioned in Vaca de Castro (1908 [1543]).

[8] The modern location is unknown. A place called Parocay is mentioned in the 1568 will of Diego Condor Guacho (ADC, Notariales de Andahauyalas, Escritura publica de Antonio Sánchez, Protocolo 1.)

[9] The modern location is unknown. A reference to a place called Quecapata has been found (ADC, Notarial de Andahuaylas del siglo XVIII, Leg. 3 [1700–1820], Registro de Pedro Julio Ojedo, Venta de Tierras).

[10] The modern location is unknown. The holdings of Hacienda of Toruro are described as being within the district of Ongoy (ADC, Notarial de Andahuaylas del siglo XVIII, Leg. 3 [1700–1820], Registro de Gregorio Antonio Pacheco [1786–1795]).

[11] Vilcaporo is listed as an *ayllu* of Andarapa in several documents (ADC, Corregimiento de Andahuaylas, Leg. 2 [1680–1699], Patrón de Indios tributarios de los indios de Andahuaylas; ADC, Corregimiento de Andahuaylas, Leg. 4 [1730–1744]). This community is also listed within Vaca de Castro (1908 [1543]). A settlement called Huicapuris is mentioned in documents as late as 1852 (ADC, Notarial de Andahuaylas del siglo XIX, Protocolo 7 [1869–1919], Registro de Hilario Cusihuaman).

---

many of the New Laws and sent Pedro de la Gasca to Peru, as the first President of the Audiencia of Peru,[8] to restore order and the rule of Castile. By 1547 La Gasca had landed in Peru, converted many previous rebels to his cause, and was marching toward Cuzco. During this long journey, he crossed into the region of the Chanka, and after a minor battle, La Gasca decided to wait for reinforcements and to spend the rainy season of 1547–1548 in Andahuaylas.[9] Agustín de Zárate describes the condition of La Gasca's troops during their time in Andahuaylas:

> And so they continued their march, suffering great shortages of food, till they reached Andaguairas [Andahuaylas], where the President stayed for a large part of the winter. All that time there was much heavy rain. Indeed it never stopped by day or night, and all the tents rotted since there was no opportunity of drying them. The maize they ate was soft with the damp, and many fell sick of dysentery. Some indeed died of it. The President was very solicitous for the nursing of the sick, which he entrusted to Fray Francisco de la Rocha of the Trinitarian order. There were more than four hundred sick, and they were as well provided with doctors and medicaments as if they had been in a healthy, populous and well supplied place. Thanks to this almost all recovered.[10] (Zárate 1981: 251 [1555: Bk. 7, Ch. 5])

Traveling with La Gasca was a cavalryman named Pedro de Cieza de León, who would become one of Peru's best-known early colonial writers. During his months in Andahuaylas, Cieza de León conducted several interviews with a man

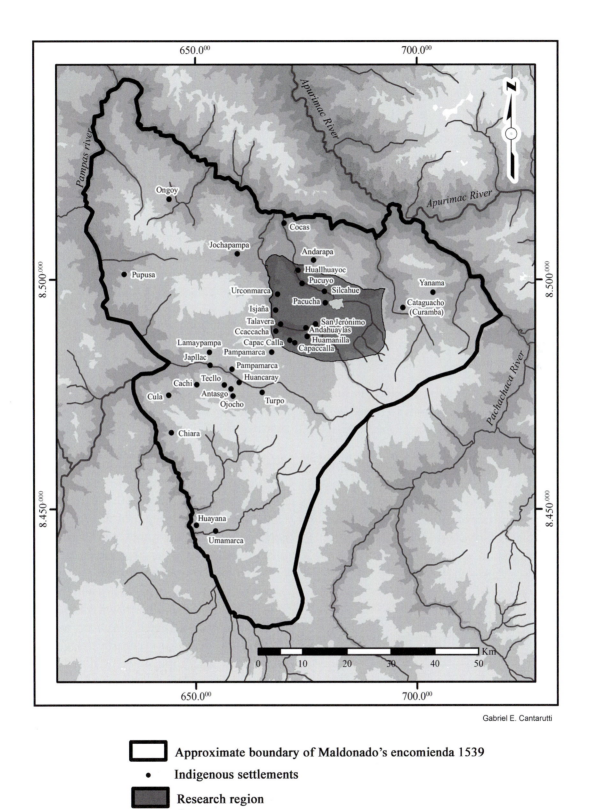

Gabriel E. Cantarutti

☐ **Approximate boundary of Maldonado's encomienda 1539**

● **Indigenous settlements**

■ **Research region**

FIGURE 2.2. The approximate area of the Andahuaylas (Chanka) encomienda granted to Diego Maldonado in 1539.

named Guasco,[11] the leader of the Chanka.[12] Among other things, Cieza de León noted the important role that Guasco played in helping La Gasca's troops recover from their sicknesses and injuries:

> We spent many days there [in Andahuaylas] with President La Gasca when he set out to put down the rebellion of Gonzalo Pizarro, and these Indians suffered much from the importunity of the Spaniards, and were of great service to them. That good Indian, the lord of this valley, Huasco, handled the matter of provisions with great care.[13] (Cieza de León 1976: 132–133 [1553: Pt. 1, Ch. 90])

Cieza de León was impressed with both the region of Andahuaylas and its people and was especially drawn to the legendary accounts of the Chanka-Inca War:

> When I first came to this province, its lord was an Indian chieftain called Huasco and the natives were known as Chancas. They went clothed in blankets and shirts of wool. In times gone by they were so brave, it is said, that they not only won lands and domains, but were so strong that they besieged the city of Cuzco and great battles were fought between them and those of the city, until in the end the bravery of [Pachacuti] Inca Yupanqui defeated them.[14] (Cieza de León 1976: 130 [1553: Pt. 1, Ch. 90])

Cieza de León also noted a few of the customs of the Chanka as well as the rich agricultural setting of the valley:

> Their burials were like those of others, and Fthey believed in the immortality of the soul, which they call *xongo*, which is also the word for heart. They buried with their lords living women and treasure and clothing. They had set days, and probably still have, to celebrate their feasts, and places to hold their dances. As there have been priests in this province uninterruptedly, teaching the Indians, some of them have become Christians, especially the younger ones. Captain Diego Maldonado has always held an *encomienda* over them. They all wear their hair long and finely plaited, tied with woolen strings that fall below their chins.[15] Their houses are of stone. In the center of the province there were great lodgings and storehouses for the rulers. In olden times there were many Indians in this province of Andahuaylas, but the wars have reduced their numbers as in the rest of this kingdom. It is very long, and there are quantities of domestic flocks, and the wild ones are innumerable. It is well supplied with food and wheat is raised, and in the warm valleys there are many fruit trees.[16] (Cieza de León 1976: 132 [1553: Pt. 1, Ch. 90])

At the end of the rainy season (April 1548), Cieza de León and the rest of La Gasca's men left Andahuaylas and advanced toward Cuzco. A short time later, they defeated Gonzalo Pizarro on the great plain of Jaquijahuana west of Cuzco, the same plain where it is believed that the Inca had defeated the Chanka a century earlier. With the subsequent execution of Gonzalo Pizarro, the rebellion was quelled.

Once the king's rule was reestablished, La Gasca ordered inspections of all the encomiendas of Peru, and a new system of divisions, called *repartimientos* (new divisions), was begun. During this process, some of the largest encomiendas were reduced and those of rebels were seized outright. Many of the newly created divisions were then granted to loyalists of the crown. Although Diego Maldonado had attempted to remain neutral during the civil war, he was eventually dragged into the conflict, and after some missteps, declared his loyalty to the king. Perhaps because of his initial hesitation to take sides, it appears that Maldonado's immense holdings were reduced by La Gasca in 1548. Maldonado was able to retain control of the central and highly populated Andahuaylas Valley; however, the eastern area of Curamba, with its large community of Huancarama, was granted to Alonso de Alva. The regions to the north and west, including the communities of Uripa and Ocobamba, were granted to Martín de Lezaña and Pero Ortiz, respectively (Figure 2.3). The smallest repartimiento of the region, called Cayara, which included the communities of Cocharcas and Uranmarca, was given to the crown (Toledo 1975: 275, 281, 282 [1570–1575]).[17]

Francisco Hernández Girón and the Chanka
The capture and execution of Gonzalo Pizarro (1548) did not bring a lasting peace to the turbulent situation in Peru. Tension over the modified New Laws continued, and new revolts against the king again broke out in 1553. This time the rebels were led by Francisco Hernández Girón. In May of 1554, one of the major battles of this revolt was fought south of Andahuaylas on the plain of Chuquinca, near the village of Chalhuanca. Once

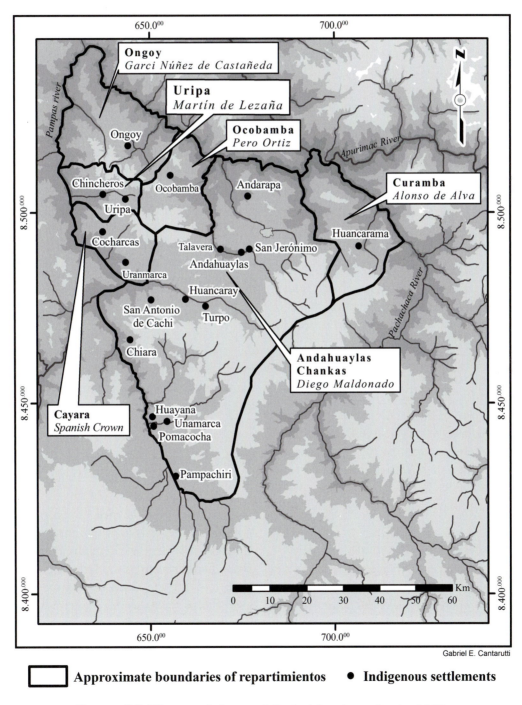

Approximate boundaries of repartimientos   ● **Indigenous settlements**

FIGURE 2.3. The repartimientos of the Andahuaylas region (ca. 1548).

more the Chanka were drawn into a Spanish civil war, fighting on the side of the Spanish crown.

The famed indigenous writer Guaman Poma de Ayala suggests that his father, Martín Guaman Malque de Ayala, held a major role in the battle of Chuquinca, leading the indigenous forces against Hernández Girón. Guaman Poma de Ayala also indicates that the two leaders of the Chanka fought beside his father in service of the king. According to Guaman Poma de Ayala, the leader of the Hanan Chanka (Upper Chanka) was named León Apo [G]uasco (sic Diego Guasco).[18] This was most likely the same man whom Cieza de León had interviewed six years before and was simply called Guasco. Guaman Poma de Ayala (1980: 401 [1615:432(434)]) also indicates that the leader of the Hurin Chanka (Lower Chanka) was named Juan Guaman Guachaca.[19]

Even more remarkable for the context of this study is that Guaman Poma de Ayala provides a drawing of the battle (Figure 2.4). In this drawing he shows the indigenous forces being led by his own father, who wears a decorated tunic. Behind him are the leaders of the Hanan and Hurin Chanka, Lord Guasco and Guaman Guachaca. To the right, Francisco Hernández Girón and his men are shown fleeing the battle on horseback.[20]

Although Hernández Girón's forces suffered badly, he emerged victorious from this battle, and for a brief period his rebels traveled with impunity across the central highlands. Hernández Girón was captured later that year (1554) near Ayacucho, but not before he had exacted revenge on the Chanka. Garcilaso de la Vega tells of the destruction that Hernández Girón brought to the Andahuaylas region following his victory at the battle of Chuquinca:

> Francisco Hernández Girón, whom we left on the battlefield at Chuquinca, stayed there a month and a half, delayed by the large number of wounded men he had taken from the marshal. At the end of this long period he traveled with them as best he could to the valley of Antihuailla [i.e., Andahuaylas]. He had been very angry with the Indians of the Chancas, who had harassed him in the battle of Chuquinca by boldly fighting his

army and discharging showers of stones from their slings, which sufficed to crack the skulls of some of his men. As soon as he got to these parts he therefore ordered his soldiers, black and white alike, to sack and burn the Indian villages and lay waste the fields and do all the harm they could.[21] (Garcilaso de la Vega 1966: 1382 [1609: Pt. 2, Bk. 7, Ch. 21])

Documents from Andahuaylas also record some of the damage that Hernández Girón brought upon the region. Most importantly, it is noted that some buildings owned by Maldonado near the town of Talavera were burned and that cattle were stolen from his holdings (AGN, Derecho Indígena, Leg. 3, Cuaderno 17).

Although the crown eventually won the wars of resistance over the New Laws, the king's rule in the colonies had been sorely tested. While the newly established repartimientos were meant to be more humane and Indian labor service was to be more strictly supervised by the crown, native groups continued to be controlled by Spanish landlords with little oversight. In the end, the native groups frequently found themselves having to pay tribute obligations to both the holder of the repartimientos as well as to the crown. In the case of the Chanka, their greatest labor obligation was to provide men to work in the dreaded Huancavelica mercury mines. The difficulty of fulfilling this exacting labor obligation was made even more overwhelming in the wake of dramatic population declines throughout the seventeenth and eighteenth centuries (Stern 1982; Hyland and Amado González n.d.).

Despite the turbulence of the times, Diego Maldonado was able to maintain control of the Andahuaylas region throughout his lifetime (Busto Duthurburu 1963; Hemming 1970). At his death in 1570, the estate passed to his Spanish-born widow, Francisca de Guzmán. Because Maldonado and Guzmán had produced no children, Juan Arias Maldonado, his son by an indigenous woman of noble Inca birth, helped to run the estate.[22] With the death of Francisca de Guzmán in 1579, the repartimiento of Andahuaylas was declared vacant and reverted to crown control

FIGURE 2.4. The battle of Chuquinca by Guaman Poma de Ayala. The title of the figure reads: "Conquest. The battle fought in service of your Majesty [by] the most excellent knight, Royal Lord, Don Martín de Ayala, father of the author, [lord of] Chinchaysuyo, and Guasco [and] Guaman [G]uachaca, Lords of the Hanan [and] Hurin Chancas, with one hundred soldiers and Francisco Hernández [with] three hundred soldiers. He was defeated but he escaped" (Guaman Poma de Ayala 1980: 400 [1615: 432 (434)]). *Courtesy of Det Kongelige Bibliotek.*

(Toledo 1975: 115 [1570–1575]). Although the holdings had been diminished by the actions of Pedro de la Gasca, the repartimiento was still substantial, and it remained a royal hacienda well into the Colonial Period.

Moiety Organization of the Chanka

In Guaman Poma de Ayala's description of the battle of Chuquinca, he clearly states that the Chanka were divided into two groups (Hanan Chanka and Hurin Chanka), each of which was led by a different individual. In this way, the Chanka were not unusual. In fact, most central Andean ethnic groups divided themselves into two groups, or what anthropologists call "moieties." This is to say, that they functioned under systems of dual social organization, where the community or polity as a whole was divided into two equal, but opposing descent groups (Turner 1984; Moore 1995). In the Quechua-speaking sectors of the Andes, these pairs were most frequently called the Hanansaya (upper division) and the Hurinsaya (lower division). For example, the chronicler Cobo writes:

> The Incas made the same division throughout all of their kingdom that they had made in dividing Cusco into Hanan Cusco and Hurin Cusco. Thus they divided each town and cacicazgo into two parts, known as the upper district and the lower district, or the superior part or faction and the inferior; and even though these names denote inequality between these two groups, nevertheless, there was none, except for this preeminence and advantage, which was that the group of hanansaya got preference in seating and place over those of hurinsaya; this is the same thing done at court, where some cities precede others in place and in speaking first. In everything else they were equal, and the hurinsaya people were considered to be as good as the hanansaya people.[23] (Cobo 1979: 195 [1653: Bk. 12, Ch. 24])

The two moieties were represented by two different authorities, or *curacas* (also called *caciques*[24]

by the Spaniards). As noted above by Cobo, while the two leaders held similar political positions, the leader of the upper moiety carried more prestige than did his counterpart. Below each of the moiety leaders, a series of subordinate authorities represented the lesser levels or divisions within each half. The exact number of these lower authorities depended on the internal complexity of the moieties.

Because the moiety pairs were considered to be ranked, with the Hanan authority holding more stature than the Hurin, the leader of the upper moiety at times spoke for the group as a whole. Across the Andes, the more expansive weight of the Hanan authority is reflected in the fact that the leader of the upper part was frequently referred to by the Spaniards as the *cacique principal* (principal leader), while the leader of the lower part was commonly called the *segunda persona* (second person).[25] We know that this structural imbalance of social prestige between the moieties existed within Chanka society, since many early colonial documents refer to the leader of the upper moiety as the leader of all the Chanka, while at the same time noting that another, presumably slightly lesser-ranked, individual was the leader of the lower moiety.[26] For example, in a 1604 inspection document, León Apo Guasco, the leader of the Hanan Chanka, is referred to as the cacique principal, and Tomay Guaraca, the leader of the Hurin Chanka, is described as the segunda persona (AGN, Derecho Indígena, Leg. 3, Cuaderno 50).[27] Competition among families in the Andahuaylas region to control these prestigious positions remained high throughout the Colonial Period (Hyland and Amado González n.d.), and we can presume that it was even greater in the prehistoric past when these leaders may have held even greater political authority over their populace.

THE MYTHICAL ORIGIN OF THE CHANKA MOIETIES

Most groups in the Andes traced the origins of their dual social system back in time to the primordial actions of two mythical individuals who were thought to be the founders of the separate divisions. The mythical founders of the moieties were frequently believed to have been two siblings, most commonly an older brother (founding the upper moiety) and younger brother (founding the lower moiety). True to this cultural tradition, the Chanka believed that their moiety system had been established by a pair of brothers. The older of these two mythical founders was named Uscovilca, and he is said to have established the upper division, whereas the younger was named Ancovilca, and he was believed to have been responsible for the lower division.[28] These brothers are said to have arrived together in Andahuaylas and founded the first Chanka settlements. Sarmiento de Gamboa provides the most detailed retelling of the Chanka moiety origin myth:

> Thirty leagues to the west of Cuzco is a province called Andahuaylas, whose natives are called Chancas. In this province there were two *cinchis*, named Uscovilca and Ancovilca, [who were] thieves and cruel tyrants. They came pillaging with certain bands of thieves from the area of Guamanga. They had come to settle in the Andahuaylas Valley and had formed two groups there. They were brothers, and Uscovilca, who was the eldest and most important, founded one of the groups and called it Hanan Chancas, which means "the upper Chancas." Ancovilca formed the other group and named it Hurin Chanca, which means "the lower Chancas." [29] (Sarmiento de Gamboa 2007: 104–105 [1572: Ch. 26])

Although the founding of the moieties took place in the mythical past, the Chanka had highly venerated statues of Uscovilca and Ancovilca.[30] These idols were kept and worshiped in their own separate temples in the Andahuaylas region; at times of war, however, they could also be carried into battle by members of their separate moieties. These totems played such dominant roles in battles, and so fully represented their respective moieties, that colonial writers occasionally use the names of the idols in references to the actions of the moiety leaders (for example, Betanzos 1996: 30

[1557: Pt. 1, Chs. 6–30]). While unquestionably inspirational, the use of the idols in battles did present certain risks. Sarmiento de Gamboa records the capture of the moiety statues by enemy forces during the climax of the Chanka-Inca War:

> Inca Yupanqui was so swift and skilled in his attack that those who carried the statue of Uscovilca were alarmed by his speed and prowess. The Chancas started to flee, leaving the statue of Uscovilca, and they say even that of Ancovilca, because they saw a large number of people come down from the sides of the hills. (Sarmiento de Gamboa 2007: 109 [1572: Ch. 27])

We can also presume that, besides being used in warfare, the Uscovilca and Ancovilca idols held important roles within the ritual festivals that took place in the Andahuaylas region. Like many other shrines of the Andes, these sacred objects most likely also had lands and servants assigned to them for the maintenance of their cults.

The Andean tradition of shrine worship continued well into the Colonial Period, and it became the focus of several, large-scale, anti-idolatry campaigns. Spanish priests waged a prolonged war against the idols and ancestral mummies of the Andes in the mid- to late 1500s. During one of the best-known campaigns (1569–1571), led by Cristóbal de Albornoz, tens of thousands of Andean shrines and mummies were destroyed. Albornoz personally visited the Andahuaylas area (Millones 1990: 180) and reports destroying more than 2,000 shrines in that region alone. In his account, Albornoz specifically records the names of three of the most important shrines of the Chanka. The first two of these were named Uscovilca and Ancovilca.[32] Albornoz (1984: 207 [1582]) writes:

> Uscovilca is a shrine of the [H]anan Chankas. It is a dressed rock in the shape of an Indian. It had a house in the town of Andahuaylas. Ancovilca was a shrine of the Hurin Chankas. It was a stone that they carried with them wherever they went and it had a house.[33] (translation by the authors)

Table 2.2
Population of Hanan and Hurin Chankas

	Tribute Payers	Older Males	Young Males	All Females	Total
Hanan	3,201 (60%)	1,366 (56%)	3,852 (62%)	8,669 (58%)	17,088 (59%)
Hurin	2,109 (40%)	1,062 (44%)	2,410 (38%)	6,142 (41%)	11,723 (41%)
Total	5,330 [5,310]	2,428	6,271 [6,262]	14,811	28,840 [28,811]

Source: Toledo 1975: 115–116 [1570–1575].   Note: Square brackets indicate actual total.

Thus, Albornoz not only confirms the names of the mythical ancestors of the Chanka moieties, but indicates that they continued to be worshiped in their own temples in Andahuaylas long after the establishment of the encomiendas.

Reconstructing the Moieties of the Chanka

Although researchers have suspected that the Chanka functioned under a system of dual social organization, few have attempted to understand the internal composition of the moieties.[34] Published colonial censuses and archival documents recovered during the course of our project can provide some insights into the particular composition of the Hanan and Hurin divisions of the Chanka. For instance, the earliest known census of the Chanka dates to the mid-1570s and lists a total of 28,830 individuals (Toledo 1975: 115–116 [1570–1575]). The census is divided into Hanan and Hurin Chankas and is further subdivided into different classes of individuals, including tax-paying adult males, older men, boys, and all females (Table 2.2). Within each of these classifications, we find that the population ratio of Hanan Chanka and Hurin Chanka is about 60% versus 40%, respectively. Such population imbalances between moieties are not uncommon and can be found in other colonial records as well (for example, Diez de San Miguel 1964 [1567]).

A combination of dramatic post-European contact events makes the physical reconstruction of prehispanic Andean moieties on the landscape difficult.[35] It is well known that indigenous population levels dramatically declined in the wake of the various European diseases that swept through the Americas at the time of contact (Cook 1998). So even before the first European census was taken, the general population level and the distribution of native settlements across South America had been inalterably changed (Cook 1981). A further shifting of local settlement patterns came with the establishment of the encomiendas, as natives struggled against the labor and tributary demands of the Spaniards. We know, for instance, that Juan Arias Maldonado, the son of Diego Maldonado, specifically states that his father resettled many villagers away from their settlements in the *puna* (highlands) and remote valleys, to the central valley of Andahuaylas, for better administrative control (AGN, Derecho Indígena, Leg. 3, Cuaderno 17).

An even larger and more systematic reconfiguration of the Andean social landscape occurred during the viceroyalty of Francisco de Toledo. Starting around 1571, in an effort to more efficiently extract tribute and to increase religious indoctrination, Viceroy Toledo began to implement a massive reorganization of the Andean demographic landscape. Under his direction, the Spaniards forced hundreds of thousands of local inhabitants to abandon their traditional settlements and to relocate into newly created towns, called *reducciones*.[36] At this time, some of the former settlements were destroyed to prevent reoccupation. Following specific Spanish conceptions of town organization, the reducciones were built with a central plaza, a town hall, and a church. Despite their European form, many of the reducciones were also divided into Hanan and Hurin sectors (Gade and Escobar M. 1982; Bauer 1987,

1992: 52–53). In the Andahuaylas region, the reduccion policies resulted in the creation of a series of central towns, all of which still function as district capitals today. For example, the central core of Andahuaylas, with its church, plaza, and public buildings, was built during this period. The other two towns of the valley, Talavera (to the west) and San Jerónimo (to the east), were most likely also reorganized at this time. Although European in layout, numerous local archival documents indicate that each of these communities was established with internal Hanan and Hurin divisions (Hyland and Amado González n.d.).

Archival documents also provide insights into the internal organization of the Hanan and Hurin divisions of the Andahuaylas region and show that the structural composition of the Chanka moieties was similar to that of many of their peers across the highlands. Andean moieties were conceptually seen as being made up of a number of separate kin groups, frequently called *ayllus*. Ideally, both the Hanan and the Hurin sides contained the same number of ayllus. Furthermore, each of the ayllus carried a certain rank within its respective moiety, based on its population and historic social position. Generally, the leader of the largest and most important ayllu of each moiety also served as the head of the moiety. Archival records indicate that the Chanka followed this same cultural tradition (Table 2.3). For example, a tribute list dating to the early 1570s indicates that the Hanan Chanka and the Hurin Chanka each contained five ayllus (AGN, Derecho Indígena, Leg. 3, Cuaderno 17). At that time, the most powerful ayllu of the upper moiety was Guasco Ayllu, and its leader, Francisco Condor Guacho, served as the head of the Hanan Chanka.[37] Similarly, the most powerful ayllu of the lower moiety was Guaracas Ayllu, and its leader, Luis Tomay Guaracas, served as the head of the Hurin Chanka.

Our next relatively complete tribute list dates to 1594. It reveals that a slightly more complex social arrangement of ayllus had developed in the intervening years (AGN, Derecho Indígena, Leg. 3, Cuaderno 50). The 1594 tribute list contains each of the "original" five Hanan and Hurin ayllus; however, the total number of ayllus included in each division had grown (Hyland and Amado González

TABLE 2.3. Moieties and Ayllus of the Chanka 1568, 1573, and 1594

1568[1]	
HANAN CHANKA	HURIN CHANKA
(Diego Condor Guacho: Cacique Principal)	
Malma	?
Guasca	?
Apras	?
Moros	?
Pachuacarua	?

1573[2]	
HANAN CHANKA	HURIN CHANKA
(Francisco Condor Guacho: Cacique Principal)	(Luis Tomay Guaracas: Segunda Persona)
Malma	Quichuas
Guasco	Guaracas
Apes	Guachaca
Moros	Caha
Pachacaruas	Yana (also called Yanec)

1594[3]	
HANAN CHANCA	HURIN CHANCA
(León Apo Guasco: Cacique Principal)	(Luis Tomay Guaraca: Segunda Persona)
Guasco	Guaraca
Macma	Guachaca
Moros	Yanac
Pachacarua	Cachacc
Abras	Marma
Inga	Achan Quichua
Churichayo	Bilca Poros
Yunga	

[1] ADC, Notariales de Andahauylas, Escritura publica de Antonio Sánchez, Protocolo. 17.
[2] AGN, Derecho Indígena, Leg. 3, Cuaderno 17.
[3] AGN, Derecho Indígena, Leg. 3, Cuaderno 50.

n.d.). In 1594, the Hanan Chanka, led by León Apo Guasco, the son of Francisco Condor Guacho, had increased to seven ayllus. The Hurin Chanka were still being led by Luis Tomay Guaracas, but their ayllu number had increased to six. We do not believe that this increase in the number of ayllus reflects a population growth in the region, since native populations in the central highlands were dramatically decreasing during this period (Stern 1982). Instead, it seems far more likely that the increased number of Hanan Chanka and Hurin Chanka ayllus reflects the collapse of other neighboring systems and the incorporation of their populations into the Andahuaylas tributary system.

While the population of the Andahuaylas region continued to be called the Hanan and Hurin

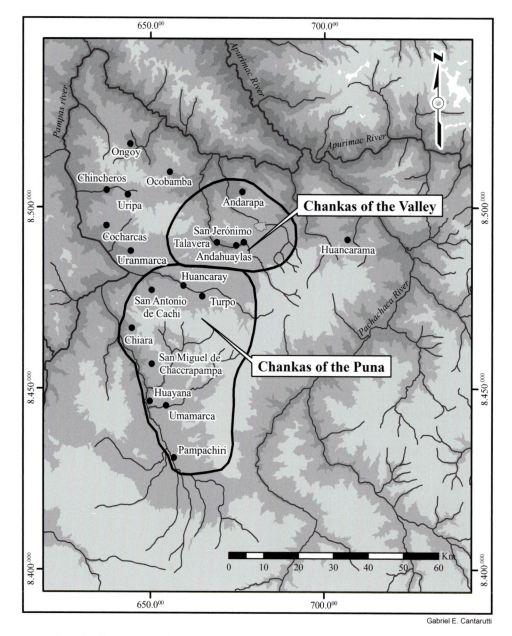

Gabriel E. Cantarutti

● **Indigenous settlements**

FIGURE 2.5. In the late 1600s, the southernmost Chanka were called "Chankas of the Puna" while the northern populations were called "Chankas of the Valley." It is currently not known if these divisions were newly introduced or were built on the older Hanan and Hurin divisions of Chanka.

Chanka well into the eighteenth century, beginning sometime in the mid- to late 1600s we also see the introduction of slightly different terms (ADC, Corregimiento de Andahuaylas, Leg. 1 [1626–1672]; ADC, Corregimiento de Andahuaylas, Leg. 2 [1680–1699], Visita de 1684; AGN, Superior Gobierno, Legajo 10, Cuaderno 210). The four southernmost districts, including Huancaray, Cachi, Huayana, and Pampachiri, begin to be collectively referred to as the *Chankas de la puna* (Chankas of the Puna]), while the northern districts are called *Chankas del valle* (Chankas of the Valley). It is currently not known if these divisions were newly introduced or were built on the older Hanan and Hurin moieties of region[38] (Figure 2.5).

Such a cultural and economic division between agriculturalists (*Huari*) and pastoralists (*Llacuaz*) in the central Andes during the seventeenth century has been discussed in detail by Duviols (1973). While it is not clear if the "Chankas of the Puna" and the "Chankas of the Valley" designations were built directly on the older moiety divisions of the region or introduced by the Spanish, it may have some relation to Duviols's (1973) herder/agriculturalist dichotomy. In fact, Parsons, Hastings, and Matos Mendieta (1997) have offered a convincing argument for the existence of distinct groups of pastoralists and agriculturalists in the Tarama/Chinchaycocha region during the Late Intermediate Period, as well as of their economic and ritual integration. While at present we cannot endorse a similar view of specialized Chanka pastoralists and agriculturalists in the Andahuaylas Valley, current survey and excavation data (Kellett 2008, 2010) support the notion that the Chanka were engaged in a broad range of agropastoral subsistence activities, which may have been dependent on local topography and the availability of suitable agricultural and/or pastoral land, as well as other critical resources.

SUMMARY

The goal of this chapter has been to provide an introduction to the physical location and the social organization of the Chanka at the time of European contact and to highlight some of the major events that occurred in the Andahuaylas region after the establishment of Spanish rule in the Andes. We have seen that there is ample evidence to suggest that the Andahuaylas region was the homeland of the Chanka and that this ethnic group was organized within a traditional regional moiety system. Furthermore, despite a series of reorganizational policies by the Spaniards, which included the encomiendas of the late 1530s, the repartimientos of the late 1540s, and the reducciones of the early 1570s, it is clear that the indigenous Hanan and Hurin divisions of the Chanka remained strong for at least a century into the Colonial Period. The full story of Andahuaylas and the Chanka begins, however, long before these events. To gain a more complete understanding of the Chanka, we must turn to the distant past and the arrival of the first hunters and gatherers to the central Andes.

NOTES

1 "El Inca, habiendo dejado los ministros necesarios, pasó adelante en su conquista a otra provincia que llaman Uramarca, que también es del apellido Chanca. . . . De allí pasó el Inca a la provincia y nación llamada Hancohuallu y Uillca, que los españoles llaman Vilcas, y con la misma pesadumbre se sujetaron a su imperio; porque estas naciones que también son chancas, eran señores de otras provincias que habían sujetado con las armas. . . . DeUillca [el Inca] torció el camino a mano izquierda al Poniente, que es hacia la costa de la mar, y llegó a una de dos provincias muy grandes, ambas de un mismo nombre, Sulla; aunque para diferenciar la una de la otra llámanla una de ellas Utunsulla. Estas dos provincias abrazaban entre sí muchas naciones de diversos nombres, unas de mucha gente y otras de pocas. . . . En las últimas dos provincias que conquistó este Inca llamadas Sulla y Utunsulla, se han descubierto de treinta dos años a esta parte algunas minas de plata y otras de azogue, que son riquísimas y de grande importancia para fundir el metal de plata" (Garcilaso de la Vega 1960 [vol. 1]: 135–136 [1609: Pt. 1, Bk. 4, Ch. 15]).

2 "Tanto la información que nos proporcionan los documentos, como la evidencia arqueológica, nos lleva a concluir que cuando hablamos de la nación Chanka y quienes la integraban, estamos ante un conjunto de grupos con similares condiciones de vida material, dominio y ocupación de un determinado territorio; con uso probablemente de una misma lengua y un

conjunto de rasgos y características que se expresan en la peculiaridad regional de su cultura" (González Carré 1992a: 87).

3 Pizarro's forces first passed through Andahuaylas on their way to Cuzco in early November 1533 (Sancho 1917: 78 [1534: Ch. 8]).

4 Vilcaparo was located near the modern community of Andarapa (ADC, Corregimiento de Andahuaylas: Leg. 2 [1680–1699], Padrón de Indios tributarios de los Indios de Andahuaylas [1684]).

5 Diego Maldonado was a principal member of Pizarro's expeditionary force and had been with Pizarro during the fateful events in Cajamarca. He had already been given a large lot on the central plaza of Cuzco (Bauer 2004) as well as several other tracts of land near Cuzco (La Lone 1985: 179).

6 It seems that the Ongoy area was granted to Núñez de Castañeda after 1539, since part of this encomienda appears to have been carved out of the territory originally controlled by Maldonado.

7 Some of the village names listed in the 1539 document are common Quechua toponyms and have more than one possible location.

8 Also known as the Viceroyalty of Peru.

9 Also see Fernández (1963: 219–233 [1571: Pt. 1, Bk. 2, Chs. 83–85]) for a detailed description of La Gasca's stay in Andahuaylas.

10 ". . . y assí continuaron su camino padeciendo gran necessidad de comida hasta llegar a Andaguaylas, donde el Presidente se detuuo mucha parte del inuierno, que fue de muchas y muy rezias aguas que de día ni de noche cessaua de llouer, tanto que los toldos se podrían por no auer lugar de enxugarse, y por estar el maíz que comían tierno. Con la mucha humidad adolecieron muchos y algunos murieron del fluxo del vientre, caso que el Presidente tenía especial cuydado de hazer curar los enfermos por medio de fray Francisco de la Rocha, frayle de la Orden de la Santíssima Trinidad, que tenía cargo y por copia más de quatrocientos dellos, y los proueya de médicos y medicinas como si estuuieran en vn lugar muy bueno y bien proueydo y poblado, y por su buena diligencia conualecieron casi todos" (Zárate 1995: 365 [1555: Bk. 7, Ch. 5]).

11 Betanzos (1996: 239 [1557: Pt. 2, Ch. 18]) indicates that the principal leader of the Chanka during the Inca civil war between Atahualpa and Huascar, which took place on the eve of the Spanish invasion, was a man named Guasco and that the Chanka sided with Huascar during that conflict. Although Huascar's army was defeated while defending Cuzco, Guasco survived the battle and was granted a pardon by Atahualpa's generals. It is likely that Guasco returned to Andahuaylas after the civil war, and it is certainly possible that this was the same Chanka leader interviewed by Cieza de León approximately 15 years later.

12 Although Cieza de León suggests that Guasco was the lord of all the Chanka, we can assume that Guasco was the head of the Hanan Chanka and was thus per-

ceived by the Spaniards as the spokesperson for both divisions.

13 "Aquí estuuimos muchos días con el presidente Gasca: quando yua a castigar la rebelión de Gonçalo Piçarro: y fue mucho lo que estos Indios passaron y siruieron con la importunidad de los Españoles. Y este buen indio señor deste valle Guasco entendía en este proveymiento con gran cuidado" (Cieza de León 1996: 255 [1553: Pt. 1, Ch. 90]).

14 "Quando yo entré en esta prouincia, era señor della vn Indio principal llamado Basco: y los naturales han por nombre Chancas. Andan vestidos con mantas y camisetas de lana. Fueron en los tiempos passdos tan valientes (a lo que se dize) estos, que no solamente ganaron tierras y señoríos más pudieren tanto, que tuuieron cercada la ciudad del Cuzco y se dieron grandes batallas entre los de la ciudad y ellos, hasta que por el valor de Inga Yupangue fueron vencidos" (Cieza de León 1996: 254 [1553: Pt.1, Ch. 90]).

15 Cobo, using information originally provided by Polo de Ondegardo, also describes the headwear of the Chanka, writing, "The Indians of Andaguaylas wrapped around their heads wool cords that came down under the chin" (Cobo 1979: 197 [1654: Bk. 12, Ch. 24]); "Los de Andaguaylas liaban la cabeza con unas cuerdas de la lana que les venían a caer por debajo de la barba" (Cobo 1964: 113 [1653: Bk. 12, Ch. 24]).

16 "Vusaron los entierros como los demás: y assí creyan la immortalidad del ánima, que ellos llaman Xongon que es también nombre de coraçon. Metían con los señores que enterrauan mugeres biuas, y algún thesoro, y ropa. Tenían sus días señalados, y aun deuen tener agora para solemnizar sus fiestas, y plaças hechas para sus bayles. Como en esta prouincia ha estado a la contina clérigo, industriando a los Indios, se han vuelto algunos dellos Christianos, especialmente de los moços. Ha tenido siempre sobre ella encomienda el capitán Diego Maldonado. Todos los más traen cabellos largos entrançados menudamente, puestos vnos cordones de lana que les viene a caer por debaxo de la barba. Las casas son de piedra. En el comedio de la prouincia auía grandes aposentos y depósitos para los señores. Antiguamente ouo muchos indios en esta prouincia de Andabaylas, y la guerra los ha apocado como a los demás deste reyno. Es muy larga, y poseen gran número de ganado doméstico: y en sus términos no tiene quenta lo que ay montes. Y es bien bastecida de mantenimientos: y dase trigo. Y por los valles calientes ay muchos árboles de fructa" (Cieza de León 1996: 254–255 [1553: Pt. 1, Ch. 90]).

17 The four smallest repartimientos of the Andahuaylas region (Ongoy, Uripa, Ocobamba and Cayara) are collectively called los cuarto repartimientos (the four repartimientos) in various colonial documents, and they are treated as politically distinct from the larger, more powerful, repartimiento of Andahuaylas. During late Inca and early colonial times, the center of these four territorial units may have been located in the town of Uranmarca.

18 The names that Guaman Poma de Ayala assigns to the Chanka leaders are interesting. He suggests that Juan Guaman Guachaca was the leader of the Hurin Chanka in the 1550s. This may have been the case, since the earliest named ruler of the Hurin Chanka that we have is Juan Guaman Lurinchanga; however, this information is from a 1570 document (AGN, Derecho Indígena, Leg. 3, Cuaderno 17). Guaman Poma de Ayala also states that the leader of the Hurin Chanka at the time of Hernández Girón's revolt was named León Apo Guasco. This was not the case. We know from a 1552 Chanka tribute list that Diego Guasco was the leader of the Hanan Chanka during the 1550s (AGN, Derecho Indígena, Leg. 3, Cuaderno 17), and that León Apo Guasco, who was the grandson of Diego Guasco, did not become the head of the Hanan Chanka until the earlier 1600s (BN, Ms. B-28). In short, it appears that Guaman Poma de Ayala used the name of a contemporary leader (León Apo Guasco), rather than the historical one (Diego Guasco) when discussing the Hanan Chanka.

19 Guaman Poma de Ayala writes:

> Don Martin Guaman Malque de Ayala, capac apo [royal lord], second person to the Inca and his viceroy in these kingdoms, the most excellent lord, Duke of this Kingdom, as well as Don León Apo [G]uasco, [of the] Hanan Chanka and Don Juan Guaman [G]uachaca, [of the] Hurin Chanka of the town and province of Andahuaylas along with their people fought against the traitor Francisco Hernández Girón in service of your Majesty (translation by the authors)

> Don Martín Guaman Malque de Ayala, capac apo, segunda persona del Ynca y su bizorrey destos rreynos, el excelentícimo señor, duque deste rreyno, y don León Apo Uasco, Hanan Changa, y don Juan Guaman Uachaca, Lurin Changa del pueblo de Andaguaylas y de su prouincia, dieron la batalla con sus personas en seruicio de su Magestad con Francisco Hernandes Girón, traydor. (Guaman Poma de Ayala 1980: 400 [1615: 433 (435)])

20 The title to the drawing reads, "Conqvista Batalla qve hizo en servicio de su Magestad el excelentícimo señor capac apo don Martín de Ayala, padre del autor, Chinchaysuyo, y apo uasco, apo Guaman Uachaca, Hanan, Lurin Chanca, con cien soldados y Francisco Hernandes, trecientos soldados. Fue uencido y se huyó" (Guaman Poma de Ayala 1980: 400 [1615: 432 (434)]).

21 "Francisco Hernández Girón, que lo dejamos en el sitio de la batalla de Chuquinca, estuvo en él cerca de mes y medio por los muchos heridos que de parte del mariscal quedaron. Al cabo de largo tiempo caminó con ellos como mejor pudo hasta el valle de Antahuailla con enojo que llevaba de los indios de las provincias de los Charcas [sic Chancas] por la mucha pesadumbre que en la batalla de Chuquinca le dieron, que se atre-

vieron a pelear con los suyos y les cargaron de mucha cantidad de piedras con las hondas y descalabraron algunos de los de Francisco Hernández. Por lo cual, luego que llegó a aquellas provincias, mandó a sus soldados, así negros como blancos, que saqueasen los pueblos y los quemasen y talasen los campos e hiciesen todo el mal y daño que pudiesen" (Garcilaso de la Vega 1960 [vol. 4]: 107 [1609: Pt. 2, Bk. 7, Ch. 21]).

22 Juan Arias Maldonado indicates that his mother was a full sister of Atahualpa, who was later baptized as Lucia Clara Coya. He also suggests that she had been given to his father in Cajamarca at the time of Atahualpa's execution to prevent her from committing suicide (Hemming 1970: 597; Busto Durthurburu 1963).

23 "Hicieron en todo su reino estos Incas la misma división en que estaba repartida la ciudad del Cuzco, de Hanan Cuzco y Hurin Cuzco; dividiendo cada pueblo y cacicazgo en dos partes o bandos dichos hanansaya y hurinsaya, que suena el barrio alto y el barrio bajo, o la parte y bando superior y el bando inferior; y puesto caso que los nombres denotan desigualdad entre estos dos bandos, con todo eso, no la había más que en esta preeminencia y ventaja, que era ser preferido en asiento y lugar el bando de hanasaya a el de hurinsaya; al modo que en cortes unas ciudades preceden a otras en lugar y en hablar primero. En todo lo demás eran iguales, y por tan buenos eran tenidos los hurinsayas como los hanansayas" (Cobo 1964: 112 [1653: Bk. 12, Ch. 24]).

24 *Cacique* is the Carib term for chief, which the Spaniards used across the Americas.

25 Very often the term *segunda persona* is also used to denote a *kuraka's* second in command from the same moiety, but possibly from a different *ayllu*. Also, lower-ranking kurakas could have segunda personas as well. So the meaning shifts slightly according to the context. The terms *principal* and *segunda persona* reflect more the desire of the invading Spanish to identify and develop a single line of authority within the Andean setting, rather than the symmetrical power relationship that actually existed between the local-level authorities.

26 During later colonial times, the Chanka also represent a rare case where the traditional prestige relationships between the upper and lower moieties were reversed because of particular historic events. In 1606/07, as a result of a census that revealed significant errors in the recorded number of tributary Indians, the leader of the upper moiety was removed and replaced by his nephew. At the same time, the leader of the lower moiety was elevated and made head of all the Chanka. This reversal of power (between Hanan and Hurin) was instituted by the Spanish colonial government, and following this action, members of the upper moiety were never again able to gain the dominant voice in local affairs (Hyland and Amado González n.d.).

[27] The exact quote reads as follows: "En el dicho pueblo de Andaguaylas el dichodía 9 de septiembre por la mañana año de 1604, el dicho Juez y escribano leí y notifique este dicho auto en el contenido y el testimonio en el referido de los indios muertos y reservados como en ellos se contiene a los dichos Don León Apo Guasco Cacique Principal de esta provincia y al dicho Don Luis Tomay Guaraca cacique Principal Segunda Persona en ella, caciques de las parcialidades de Anansaya y Urinsaya y ayllos de ellas . . ." (AGN, Derecho Indígena, Leg. 3, Cuaderno 50).

[28] Cieza de León (1976: 207 [1554: Bk. 2, Ch. 38]) called the mythical founders Uasco and Guaraca, using the traditional Chanka names which are associated with the leaders of Hanan and Hurin divisions, respectively.

[29] "Treinta leguas del Cuzco al poniente es una provincia llamada Andaguay(l)las, cuyos naturales llaman Chancas. En esta provincia hobo dos cinches, ladrones y crueles tiranos, llamados Uscovilca y Ancovilca, que viniendo robando con ciertas compañas de ladrones desde los términos de Guamanga, habían venido asentar al valle de Andaguayllas y allí habían hecho dos parcialidades. Uscovilca que era el mayor y más principal, ca hermanos eran, instituyó la una y llamóla Hananchancas, ques decir, 'los Chancas de arriba', y Ancovilca hizo la otra parcialidad y nombróla Hurinchanca, que suena 'los Chancas de abajo'" (Sarmiento de Gamboa 1906: 59–60 [1572: Ch. 26]).

[30] Unfortunately, this quote from Sarmiento de Gamboa, which recounts the mythical establishment of the Chanka moieties in Andahuaylas, and which contains no more historical truth than the origin myths of other cultures (such as the Judaeo-Christian Adam and Eve myth), has been read by some researchers as reflecting historical events. This is most frequently reflected in the literature by researchers suggesting that the Chanka first developed in the Huamanga region and that they later expanded into the Andahuaylas region (González Carré, Pozzi-Escot, and Vivanco 1988; González Carré 1992a, 1992b; González Carré and Rivera Pideda 1988).

[31] "Inga Yupangui fué tan presto y diestro en el acometer, que, turbados con su presteza y destreza, los que traían la estatua de Uscovilca y porque vieron bajar de los cerros de los lados mucha suma di gente... empezaron á huir los Chancas, dejando la estatua de Uscovilca, y aun dicen que la de Ancovilca" (Sarmiento de Gamboa 1906: 63 [1572: Ch. 27]).

[32] Albornoz (1984: 207 [1582]) also names a third shrine of the Chanka, writing, "Llahapalla shrine of the Chanka Indians. It was a dressed stone in the shape of a man and had a house [Llahapalla guaca de los indios chancas era una piedra bestida y tenía un agujero en el hombro y tenía casa]."

[33] "Uscovilca es guaca de los indios ananchankas. Es una piedra a manera de indio bestido. Tenía casa en el pueblo de Andaguailas. Ancovilca era guaca de los indios hurinchangas. Era una piedra que traían consigo donde quiera que iban y tenía casa" (Albornoz 1984: 207 [1582]).

[34] The earliest detailed account that describes the Andahuaylas region dates to 1539, and it confirms that the Chanka were divided into upper and lower moieties (AGI, Patronato 93, No. 11, Ramo 2). Unfortunately, even though the document includes a detailed list of 63 villages and the names of their leaders, it does not record how the moieties were distributed across the Andahuaylas region.

[35] At the beginning of our project, we had hoped to be able to determine the exact Hanan and Hurin divisions of the Chanka using the 1539 *Andahuaylas Encomienda Document*. Unfortunately, like Julien (2002), we have not been able to do so.

[36] It is worth noting that these reducciones sometimes combined communities that had not previously shared common social affiliations.

[37] The tribute list of Hanan Chanka *ayllus* matches a list recorded in the 1568 will of Diego Condor Guacho, the father of Francisco Condor Guacho (ADC, Notariales de Andahuaylas, Escritura publica de Antonio Sánchez).

[38] It seems clear, however, that the Spanish divisions did not exactly correspond to the prehistoric Chanka moieties, since the Pampachiri area, which was traditionally part of the Soras ethnic group, falls with the "Chanka de la Puna" during late Colonial times.

CHAPTER 3

THE EARLY PEOPLES OF ANDAHUAYLAS: THE ARCHAIC (9500–2100 BC) AND MUYU MOQO (2100 BC–300 BC) PHASES

THE ARCHAIC PHASE

The Archaic Period of the Andean highlands is a vast and largely understudied time period. Until recently, only a small number of preceramic sites or artifacts had been identified in the Department of Apurimac, a fact that reflects the general lack of research conducted in the region rather than the actual activities of Archaic Period peoples. Our work in the Andahuaylas region has recorded a few small lithic scatters, several Archaic Period projectile points, and a large number of petroglyphs, some of which may date to Archaic times (Appendix 2).

Paleoclimatic data indicate that the mountains of Peru were suitable for human occupation soon after the end of the Pleistocene, between 10,000 BC and 8,000 BC, and there is some evidence suggesting that small groups ventured into the Andes at this early time. There is, however, more substantial evidence documenting that the highlands were inhabited after 8000 BC (Dillehay, Bonavia, and Kaulicke 2004). The earliest Archaic peoples of the Andes lived in small, highly mobile bands. The large caves of the central highlands served as excellent base camps for these small bands, and extant data suggest that groups were moving seasonally across a wide range of elevations and ecological zones to hunt, gather, and acquire lithic and fiber materials. Research conducted in the Ayacucho Basin, directly west of Andahuaylas, as well as at several sites farther north, in the Callejon de

FIGURE 3.1. Possible Middle Archaic Period point from the Andahuaylas Municipal Museum.

Huaylas and the Junín regions, has revealed various cave sites with hunting and foraging remains dating between 8000 and 7000 BC (MacNeish et al. 1980; Rick 1980, 1988; Lynch 1980, 1999; Dillehay 1997; Dillehay, Bonavia, and Kaulicke 2004). Recent excavations in the Cuzco Valley have recorded open-air hunting camps dating to 4000 BC, and surface surveys have yielded projectile points dating to earlier times (Bauer 2004, 2007). The most intensive preceramic archaeological research in the highlands has taken place farther south, in the Lake Titicaca region, where there is ample evidence that groups were living in the area after 8000 BC (for example, Klink 2005; Klink and Aldenderfer 2005; Cipolla 2005).

Unfortunately for the archaeologist, these small early sites are difficult to locate. Furthermore, thousands of years of erosion and cultivation, as well as the establishment of later, larger, and more permanent occupations, can easily destroy the delicate archaeological remains of the Archaic Period. Nevertheless, because evidence of Archaic occupations had been reported near Cuzco and Ayacucho, we were optimistic that our archaeological survey would provide new information on these early peoples. We also speculated that the Archaic Period sites would contain numerous lithic artifacts made from obsidian, since research on prehistoric obsidian use in Peru had documented the presence of several obsidian sources in Apurimac and neighboring departments (Burger, Chávez, and Chávez 2000; Burger, Fajardo Ríos, and Glascock 2006).

Our survey of the Andahuaylas region did identify a few (n < 5) small (< 0.25 ha) sites that contained exclusively lithic debris. Yet, since none

of these sites yielded diagnostic Archaic Period projectile points, they cannot be definitively dated to this time period. Other evidence suggestive of Archaic Period activities in the region was provided by the recovery of several isolated, possible Archaic Period projectile points during the survey. Unfortunately, most of the recovered projectile points were not complete, which precluded our ability to reliably type these artifacts. However, the most impressive Archaic projectile point from the region is included within the holdings of the Andahuaylas Municipal Museum (Figure 3.1). This is an exceptionally well-made obsidian point with fine pressure retouching and serrated edges. Based on other projectile points found in the central Andes, this point appears to date to Middle Archaic times (Cynthia Klink, pers. com. 2005).[1]

As the mild climate and gently rising slopes of the Andahuaylas region seem to provide a nearly ideal setting for early hunters, we had expected to find more evidence of Archaic camps. Even accounting for erosion and site loss by more recent occupations, the small number of lithic scatters recorded during our survey seems surprisingly low. Currently, our best explanation is that there may be other sites still to be found in the high and expansive *puna* (4,000–4,500 masl) to the south of Andahuaylas, an area not included within the survey area. These high, open grasslands are the favored environment for wild Andean camelids, and it is possible that they held a much greater density of hunting camps during the Archaic Period than the lower valley areas (Rick 1980). Alternatively, perhaps there were areas of the Andean highlands, like Andahuaylas, that were simply not heavily exploited by mobile groups.

THE MUYU MOQO PHASE

Relatively early in prehistory, the coastal valleys of Peru became densely occupied, and a series of large polities developed, some numbering in the tens of thousands of people (Haas and Creamer 2006). Ritual cults thrived and centers with impressive architectural features were built. Ranked societies, or chiefdoms, developed, as powerful individuals and their clans began to dominate the emerging social hierarchies (Burger 1992). The course of cultural development in the highlands took, however, a slower pace and a far more humble trajectory. It is generally believed that around 2500 BC, populations in the central highlands gradually began shifting from a mobile or semi-mobile lifestyle to a sedentary one (Dillehay, Bonavia, and Kaulicke 2004). This is marked in the archaeological record with the appearance of several important features, including the construction of permanent residential structures, an increased reliance on domesticated plant and animal resources, and the widespread use of ceramics. Over time, the populations aggregated into hamlets and villages, centered in the best regions for agricultural production. Innumerable communities were gradually established in the highlands, focusing on grain and tuber production as well as pastoralism. Hunting continued, but its role in subsistence gradually declined and was increasingly replaced by small-scale agriculture. In the higher reaches of the mountains (4,000+ masl), the communities were smaller and widely scattered, concentrating on camelid herding (Rick 1980). The lower reaches of the mountain valleys witnessed the slow development of agriculture supported by rudimentary systems of terraces and irrigation agriculture. In the central and south central highlands, the time during which these first agricultural communities developed is frequently called the Formative Period.[2] While we will use this term for comparative purposes, we will also detail the specific events that took place within the Andahuaylas region during what we have termed the Muyu Moqo Phase.

Although widely believed to be a period of fundamental economic and social changes in the highlands, there has been little work on the early sedentary societies in the departments of Ayacucho, Cuzco, and Apurimac. Several Formative Period sites have been excavated near the city of Ayacucho, and a number of local ceramic styles have been defined (Ochatoma Paravicino 1992, 1998). Nevertheless, additional excavations and regional surveys are needed before a full description of the early village settlement patterns in the Ayacucho region can be developed.

In comparison, the Cuzco region has a far greater number of known Formative Period sites (Bauer 2004). The first Formative site in the Cuzco Basin, Chanapata, was recorded by Rowe (1946). Currently the best-documented early village site in the basin is Marcavalle, which was occupied as early as 1200 BC (Chávez 1980, 1981a, 1981b, 1982). Excavations by Chávez at Marcavalle provided important information on the lifeways of the early villagers who lived in the Cuzco region during this time. The sizes and ages of the camelids recovered at the site indicate that they were domesticated and were being used for a variety of purposes (Chávez 1980: 246–248). Other domesticated animals included guinea pig (*cuy*) and dog. Wild faunal resources included deer, puma, small rodents, birds, and toads, in decreasing percentages, respectively (Chávez 1980: 244, 247). Chávez (1980: 243–244) also recovered direct evidence of agriculture, with remains of common beans dated at 800 BC and maize at 200 BC.

More recently, Bauer (2004) has examined the site sizes and distribution patterns of more than 80 Formative Period sites documented during a systematic survey of the Cuzco Valley. These sites fall within several site-size categories, including hunting stations, homesteads, hamlets, and villages. The hamlet- and the village-level sites contain dense trash middens and most likely held populations from a few dozen to several hundred persons each. Among the most intriguing of the Formative Period occupations of the Cuzco Valley is the large site of Wimpillay, situated on a broad river terrace just south of Cuzco. Bauer (2004) suggests that this large site was the paramount village of a valley-wide chiefdom during late Formative times (500 BC–200 AD).

Previous Muyu Moqo Phase Research in the Andahuaylas Region

Before our work began, only two early ceramic period sites had been described in the Andahuaylas region. These were the sites of Waywaka (PAA 72)[3] and Muyu Moqo (PAA 76).[4] Located immediately south of the city of Andahuaylas, both of these sites were documented by Rowe (1956: 143) during his brief visit to the region in the mid-1950s. The site of Waywaka (3,040 masl) is situated at the end of a prominent ridge that dominates the center of the Andahuaylas Valley (Figure 3.2). The Chumbao River runs along the base of the ridge, and some of the best maize fields of the region surround it. The site of Muyu Moqo (3,311 masl) is on a higher spur of the same ridge, located about 4 km to the east.

In 1970, Grossman (1972a) conducted excavations at Waywaka. His work confirmed the site's long occupational sequence, which begins in Formative times and continues without interruption into the Inca Period. The lower stratum of the site contained pottery similar to the Marcavalle and Chanapata ceramics already defined in the Cuzco region. Grossman called the local Andahuaylas Formative pottery style "Muyu Moqo" and divided it into three temporal phases (from earliest to latest: Muyu Moqo A, Muyu Moqo B, and Muyu Moqo C/D) based on the stratigraphy of the site. A carbon sample recovered from the lowest excavation strata yielded an uncalibrated date of 1490 ± 100 BC.[5] At the time of Grossman's research, this was the earliest date for ceramic production in the central highlands. Additional radiocarbon dates provided by Grossman (1983) confirmed the early production period for Muyu Moqo ceramics (see Appendix 1).

During his research at the site, Grossman found evidence of camelids, deer, guinea pigs, and a few fragments of mussel shell, the latter of which appear to have been imported from the Peruvian coast. His excavations also revealed 15 burials, many of which contained beads. The beads were made from various materials, including nonlocal lapis lazuli, which may have originated in northern Chile or southern Peru. Grossman (1972b) also recovered numerous small pieces of gold foil and a goldworker's kit (consisting of two small stone bowls, a small anvil, and three hammer stones) during his excavations at Waywaka. The recovery of early ceramics at the site, as well as evidence of metalworking, gave the site a certain notoriety, and references to Waywaka can be found scattered through the 1970s and 1980s archaeological literature.

FIGURE 3.2. The ridge of Waywaka looms above the Andahuaylas Valley.

Further inferences on the nature of the Muyu Moqo Phase in the Andahuaylas region comes from an analysis of obsidian samples collected during Grossman's excavations (Burger and Asaro 1979; Grossman 1983). Burger et al. (Burger, Chávez, and Chávez 2000; Burger, Fajardo Ríos, and Glascock 2006) note that during the Formative Period, obsidian was coming into the Andahuaylas region from a wide range of distance sources. Obsidian used during the early Formative (Muyu Moqo A and B) came from sources located in southwest Apurimac (source: Petreropampa) and Ayacucho (sources: Quispissisa and Jampatilla). In later Formative times (Muyu Moqo B, C, and D), there appears to have been an increased dependence on Ayacucho sources (Quispissisa), with some obsidian still coming from southwest Apurimac (source: Luisahucho) and even as far away as Arequipa (source: Alca). These data may provide evidence of emerging trade networks in the central Andean highlands.

Muyu Moqo and Chacamarca Ceramics

During our work in the Andahuaylas region, we recognized two distinct early pottery styles. The dominant style was Muyu Moqo (see Appendix 5). This ceramic style was first recorded by Rowe (1956: 143) during his brief stay in Andahuaylas and, as noted above, it was later more fully defined by Grossman (1972a) based on his work at the site of Waywaka. It is similar to other early ceramics found throughout the central highlands, particularly those of the Cuzco region (Rowe 1944; Zapata 1998; Bauer 1999, 2002; Bauer and Jones 2003). Found at about 25 sites, the Muyu Moqo style contains distinctly burnished vessels and relatively thick rim forms and is frequently made with a micaceous paste (Figures 3.3, 3.4).

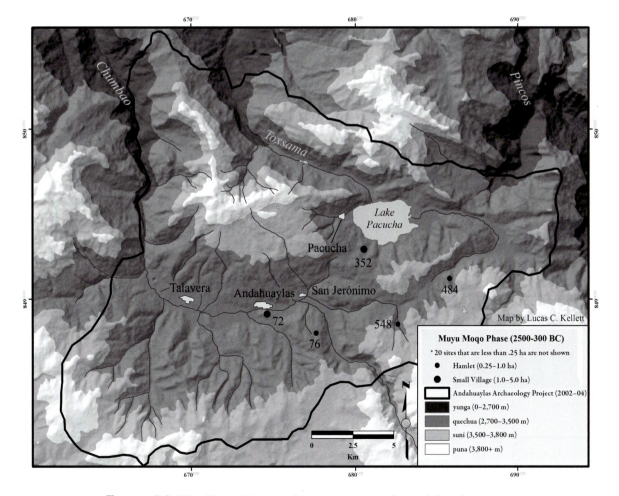

FIGURE 3.3. The Muyu Moqo settlement pattern in the Andahuaylas region.

During our ceramic analysis, a thin pottery style was noted which occasionally contained incised and/or small appliqué designs (Figure 3.5; see also Appendix 6). Termed "Chacamarca" by the project, these fragments represent a new style for the region that appears to be similar to styles, such as San Blas, that have been reported from areas northwest of Apurimac (Morales Chocano 1998). Chacamarca ceramics were found in relatively light densities at thirteen sites, three of which also

FIGURE 3.4. Two examples of Muyu Moqo ceramics. Note the well burnished surfaces and the raised horizontal bands on both of these sherds.

FIGURE 3.5. Chacamarca ceramics recovered in the Andahuaylas region.

contained examples of Muyu Moqo. The sites containing Chacamarca ceramics were generally very small, most measuring less than 0.25 ha.

Dating the Early Ceramics of the Andahuaylas Region

Grossman (1983: 58) processed six carbon samples from his excavations at Waywaka to help date the production of Muyu Moqo ceramics.[6] The four oldest samples produced uncalibrated dates between 1600 BC and 1235 BC.[7] These dates are supported by those recovered by other research projects in the south central highlands, especially in the region of Cuzco (Bauer 2004) and Lake Titicaca (Stanish 2003), which document that village cultures were flourishing during the second millennium BC. A fifth uncalibrated date of Muyu Moqo ceramics, 710 ± 250 BC,[8] suggests, despite its large standard deviation, that Muyu Moqo ceramics were produced for nearly a millennium. It is not clear, however, when Muyu Moqo ceramics stopped being made. As Grossman notes, his samples were all collected in the lower strata of his Waywaka excavations and thus were not expected to define the upper terminal era of the pottery style. This issue is not aided by the fact that the youngest carbon sample submitted by Grossman provided an exceptionally large standard deviation, which renders it of limited value (see Appendix 1).[9]

During the course of our work in the Andahuaylas region, carbon samples were collected from the exterior of Chacamarca sherds recovered at three different sites. These samples yielded uncalibrated dates that clustered within a relatively narrow time range, between 544 BC and 785 BC.[10] Based on these findings, we currently believe that both Muyu Moqo and Chacamarca ceramics were still being produced in the Andahuaylas region during the early half of first millennium BC (see Figure 1.11).

Overview of the Muyu Moqo Phase in the Andahuaylas Region

Muyu Moqo and Chacamarca ceramics have been found at a total of 35 sites in the Andahuaylas region (Table 3.1). No architectural remains were

observed at these sites, and they were all recorded as densities of surface pottery. As in the Cuzco region (Bauer 2004), sites of this period tend to be located above the valley floor, frequently on knolls or the ends of ridges, with excellent views of the valley bottom. The reconstruction of the Muyu Moqo Phase settlement pattern is complicated by the fact that the sites dating to this era are relatively small and are frequently built in locations that continued to be occupied or farmed for millennia. The continuous use of these site locations has undoubtedly disturbed many of the Muyu Moqo Phase settlements and rendered them difficult to identify in surface collections.

Noting these limitations, the two largest Muyu Moqo Phase sites in the Andahuaylas region include the well-known site of Waywaka, near the city of Andahuaylas, and the newly found site of Muyupata (PAA 352; 3,330 masl)[11] along the southern shore of Lake Pacucha (see Figure 3.3). While these two Muyu Moqo Phase sites are described as the largest of their kind in the region, it should noted that with site-size estimates of just over 1 ha each, they were only large hamlets or, at best, small villages.[12] Three additional sites were found to be slightly smaller, but of notable sizes. These include the type site for Muyu Moqo pottery (PAA 76) located a short distance from Waywaka, the site of Pumayhuirca (PAA 484; 3,550 masl),[13] and the site of Ayapata (PAA 548; 3,600 masl).[14] The latter of these sites, located on a small, low ridge east of San Jerónimo in the petroglyph-rich area of the valley, provided some of the best Muyu Moqo ceramics in our sample. Unfortunately, house construction is currently occurring at this site, and it may not survive much longer.

Grossman argues that the Muyo Moqo Phase witnessed the integration of an agro-pastoral economy supplemented with hunting, most likely conducted in the upper reaches of the valleys. During his excavations at Waywaka, Grossman recovered the carbonized remains of domesticated beans as well as possible quinoa remains. Presumably, the agricultural fields that supported these crops were watered by seasonal rains, and, perhaps in some cases, small irrigation ditches were constructed to bring water from adjacent

Table 3.1
Elevations and sizes of Muyu Moqo Phase sites in the Andahuaylas region

Ecological Zones	House-hold < 0.25 ha	Hamlet 0.25–1 ha	Small Village 1–5 ha	Medium Village 5–10 ha	Large Village > 10 ha	Total
Yunga (0–2,700 masl)	0	0	0	0	0	0
Quechua (2,700–3,500 masl)	13	1	2	0	0	16
Suni (3,500–3,800 masl)	13	2	0	0	0	15
Puna (3,800+ masl)	2	0	0	0	0	2
Total	28	3	2	0	0	33

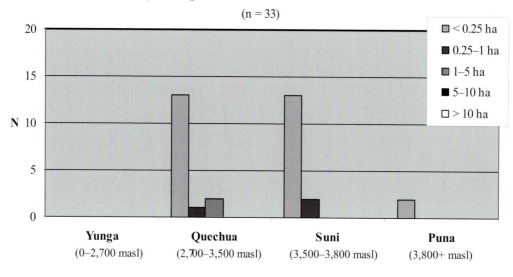

Muyu Moqo Phase Settlement Distribution
(n = 33)

springs or streams. These findings that document agricultural practices during Muyu Moqo times are strengthened by recent research conducted in the Cuzco region. Cores taken from Lake Marcacocha suggest that the production of quinoa in the south central highlands reached a peak at around 800 BC, and thereafter experienced a massive decline (Chepstow-Lusty et al. 2003).

Grossman also suggests, based on the recovery of a diverse set of food remains, that the Muyu Moqo Phase in the Andahuaylas region saw some integration of vertically distributed production zones. Although currently undocumented, it is reasonable to assume that tuber crops were also being grown on the upper valley slopes during this time. Hunting also continued throughout this period, as evidenced by the projectile points found on the surfaces of the Muyu Moqo Phase sites and by the deer remains found during Grossman's excavations. We can also presume that camelid herds were kept in the upper elevations of the valley during this era.

In sum, the occupations of this period represent the formation of small independent villages, surrounded by scattered hamlets and clusters of households. All of the staple crops that would support Andean populations for thousands of years had already been domesticated by this time. While living an agricultural and largely isolated existence, the early villagers of the Andahuaylas region did have limited long-distance contact and exchange with other areas of the Andes, as documented by imported lapis lazuli stone beads and obsidian as well as the remains of marine mussel shell. Craft production included the working of gold, but there is no evidence to suggest that this occurred on a large scale or that it was controlled above the household level. Furthermore, there is no current evidence of public architecture or differences in social ranking within or among villages. In other words, while some settlements may have been larger than others, and may have even served as the central loci for ritual, ceremonial, and trading activities, no single site appears to have held disproportionate power or controlled the activities of the smaller settlements that surrounded it.

NOTES

1 Unfortunately, the specific provenience of this projectile point is not known.
2 Some researchers, especially those working in the northern parts of Peru, refer to the period between 1800 BC and 800 BC as the Initial Period, and the time between 800 BC and 100 BC as the Early Horizon. These two periods are generally associated with the appearance and spread of the Chavín material culture across parts of northern Peru. In contrast, some researchers working in the central and south central highlands tend to refer to this time as the Formative Period.
3 18L 0674597, 8489136 (all coordinates are in WGS 1984, UTM Zone 18S projection).
4 18L 0677609, 8488010.
5 Sample UCLA 1808A.
6 Samples UCLA 1808F, UCLA 1808I, UCLA 1808E, UCLA 1808A, UCLA 1808J, and UCLA 1808D.
7 Calibrated dates of these samples are provided in Appendix 1.
8 Sample UCLA 1808F.
9 Sample UCLA 1808D (2200 ± 430 BP).
10 Samples AA 56640, AA 56642, and AA 56652.
11 18L 0680518, 8492930.
12 While both Grossman's research and our survey results suggest Waywaka was the largest Muyu Moqo Phase site in the region, we differ somewhat in our site-size estimates. Grossman suggests that Waywaka was about .50 ha during Muyu Moqo times, while we estimate its size to be about 1.5 ha. Whatever its actual size was, it is clear that it was little more than a village.
13 18L 0685782, 8491237.
14 18L 0682590, 8488537.

CHAPTER 4

THE QASAWIRKA PHASE (300 BC–AD 1000) IN THE ANDAHUAYLAS REGION

The Qasawirka Phase of the Andahuaylas region is a long temporal period, the beginning of which is defined by the appearance of Qasawirka ceramics, currently estimated to have occurred around 300 BC. The period ends with a massive abandonment of valley slope and bottom settlements in the region and the widespread establishment of new aggregated settlements on ridgetops (see Chapter 6). Current research suggests that the settlement shift from the valley floors to the ridges occurred sometime between AD 1000 and 1100. Therefore, the Qasawirka Phase overlaps with the time traditionally assigned to the Early Intermediate Period (ca. 100 BC–AD 600) and the Middle Horizon (ca. AD 600–AD 1000). It is a period of major sociopolitical development and population growth, and

includes increased contact with the Wari state of the Ayacucho region. In this chapter, we briefly discuss the ceramic styles associated with the Qasawirka Phase and the overall settlement pattern. In the following chapter, we examine some of the changes that occurred in the Andahuaylas region during the latter half of this period, when it was under the influence of the Wari.

PREVIOUS RESEARCH IN THE AYACUCHO AND CUZCO REGIONS

While Formative Period ceramics in the central and south central highlands share many similarities, the populations of the subsequent era produced a host of different ceramic styles, many of which have proven difficult for archaeologists to define and describe. The general paucity of research focused on the cultures of this time period make this era one of the least understood in the Andes. Research indicates that the Huarpa culture developed in the Ayacucho region before the rise of the Wari (González Carré and Cruzatt Añaños 1966; González Carré 1967). Huarpa ceramics are generally characterized by black or, less frequently, red geometric designs painted on a cream or white slip. Although Lumbreras (1974a: 133–138) has proposed a four-phase ceramic sequence for Huarpa ceramics, additional research is needed to confirm the sequence and to ground it with absolute dates. Only three carbon dates are currently available for Huarpa pottery. They include a sample provided by Knobloch (n.d.) from a road cut at the site of Wari, with an uncalibrated date of AD 237 ± 120, as well as two samples from the site of Ñawinpukyo, with uncalibrated dates of AD 350 ± 70 and AD 367 ± 34 (Leoni 2006: 286). Later, perhaps around AD 500, the Ayacucho region began a period of close contact with the Nasca culture on the central south coast of Peru, and the local ceramic sequence began to reflect this interaction (Knobloch 1991; Leoni 2006).

Huarpa ceramics are widely distributed across the Ayacucho Basin. There may be hundreds of Huarpa sites in the region, most of which are thought to represent small villages, hamlets, or isolated households (Lumbreras 1974a). The sites are generally distributed between 2,600 and 3,600 masl and tend to be situated near good agricultural lands. There is also widespread evidence of terraces and traces of irrigation systems surrounding some of the larger sites. Lumbreras (1974a: 135) proposes that with the use of these agricultural technologies, significantly more land in the Ayacucho Basin was under cultivation during Huarpa times than is the case today.

The largest known site in the Huarpa settlement system is Ñawinpukyo, located south of the modern city of Ayacucho. Surface inspections and excavations indicate that the site contained a dense concentration of residential buildings, some possible elite structures, and numerous patios or plazas (González Carré 1972). Lumbreras (1974a: 134) calls Ñawinpukyo a city and

proposes that it served as the capital of an early state in the region. Schreiber, having access to more recent data, provides an alternative overview of the settlement pattern in the region:

> The Huarpa phase of the Early Intermediate period was characterized by a broad regional distribution of sites, with no evidence of strong centralized control from any single site. . . . I suggest that the overall settlement data indicate political organization no more complex than a series of complex chiefdoms during the Early Intermediate period. (Schreiber 1992: 87)

While Lumbreras's identification of a Huarpa state appears to have been overly enthusiastic, the large size of Ñawinpukyo, apparently dwarfing many other contemporary sites within the local settlement system, does suggest that it played an important role. Recent excavations at the site by Juan B. Leoni have exposed various buildings and a circular ceremonial area on the summit of the site. Seeing the site as the center of a local chiefdom, Leoni (2006: 303) writes, "It seems clear, however, that even though the site might have had some regional projections as a ceremonial center, Ñawinpukyo was not the dominant urban or proto urban capital once believed, but more probably one of many more of less equivalent centers [of the greater Ayacucho region]."

During this same period in the Cuzco region, another culture, now called Qotakalli, was developing, which also contained a strong tradition of black-on-cream ceramics (Bauer 2002, 2008: 385–393; Bauer and Jones 2003). The origins of this local style are unclear; however, excavations suggest that there was a rapid transformation in local ceramic production from the burnished, earthen Marcavalle and Chanapata styles of the Formative Period to the distinctly different Qotakalli style sometime after the beginning of the modern era (Bauer 2004; Bauer and Jones 2003).

The Qotakalli settlement pattern suggests that population growth occurred in the Cuzco region during this period and that there was a shift from a mixed agro-pastoral economy toward more intensive agricultural production, centered on maize (Bauer 2002, 2004). Small irrigation and terrace projects may have been initiated at this time to increase maize production. A settlement survey suggests that the center of political power in the Cuzco Basin rested near its western end, localized in a dense cluster of large villages (Bauer 2004). While this polity cast its control over the inhabitants of the Cuzco Basin, its influence was most likely limited to the east and west by similarly sized polities in the plain of Anta and the Lucre Basin, respectively. To the north and south, however, smaller, weaker entities may have come under its sway, if not its direct control.[1]

RESEARCH IN THE ANDAHUAYLAS REGION

Qasawirka pottery was first identified by Rowe (1956: 143) during his brief visit to the Andahuaylas area in 1954. Grossman's excavations at Waywaka found a thick stratum of Qasawirka ceramics directly above the Muyu Moqo remains. Using collections from Waywaka as well as information collected during his explorations of the valley, Grossman (1972a) provided an expanded description of this largely unknown ceramic style. He also noted that there appears to have been population growth in the Andahuaylas region during this time, with settlements scattered across various altitudes and ecological zones (Grossman 1983). During our survey work in Andahuaylas, it became immediately clear that Qasawirka ceramics were the most widely distributed pottery style in the valley. Sites containing this ceramic style, which is easily identified by a dark red paint covering all or parts of the vessels (Figure 4.1), dominate the valley floor as well as the hills and lower valley slopes of the region. During the classification of our ceramic materials, we recorded a general class of Qasawirka pottery, with several subdivisions, as well as Qasawirka Fine Ware and Qasawirka Polychromes (see Appendix 7).

In describing this new style, Rowe (1956) suggested that Qasawirka ceramics span the Early Intermediate Period. Grossman also felt that these ceramics date largely to the Early Intermediate Period, but he also suggested that they continued into the Middle Horizon:

No radiocarbon determinations have been run on Qasawirka-associated material but stylistic and stratigraphic considerations would indicate that Qasawirka at least spans the Early Intermediate period. Furthermore, the Qasawirka style appears to have continued until the advent of Huari influence in the region in Epoch 1B of the Middle Horizon. A few Qasawirka sherds utilized some Huari motifs and one sherd with distinct Huari paste is decorated with a Qasawirka design. (Grossman 1983: 59–60)

During our fieldwork, we independently reached a similar conclusion, based on the fact that many of the sites that contained large amounts of Qasawirka ceramics also contained a light scatter of Wari pottery. Our impression is that many of these sites were villages well before the Wari expanded across the central Andes and that they continued to be occupied during the period of Wari influence. We believe that as a result of increased contact with the Ayacucho region, their occupants gradually began to use imported Wari vessels as well as locally produced Wari-influenced ceramics, along with the traditional Qasawirka pottery of the Andahuaylas region.

To document the production dates of Qasawirka ceramics and to understand their relationship with Wari influence in the Andahuaylas region, we submitted a total of seven carbon samples for AMS dating from soot-encrusted pottery and exposed midden deposits identified during the course of our regional survey. The samples came from three different sites with Qasawirka ceramics: PAA 158, PAA 140, and PAA 206. These sites were of special interest, since PAA 158 contained what appeared to be early Qasawirka ceramics, PAA 140 yielded pure Qasawirka remains, and PAA 206 provided a combination of Qasawirka and Wari vessel fragments. Later, three additional carbon samples collected during the course of Kellett's excavations at site PAA 206 were also submitted for AMS dating. Brief descriptions of these sites help to place the carbon results in context:

PAA 158 is a very small site (<0.25 hectare) located on the northern slope of the valley between Talavera and Andahuaylas.[2] This is

FIGURE 4.1. Qasawirka ceramics are the most commonly recovered ceramics in the Andahuaylas region This photograph shows a Qasawirka necked vessel (with offset handles) from the Andahuaylas Municipal Museum.

a region of thick natural clay deposits, which is currently the focus of brick production in the valley. The site was detected as a very dark stratum in the profile of a modern clay quarry, approximately 1.5 meters below the current ground surface. The ceramic fragments recovered from the profile were generally large and well preserved and several were covered with carbon. The pottery from the site is thicker and bulkier than the typical Qasawirka ceramics of the region, but it is covered with a dark red paint, a hallmark of this ceramic style. Because no fine wares or polychromes were recovered from the stratum, we felt that this site might be an early Qasawirka occupation and a sample of carbon found on the exterior of a sherd was submitted for dating. The sample provided a relatively early uncalibrated date of 312 ± 77 BC.[3]

PAA 140 is a very small site (<0.25 hectare) located west of the town of Andahuaylas, on the lower, northern slope of the valley.[4] A road cut through the site exposed a buried midden level approximately 25 cm thick. The midden contained dense quantities of well preserved Qasawirka pottery, carbon,

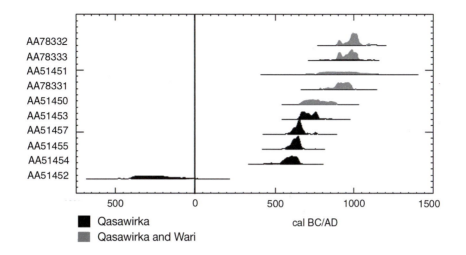

FIGURE 4.2. Calibrated radiocarbon dates from sites containing Qasawirka ceramics in the Andahuaylas region (PAA 140, PAA 158, and PAA 206).

bone, and other cultural materials. Four carbon samples from this lens yielded the following uncalibrated dates: AD 438 ± 48,[5] AD 486 ± 39,[6] AD 514 ± 41,[7] and AD 587 ± 42.[8] These dates span what is traditionally thought to be the end of the Early Intermediate Period and the beginning of the Middle Horizon.

PAA 206 is a small site (<0.25 hectare) situated approximately one kilometer north of Lake Pacucha.[9] A soil profile at the site, exposed by agricultural terrace construction, contained a midden deposit with a rich mixture of carbon, Qasawirka ceramics as well as Wari sherds. The preservation at this site appeared to be good, so it was selected by Kellett in 2005 for test excavations to increase our understanding of the Wari presence in the region. In 2001, however, we were only able to collect materials from the surface of the site and the exposed soil profile. Two carbon samples taken from the soil profile were submitted for dating and returned uncalibrated ages of AD 638 ± 55[10] and AD 810 ± 120.[11] Three additional samples from excavation contexts were later submitted for dating by Kellett. These samples provided the following uncalibrated dates: AD 775 ± 38,[12] AD 827 ± 37,[13] and AD 855 ± 38.[14]

In sum, although the exact dates for this ceramic style are still being defined, we are gaining a better idea of its production period. Our earliest sample, recovered from a deeply buried site (PAA 158) with what appears to be early Qasawirka ceramics, yielded an uncalibrated date of 312 ± 77 BC, suggesting that Qasawirka pottery production began while Muyu Moqo pottery was in decline. A suite of four other dates from PAA 140 confirms that Qasawirka pottery was being made in the Andahuaylas region in the centuries before the Wari arrived, and five other dates from the site of PAA 206 document that it continued to be produced during the height of Wari influence in the highlands (Figure 4.2).

OVERVIEW OF THE QASAWIRKA PHASE

Our archaeological survey documented more than 400 sites that contained Qasawirka ceramics (Table 4.1; Figure 4.3). This large number of sites reflects the long period during which this ceramic style was in production. The sites ranged widely in size and in elevation. A large percentage (~ 70%) of Qasawirka sites consisted of light scatters of ceramics, less than 0.25 ha in size. At the other end of the size spectrum, the largest Qasawirka site in the Andahuaylas region is site PAA 120.[15] We currently believe that this site may have reached over 10 ha; however, its exact size is difficult to determine since it is largely destroyed by the modern city of Andahuaylas.

There are 23 Qasawirka sites estimated to be 1 ha or larger. Most of these sites are situated on the lower valley slopes or at the lower ends of the long ridges that descend into the Andahuaylas Valley. None of these Qasawirka sites had standing architecture or evidence of public gathering spaces (such as platforms or plazas). Nor do they

TABLE 4.1
Elevations and size of Qasawirka Phase sites in the Andahuaylas region

ECOLOGICAL ZONES	HOUSE-HOLD < 0.25 HA	HAMLET 0.25–1 HA	SMALL VILLAGE 1–5 HA	MEDIUM VILLAGE 5–10 HA	LARGE VILLAGE > 10 HA	TOTAL
Yunga (0–2,700 masl)	3	1	0	0	0	4
Quechua (2,700–3,500 masl)	242	56	17	4	1?	320
Suni (3,500–3,800 masl)	61	11	2	0	0	74
Puna (3,800+ masl)	7	0	0	0	0	7
Total	313	68	19	4	1?	405

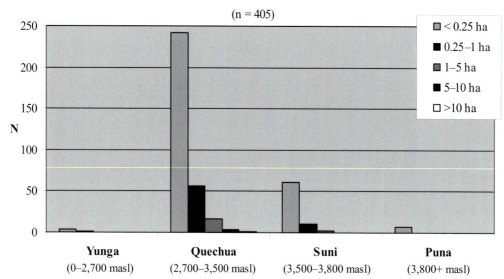

Qasawirka Phase Settlement Distribution
(n = 405)

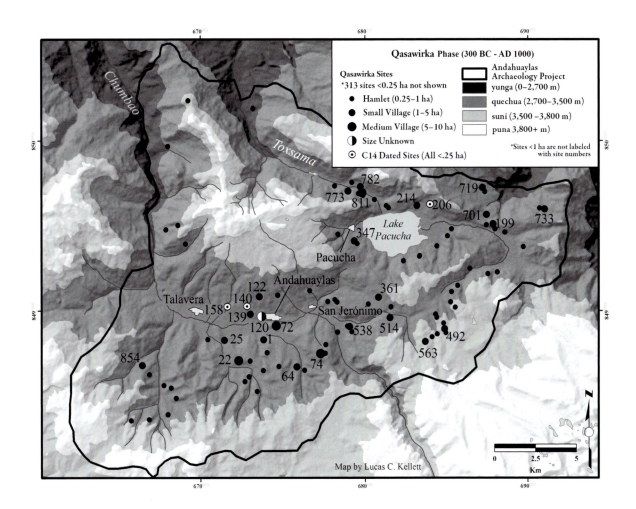

FIGURE 4.3. The Qasawirka settlement pattern in the Andahuaylas region.

contain evidence of defensive works, such as ditches or walls. In other words, although there is some size variation among these sites, there is currently no archaeological evidence to suggest that one held a qualitatively different role in the settlement pattern than the others. That is to say, we do not see evidence of a distinct settlement hierarchy that would indicate a well-developed sociopolitical structure within the valley during this time.

The smaller Qasawirka sites are scattered across all altitudinal zones of the region. They are found in especially dense quantities between 3,000 and 3,600 m, but a moderate number of these smaller sites are also located in the highest and lowest resource zones of the region. This site distribution pattern is reflective of an agricultural society, increasingly dependent on growing differ-

ent crops in various microclimates as well as on camelid husbandry in the high grassland (*puna*) areas of the region. Excavation data recovered by Grossman (1983: 83) from the site of Waywaka, and his limited settlement data, support the view that there was an expanded use of diverse resource zones during this time period. He concludes that the Early Intermediate Period was "a time of considerable population expansion in the Andahuaylas region," with numerous villages or small towns located in the mid-altitudinal zone with easy access to both the lower arable valley lands and the higher potato and grazing zones (Grossman 1983: 83).

During the course of our survey, we also identified seven Qasawirka cemetery sites that contained the remains of small, circular burial towers, generally called *chullpas*.[16] The tradition of burial towers is widespread and of great antiquity in the Andes, although the exact form and size of these towers take on many regional variations (Isbell 1997). In the Andahuaylas region, the tradition of chullpas appears to begin during Qasawirka times and becomes increasingly common through subsequent periods.

The overall Qasawirka Phase settlement pattern is suggestive of a relatively densely populated agricultural society. Like many other regions of the central Andes during this period, there were various villages situated across the grain-producing elevations of the Andahuaylas region, each of which was surrounded by a host of smaller hamlets and homesteads. Although the villages varied somewhat in size, there is currently no evidence indicating that any individual village held a disproportionate amount of influence or power over others in the region. Obsidian circulation (Burger, Fajardo Ríos, and Glascock 2006)[17] and metal production are presumed to have continued on a relatively small scale. Ceramic production in Andahuaylas during the Qasawirka Phase was locally organized and at a level that did not extend beyond the valley.

Notes

[1] It is an intriguing fact that both Ayacucho and Cuzco cultures used black-on-cream ceramics during the Early Intermediate Period, while the Andahuaylas area, which is located halfway between them, developed a distinctly different ceramic tradition.
[2] 18L 0671612, 8490251; 2,966 masl.
[3] Sample AA 51452.
[4] 18L 0672984, 8490024; 3,018 masl.
[5] Sample AA 51454.
[6] Sample AA 51455.
[7] Sample AA 51457.
[8] Sample AA 51453.
[9] 18L 0683993, 8496259; 3,336 masl.
[10] Sample AA 51450.
[11] Sample AA 51451.
[12] Sample AA 78331.
[13] Sample AA 78333.
[14] Sample AA 78332.
[15] 18L 0673719, 8489682; 2,967 masl.
[16] These sites are not included in Table 4.1.
[17] Burger, Fajardo Ríos, and Glascock's (2006) analysis of Qasawirka Phase obsidian recovered from Grossman's excavations reveals that the obsidian was from southwest Apurimac (source: Petreropampa) and Ayacucho (sources: Quispissisa and Jampatilla).

CHAPTER 5

WARI INFLUENCE IN THE ANDAHUAYLAS REGION (AD 600–1000)

When Pedro Cieza de León traveled through the Ayacucho region in the late 1540s, he noted the ruins of an ancient city with densely packed buildings. He believed, based on its ruined state and its unique architectural features, that the city must have been constructed before the Inca (Cieza de León 1996: 249 [1553: Pt. 1, Ch. 86]). The ruined city that Cieza de León saw is now called Wari,[1] and it is believed to have been the capital of the Wari state which expanded beyond the Ayacucho region sometime after AD 600. Several centuries later, when the Wari reached the height of their power, they controlled large areas of the central Andes of Peru. The end of Wari rule is thought to have occurred sometime around AD 1000. It has been suggested that their decline was accelerated by degrading environmental condi-tions which decreased opportunities for agrarian intensification in the Andes at that time (Williams 2001, 2002, 2006).

As the Wari conquered and incorporated var-ious regions into their empire, they built a series of administrative centers (Isbell and Schreiber 1978; Isbell and McEwan 1991; Schreiber 1992). With the capital of the empire located in Ayacu-cho and the second largest Wari site, Pikillacta, in Cuzco, it has long been assumed that the Wari dominated much, if not all, of the Department of Apurimac. Yet recent research has questioned the traditional model of Wari society as an expansion-istic state and has highlighted the variable nature and intensity of Wari hegemony and influence across the Andes (for example, Schreiber 1992; Jennings and Craig 2001; Jennings and Alvarez

2003; Jennings 2006). For example, archaeological surveys in the Cuzco region have shown that Wari influence was largely focused in the Lucre and Huaro basins and that it rapidly diminished in areas to the north and south (Bauer 2004). The influence of the Wari may have been even more variable in remote areas or in regions that lacked the resources the empire was interested in. The great variability in Wari influence has been noted by Schreiber (1992: 69) who writes, "The resulting mosaic of different levels of political control, ranging from very indirect to entirely imposed and direct, is documented in the archaeological records. In some areas more visible remains of the imperial occupation are to be expected, in other areas the evidence may be minimal." In other words, although the Wari certainly held considerable influence over numerous regions outside of their Ayacucho heartland, we can no longer assume that their influence on the intervening areas was continuous, even, or direct.

WARI IN THE DEPARTMENT OF APURIMAC

Wari influence in a region is commonly inferred from architectural remains and from the recovery of Wari ceramics or other portable artifacts. As witnessed long ago by Cieza de León, the Wari built many of their buildings in a distinct architectural style which included large, high-walled rectangular enclosures. Made of fieldstones and mud mortar, these enclosures generally contain a central patio and a series of distinctly elongated galleries with few doorways. Archaeologists frequently use the presence of these enclosures with their patios and galleries to identify installations built under the direction of the Wari Empire (Isbell and McEwan 1991; Schreiber 1992).

An even more common means of documenting Wari influence in a region is through ceramics. Among the various ceramic styles used to identify Wari influence are those that were produced in the Ayacucho area and then exported, including Chakipampa, Ocros, Viñaque, Black Decorated, Huamanga, and Robles Moqo (Men-

zel 1964; Knobloch 1991; Glowacki 1996, 2002). Another marker of Wari influence in a region is the development of local ceramic styles that are thought to reflect elements of Wari artistic traditions. The exact nature of these Wari-influenced styles varies widely, depending on the pre-Wari cultures of the region as well as the nature and intensity of the cultural contact and administrative control (for example, Owen 2007).

The presence of Wari materials in the Department of Apurimac was first suggested by Rowe (1956: 143) and later confirmed by Grossman (1972a). While Grossman's research was centered on earlier remains, he notes that various sites in the Andahuaylas area contain ceramic materials that appear to have been imported from Ayacucho as well as local wares that reproduced classic Wari stylistic motifs. The most extensive research on Wari influence in the Department of Apurimac has, however, been conducted near Pampachiri, some 50 km south of Andahuaylas.[2] The Pampachiri area contains the deeply incised Soras River Valley, which is flanked on either side by immense areas of highland plateaus. The valley itself is heavily terraced and produces a range of cereal crops, while the vast plateaus are used for potato production and camelid herding. Although located relatively near Andahuaylas, it is well documented that the Soras ethnic group occupied part of this region.[3] A brief visit to the Pampachiri area by project members in 2003 noted that the locally produced ceramics are similar, although distinct, from those made in Andahuaylas.

From 1978 to 1982, Frank Meddens directed a general survey of the Pampachiri area and conducted excavations at several sites to understand the extent of Wari influence in this region of the Andes. During his research, Meddens documented seven Middle Horizon sites, the largest of which was Chiqna Jota (Meddens 1985, 1991, 2001). Covering some 9 ha, this site is composed of numerous circular and semicircular structures as well as a series of large, but irregularly shaped plaza areas. Near the center of Chiqna Jota is a small, narrow, rectangular construction which deviates from the general layout of the site. Meddens (1991: 230) concludes that the informal layout of Chiqna Jota and the use of circular structures documents local village-based traditions, while its narrow rectangular building reflects Wari architectural influences. The recovery of numerous sherds from imported Wari vessels, as well as the development of a local Wari-influenced style, and even the recovery of fragments of Wari textiles, also document the influence that the Ayacucho-based empire had in this region (Meddens 2001).[4] As Meddens (1991: 230) concludes, "There can be no doubt that by Middle Horizon 2 the Chicha/Soras Valley was well inside the area of Wari domination . . . [yet] it remained culturally marginal to Wari developments. High-status goods are lacking, and architecture continued to express its traditional pattern."

WARI INFLUENCE IN THE ANDAHUAYLAS REGION

In the course of our regional survey, we recovered various samples of fine Wari ceramics, most of which can be classified as Viñaque style (Figure 5.1). These ceramics are easily identified by their fine pink and orange paste as well as their bright, well-executed polychrome designs (Figures 5.2, 5.3). Although we did not undertake any chemical analysis, we believe most of these Wari ceramics, based on their distinct pastes and colors, were imported into the Andahuaylas area from Ayacucho. The Wari ceramics found in the Andahuaylas region were most often recovered at sites that also contained locally produced Qasawirka ceramics. As noted in the previous chapter, five carbon samples

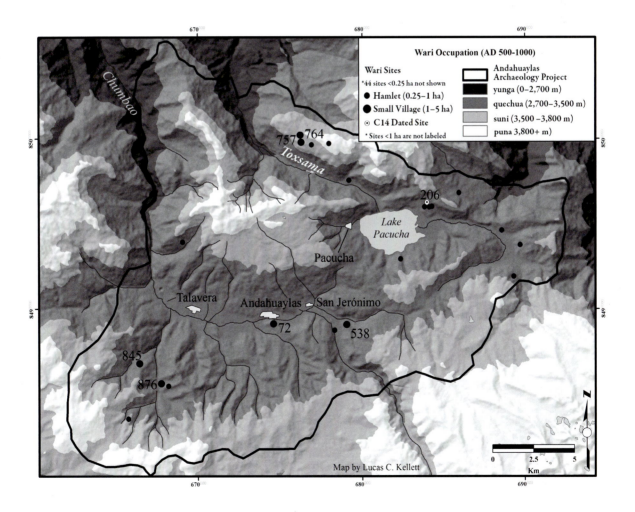

FIGURE 5.1. The Wari settlement pattern in the Andahuaylas region.

FIGURE 5.2. Fragments of Wari bowls (Viñaque style) recovered in the Andahuaylas region.

FIGURE 5.3. Fragments of Wari ceramics (Viñaque style) recovered in the Andahuaylas region.

extracted from the site PAA 206, which yielded both Qasawirka and Wari ceramics, provided a suite of uncalibrated AMS dates which fall between AD 638 ± 55[5] and AD 810 ± 120[6] (Figure 5.4). These radiocarbon samples fit within the time period generally associated with Wari influence over parts of the central Andes (Williams 2001; Bauer and Kellett 2010).[7]

During the survey we recovered Wari ceramics at about 66 sites (Table 5.1), none of which contained evidence of architectural remains. The Wari Phase settlement pattern largely overlies that of the Qasawirka Phase. This suggests to us that the expansion of the Wari into the Andahuaylas region did not bring major changes to the subsistence or settlement patterns. There

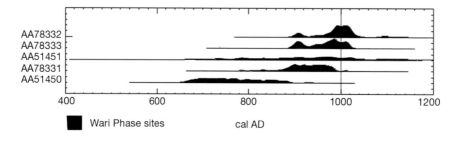

FIGURE 5.4. Calibrated radiocarbon dates from site PAA 206.

TABLE 5.1
Elevations and size of sites with Wari ceramics in the Andahuaylas region

ECOLOGICAL ZONES	HOUSE-HOLD < 0.25 HA	HAMLET 0.25–1 HA	SMALL VILLAGE 1–5 HA	MEDIUM VILLAGE 5–10 HA	LARGE VILLAGE > 10 HA	TOTAL
Yunga (0–2,700 masl)	0	0	0	0	0	0
Quechua (2,700–3,500 masl)	33	12	4	1	0	50
Suni (3,500–3,800 masl)	8	2	0	0	0	10
Puna (3,800+ masl)	3	1	2	0	0	6
Total	44	15	6	1	0	66

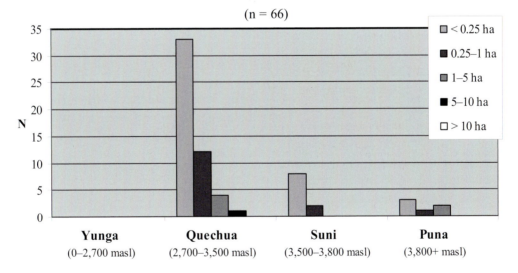

Wari Phase Settlement Distribution
(n = 66)

are, nevertheless, some important exceptions to this statement. First, the most striking difference between the Qasawirka and Wari settlement patterns is the reduced number of small sites. Although the resolution of our site-size data is not especially high, and we recognize that there are overlapping times when Qasawirka and Wari ceramics were in use, it seems that many of the smallest Qasawirka homesteads were abandoned as Wari established influence in the region.[8] A similar pattern is observable in the Cuzco Basin (Bauer 2004: 65) and in the Sondondo Valley (Schreiber 1991: 211). In the Andahuaylas region, several new settlements were also established in some of the highest reaches of the area during Wari times, particularly in the high (3,800 masl) area of Runtunpata (for example, PAA 757, PAA 764), which had seen little occupation during earlier periods (see Figure 5.1). This suggests that the Wari, or perhaps local villagers, were interested in developing what was at that time an under-utilized area of tuber cultivation and herding.

COMPARING THE WARI INFLUENCE IN THE SONDONDO AND ANDAHUAYLAS REGIONS

One of the largest known Wari administrative sites within the central Andes is Jincamocco in the Sondondo Valley (Department of Ayacucho). Located approximately 150 km south of the site of Wari and some 40 km to the west of the Soras River, Jincamocco is in the territory of the Andamarca Lucanas ethnic group (see Figure 2.1). Schreiber (1987, 1991, 1999, 2004) conducted a survey in the Sondondo Valley in the early 1980s and has written extensively on the results. The settlement pattern of the Sondondo region prior to the Wari conquest was that of widely scattered, small villages and hamlets located within the 3,300–3,600 masl elevations. At the time of Wari influence, there was a distinct shift of settlements from upper to lower slope elevations, reflecting an interest in the production of maize by the Wari state. Schreiber writes:

> Visible in the archaeological record is a change in settlement location particularly in the case of the local villages. A downward movement of village locations, coupled with the massive construction of terraces, throughout the valley, signals a major shift in subsistence focus. Whereas Kancha phase [pre-Wari period] subsistence was focused on the cultivation of tubers, maize agriculture may have formed a major component of the subsistence pursuits beginning in the Willka [Wari] phase. (Schreiber 1992: 161)

Even more notable was the construction of the site of Jincamocco, a large regional Wari center that covers some 17.5 ha. Furthermore, the Wari directed several large public works projects in the region (perhaps even importing additional labor from outside areas), including the construction of a large system of terraces to increase the production of maize in the valley. At this time the road system into the Sondondo Valley from Ayacucho was also formalized, and several small Wari installations appear to have been built along it (Schrei-ber 1992). In short, the expansion of the Wari brought major changes to the Sondondo settlement pattern and deeply affected the lives of the people in the region. Yet it is also worth noting that surveys of nearby areas show no evidence of Wari material culture, suggesting that while the Wari occupation of the Sondondo region may have been intense, it was highly localized (Schreiber 2004).

The Andahuaylas Valley is located roughly 100 km to the southeast of Wari. The people of Andahuaylas, like those of Sondondo, were affected by the development of Wari power in the central Andes; but the expansion of the Ayacucho state into Andahuaylas appears to have taken a different form than that which occurred in Sondondo. The Andahuaylas inhabitants had already developed a settlement pattern that emphasized the exploitation of cereals, including maize. Many smaller sites may have been abandoned over time, but the overall settlement pattern before and after the Wari expansion appears to be similar.[9] No new terrace systems were established, and we currently have no evidence of a Wari administrative center in the region or the construction of any other Wari installations. Some new settlements were established during this period, but these appear to have been to take advantage of areas with underexploited tuber and herding resources.

This is not to suggest, however, that the Andahuaylas region was unimportant to the Wari. After all, Andahuaylas is one of the richest agricultural valleys between Ayacucho and Cuzco and is located on the route between the Wari capital and the second largest regional center, Pikillacta. Based on the current evidence, we believe that the Andahuaylas region reflects a case of successful, and perhaps gradual, assimilation, rather than outright conquest and occupation, as appears to have been the case in the Sondondo region. Although the nature and manner in which the Wari came to control the Sondondo and Andahuaylas regions appear to be different, the decline of the Wari brought similar reactions by their indigenous populations. Schreiber (1991: 212) writes:

The most striking correlation with the fall of the Huari Empire in this region is a sudden change in settlement patterns. Nearly every village site occupied during the Middle Horizon was abandoned. New villages were established in a more restricted portion of the valley, and most of these were heavily fortified. . . . Whether there were warring factions within the valley or whether their concern was defense against invaders from other areas is unclear. What is clear, is that there was a great increase in conflict that apparently began at the time of the Huari collapse.

We will see that an equally dramatic settlement shift occurred in the Andahuaylas region with the decline of Wari, and that the majority of the population abandoned their traditional settlements and established new ridgetop villages (Bauer and Kellett 2010).

NOTES

[1] Also spelled "Huari."

[2] This area is also called the Chichas River Valley.

[3] The town of Soras is located appriximately 12 km from the town of Pampachiri.

[4] Meddens (2001) suggests that during the time of Wari influence, the people of the Pampachiri region were administered by the Wari Empire through the site of Jincamocco.

[5] Sample AA 51450.

[6] Sample AA 51451.

[7] The strong continuation of the local Qasawirka pottery style after the arrival of the Wari in the region is not surprising; however, it does complicate the settlement pattern analysis.

[8] The distribution of Wari pottery also highlights the problem of recovering nonlocal pottery within a milieu of continuing local styles. In other words, the general lack of Wari pottery at smaller sites may well also reflect the lack of distribution of Wari pottery to lower-order settlements and lower-status households in the region.

[9] This statement is speculative, given our currently imprecise chronological control over Qasawirka ceramics.

CHAPTER 6

THE CHANKA PHASE
IN THE ANDAHUAYLAS REGION
(AD 1000–1400)

The period between the decline of the Middle Horizon states (Wari and Tiwanaku) and the expansion of the Inca Empire, generally referred to as the Late Intermediate Period (AD 1000–1400), was a dynamic time of social, cultural, and ecological change (Parsons and Hastings 1988; Covey 2008).[1] Across the Andes it is characterized by profound demographic and settlement shifts, as thousands of small villages on valley floors and lower valley slopes were abandoned and new, larger settlements were established on ridges and hilltops. This period is generally associated with an increase in regional hostilities, the construction of defensive works, and the establishment of ridgetop sites (LeBlanc 1981; D'Altroy 1992; Stanish 2003; Arkush and Stanish 2005; Arkush 2006). At the same time, there appears to have been a reorganization in subsistence regimes from the maize-focused agriculture of the lower valleys (*quechua*) (which predominated during the prior Middle Horizon) to a more mixed agro-pastoral economy where potato production and camelid herding played increasingly important roles (Hastorf 1993; Parsons, Hastings, and Matos Mendieta 1997, 2000a, 2000b; D'Altroy and Hastorf 2001; Stanish 2003; Kellett 2008). Furthermore, it is widely suggested that this period included a time of climate change distinguished by drier (Thompson et al. 1985, 1986, 1995; Binford, Brenner, and Leyden 1996; Binford et al. 1997) and possibly cooler conditions (Seltzer and Hastorf 1990). There is, however, a growing recognition that there are great local variations within these trends across the Andes (Covey 2008).

In this chapter, we examine the social changes that occurred in the Andahuaylas region during this era, which is locally known as the Chanka Phase (AD 1000–1400). An analysis of our regional survey data indicates that, like elsewhere in the Andes, there were significant shifts in the local subsistence-settlement patterns during this time period. Most of the lower-elevation sites were abandoned, and a series of much larger sites were established on ridgetops. The large-scale abandonment of traditional settlements adjacent to lower agricultural lands and the construction of new, often defensibly positioned sites suggest that the Chanka Phase in the Andahuaylas area was a time of dramatic social reorganization and perhaps of regional conflict (Figure 6.1).

RELATED LATE INTERMEDIATE PERIOD RESEARCH IN THE CENTRAL HIGHLANDS

Before discussing the Andahuaylas region, it is important to outline some of the research findings of other projects that have been conducted in relatively nearby regions.[2] To date, the most intensive study of Late Intermediate Period settlement patterns in the Peruvian Andes derives from the Upper Mantaro Archaeological Research Project (UMARP), which was designed to investigate Inca expansion and consolidation practices in provincial areas of the empire (D'Altroy 1992; Hastorf 1993; D'Altroy and Hastorf 2001). Undertaken in the Department of Junín, in the Jauja region, this landmark project focused on understanding the shifting dynamics among the sociopolitical organization, settlement strategies,

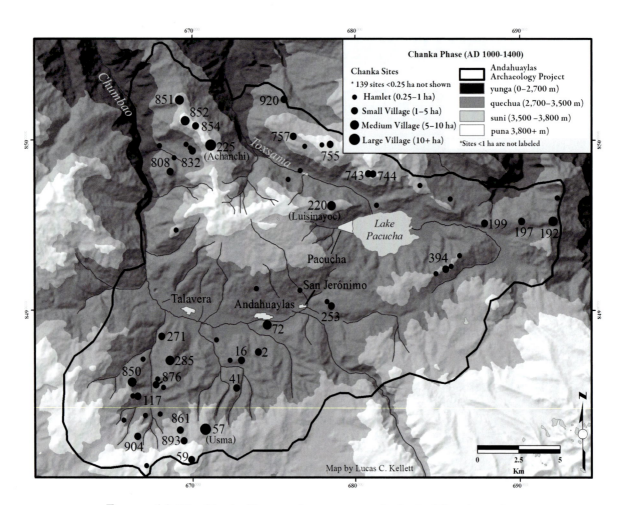

FIGURE 6.1. The Chanka Phase settlement pattern in the Andahuaylas region.

and subsistence regimes of the Wanka ethnic group before and during the Inca occupation of the region. Unlike the Andahuaylas area, the Jauja region appears to have been relatively unaffected by the development of the Wari state, and very few Wari-related artifacts were recovered during the project. Nevertheless, the region experienced many of the same radical settlement pattern shifts during the Late Intermediate Period that have been documented elsewhere in the Andes. The relocation from valley-bottom communities to ridgetop sites and the concomitant shifts in subsistence strategies appear to have begun during what is locally known as Wanka I (AD 1000–1300) times, with intense population aggregation taking place in the area at approximately AD 1350 in Wanka II times (D'Altroy 2001: 39).[3]

Besides being built at high elevations, many newly established Wanka II sites of the Jauja region were surrounded by several massive stone walls which protected large residential sectors. The Wanka II settlement pattern in the Jauja region is dominated by the immense hilltop site of Hatunmarca, estimated at more than 70 ha in size, and by several other large settlements measuring between 20 and 30 ha. These are very large sites for this period in the Andes, and they have been interpreted as representing the political centers of a series of small independent polities that competed for control of local resources (LeBlanc 1981; D'Altroy 1992; D'Altroy and Hastorf 2001). Nevertheless, social ranking within these centers appears to have been minimal during Wanka II times. As D'Altroy and Hastorf (2001: 39) note, "Despite their scale, little or no public architecture is preserved even at the largest sites. Instead, they consist largely of residential sectors comprising hundreds of architectural compounds . . . [defined by] field stone houses and patios areas, enclosed by stone walls." UMARP, however, does argue that there were likely both commoner and elite strata at Wanka II hilltop sites. This conclusion is based on the differences in quality of residential masonry, size of architectural compounds, as well as distinct differences in the quantity and quality of ceramic and food remains (D'Altroy and Hastorf 2001). In addition to the UMARP

study, the construction of Late Intermediate Period ridgetop sites has been noted across the central highlands (Covey 2008). For example, they have been documented in the Vilcanota River Valley[4] near Cuzco (Covey 2006), in Junín (Parsons, Hastings, and Matos Mendieta 2000a, 2000b), in the Asto area (Lavallée 1983), and throughout the Department of Ayacucho (Valdez, Vivanco, and Chávez 1990; Gonzalez Carré 1992a, 1992b; Schreiber 1992; Valdez and Vivanco 1994; González Carré and Pozzi-Escot 2002; Valdez 2002; Meddens and Vivanco Pomacanchari 2005).

A similar settlement pattern of hilltop sites has also been noted farther south in the Lake Titicaca region (Hyslop 1976; Stanish 2003; Frye and de la Vega 2005; Arkush and Stanish 2005). More specifically, Arkush (2006, 2008) has recently completed an extensive study of Late Intermediate Period hilltop sites in the Colla region of the northwestern Titicaca Basin which included more than 40 radiocarbon dates. In her research, Arkush proposes that the fortifications at the hilltop sites reached their maximum extent between AD 1300 and AD 1450. Her findings suggest that the development of chronic warfare in the Titicaca Basin may not have been a direct result of the fall of Tiwanaku (ca. AD 1000), but rather was brought about by later regional tensions which became gradually elevated during a prolonged period of severe climate change.

The Lake Titicaca findings are especially relevant to this study. It has long been assumed that two large kingdoms developed in the Lake Titicaca region during the Late Intermediate Period, the Colla and the Lupaqa, and that these two kingdoms were locked in a prolonged state of intraregional warfare before the Inca expanded into the region. Recent archaeological surveys in the area of the Lupaqa provide a more subtle interpretation of the social condition that prevailed during the pre-Inca times (Hyslop 1976; Stanish et al. 1997). Frye and de la Vega (2005: 173) suggest that the area of the Lupaqa was far from unified and that chronic conflict and competition existed between the separate Lupaqa groups. These researchers propose that rather than promoting the development of centralized leadership, the chronic warfare among the Lupaqa prevented regional unification. Arkush (2006: 305) presents a similar picture for the Colla in the northwest part of the Titicaca Basin: "While the [Colla] area cannot be considered politically unified, patterns of site placement and intervisibility suggest that many fortified sites relied on systems of allies for defense." Therefore, it appears that these neighboring ethnic groups (the Colla and the Lupaqa) were neither politically unified entities nor arch enemies, but were required to build and live in defensive sites during a period of actual or potential conflict.

A notable exception to the widespread pattern of Late Intermediate Period fortified hilltop sites can be found in the Cuzco Basin, the area surrounding the modern city of Cuzco, where many of the Late Intermediate Period sites are located near the valley floor (ca. 3,200–3,500 masl). Bauer (1992, 2002, 2004) and Covey (2006) have highlighted this exception, suggesting that the Cuzco Basin became politically unified very early during the Late Intermediate Period and thus was spared a prolonged period of regional conflict. Equally important, the groups living in the Cuzco Basin and some nearby areas (for example, Lucre Basin, Maras area, Xaquixaquana Valley) maintained or established subsistence systems based on valley-bottom agriculture, which promoted immigration, higher rates of population growth, greater settlement nucleation, and eventually urbanization, state formation, and the need to expand to develop new lands. Site densities also increased dramatically during the Late Intermediate Period, and within the Cuzco Basin the agricultural landscape was terraced in a way that created stable state incomes while undercutting local and individual autonomy (Bauer and Covey 2002; Covey 2006). It is becoming increasingly evident that, unlike the Lupaqa and the Colla of the Lake Titicaca region or the Wanka of the Upper Mantaro, the Inca were able to develop a political hierarchy across the Cuzco region during the Late Intermediate Period that reduced ethnic diversity and political competition and that, over the course of several centuries, resulted in the creation of a unified heartland.

The chroniclers state that the Chanka were not only early rivals of the Inca, but the initiates of territorial expansionism in the central Andes. Therefore, as we began our research in the Andahuaylas region we thought we might find evidence of political growth and regional consolidation during the Late Intermediate Period, as has been documented for the Cuzco region. It was considered possible that the early development of the Chanka paralleled, or perhaps even surpassed, that of the early Inca in the Cuzco Valley. The results of our investigations indicate, however, that the Chanka followed a course of cultural development that more closely mirrored that of the Wanka, Colla, Lupaqa, and other highland Andean groups, than the more exceptional pattern recorded for the Inca in the Cuzco area.

RESEARCH IN THE ANDAHUAYLAS REGION

While each of the Late Intermediate Period (here called the Chanka Phase) village sites in the Andahuaylas region contains unique features, they also share many similarities.[5] To begin with, they tend to be situated in prominent locations, most frequently on flat terrain at the summit of ridges (Figure 6.2). Indeed, almost every major ridge in the Andahuaylas region contains a Chanka Phase settlement. Several of the larger habitation sites also have ditches cut horizontally across the ridge near the entrances to the sites. Although the preservation of architectural features at the Chanka Phase sites is not especially impressive when compared with other regions of the central Andes, they are the best-preserved sites of any time period in the Andahuaylas region. Chanka architecture is typically built of locally available fieldstones which are rough cut and stacked with simple mud mortar, a construction technique often termed *pirca* masonry. Chanka habitation sites frequently display a dense arrangement of agglutinated circular structures that are arranged in patio groups and built on terraces (Figure 6.3). Also common are circular *chullpas*, which are frequently found in small clusters and are located

FIGURE 6.2. A typical ridgetop Chanka Phase site in the Andahuaylas region (PAA 788).

FIGURE 6.3. Agglutinated circular structures at the site of Achanchi (PAA 225).

higher on the ridge or on knolls away from hilltop settlements (Figure 6.4). Large Chanka Phase habitation sites range from 1 to 15 ha in size and contain dense concentrations of surface pottery, lithics, faunal remains, and stone grinders (*batanes*) (see Table 6.1). The sites located near large grasslands frequently also contain the remains of stone corrals. Finally, the elevated position of most of these large Chanka Phase sites provides a commanding view of the surrounding landscape and line-of-sight to other large ridgetop settlements across neighboring valleys (Kellett 2010).

The Timing of the Chanka Phase Settlement Shift

While researchers have long suggested that dramatic changes in regional settlement patterns occurred sometime between the Middle Horizon and the Late Intermediate Period (Lumbreras 1974a; Parsons and Hastings 1988), few projects have been able to provide sufficient radiocarbon dates to determine when exactly such settlement changes occurred in a specific area. The timing of the demographic shift is critical if we are to understand the political and ecological factors

FIGURE 6.4. One of the several standing chullpas at site PAA 893 dating to the Chanka Phase.

TABLE 6.1
Elevations and sizes of Chanka Phase sites in the Andahuaylas region

ECOLOGICAL ZONES	HOUSE-HOLD < 0.25 HA	HAMLET 0.25–1 HA	SMALL VILLAGE 1–5 HA	MEDIUM VILLAGE 5–10 HA	LARGE VILLAGE > 10 HA	TOTAL
Yunga (0–2,700 masl)	0	0	0	0	0	0
Quechua (2,700–3,500 masl)	98	19	10	2	0	129
Suni (3,500–3,800 masl)	24	9	5	4	0	42
Puna (3,800+ masl)	17	2	9	1	2	31
Total	139	30	24	7	2	202

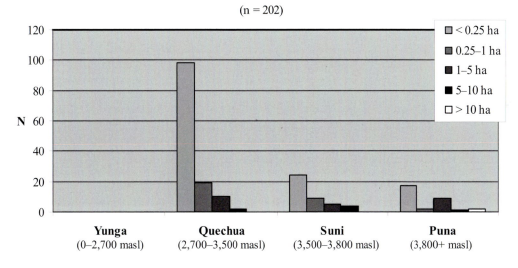

Chanka Phase Settlement Distribution

(n = 202)

that may have been involved with it and to determine if different regions underwent similar transformations at the same time (Figure 6.5).

During our research in the Andahuaylas region, as noted in the previous chapter, we processed a total of five radiocarbon samples from Anccopaccha (PAA 206), a site with Wari ceramics. These samples provided uncalibrated AMS dates ranging from AD 638 ± 55[6] to AD 855 ± 38.[7] The *calibrated dates* for these samples suggest

that the Wari occupation of the site began in the late 600s or early 700s AD and lasted until around AD 1000 (see Figure 6.5; Appendix 1). These dates match well with the currently recognized period of Wari expansionism defined elsewhere in the Andes (Williams 2001).

As discussed in greater detail below, during our survey we also collected carbon samples from various ridgetop Chanka Phase sites. Samples from seven different Chanka Phase sites within

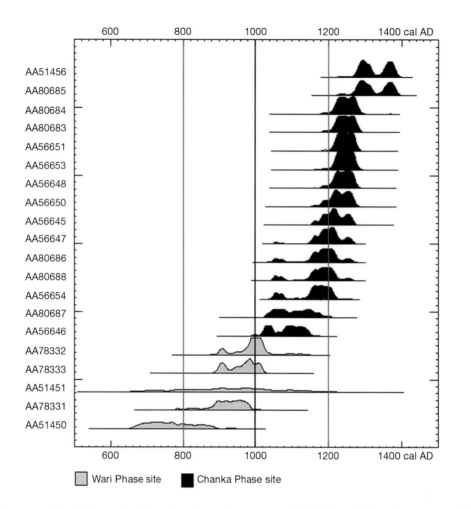

FIGURE 6.5. Calibrated radiocarbon dates from sites with Wari and Chanka ceramics. The dramatic shift in settlement patterns from the valley bottom sites of the Wari to the ridge top sites of the Chanka appear to have occurred between AD 1000 and 1100.

the Andahuaylas region and from two ridgetop sites in the nearby Uranmarca area (Socualaya Dávila 2005)[8] were submitted for dating. Although the contexts for these samples were not ideal— carbon samples and soot-encrusted ceramics from buried middens revealed in road cuts and looters' pits—the nine Chanka Phase sites provide a remarkably tight cluster of uncalibrated AMS dates, ranging from AD 934 ± 32[9] to AD 1124 ± 30.[10] These findings document that the Chanka Phase ridgetop sites were inhabited for several centuries, starting around the end of the first millennium AD (Appendix 1).

A second series of six AMS dates[11] provided from carbon samples collected during excavations by Kellett (2010) in domestic contexts at two ridgetop sites of the region (Achanchi and Luisi-

nayoc) closely match those collected during the survey phase of the project (see Appendix 1). These carbon samples also document a relatively narrow occupation period for the Chanka Phase ridgetop settlements in the Andahuaylas region, with uncalibrated AMS dates ranging from AD 982 ± 36[12] to AD 1219 ± 43.[13] Given the considerable overlap in the radiocarbon dates from these different projects, we have strong evidence to suggest that the Chanka Phase ridgetop sites were constructed and initially occupied between AD 1000 and 1100 (see Figure 6.5).

The Chanka Phase Settlement Pattern

The regional archaeological survey located approximately 200 residential sites, primarily habitation sites and corral complexes, which contained diagnostic Chanka ceramics. Of these sites, approximately 32 are considered relatively large (> 1 ha). In contrast to earlier prehistoric periods in the valley, the largest Chanka Phase occupation sites are concentrated at higher elevations (3,500–4,000 masl), frequently near the *suni*-puna ecotone at the boundary between upper agricultural lands and highland pastures.

The two largest, and certainly the most impressive, Chanka Phase sites in the Andahuay-las region are Achanchi (PAA 225)[14] and Usma (PAA 57).[15] Both sites are estimated to measure between 10 and 15 ha and are located on distant ridges on either side of the Andahuaylas Valley. Achanchi is an extremely imposing site that stretches for more than a kilometer along one of the highest ridges north of the city of Andahuay-las (Figures 6.6, 6.7). The site, located at 4,030 masl, contains more than 300 circular buildings arranged among small patios and habitation terraces. The eastern and western sides of the site

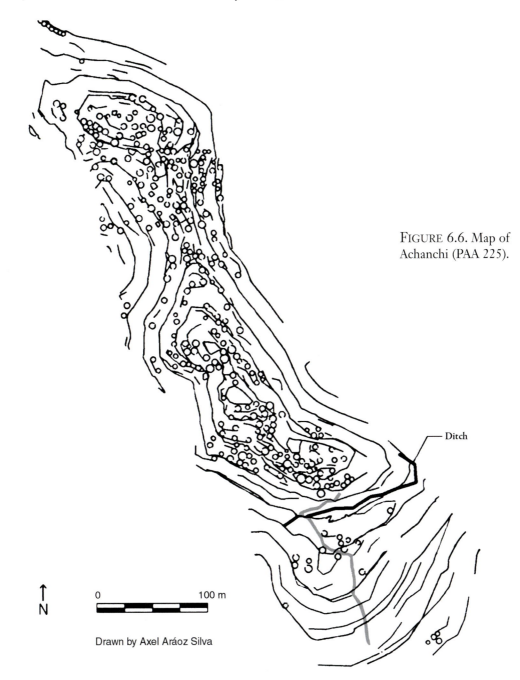

FIGURE 6.6. Map of Achanchi (PAA 225).

Ditch

↑
N

0   100 m

Drawn by Axel Aráoz Silva

ditch

FIGURE 6.7. The site of Achanchi (PAA 225) is located on top of a high, narrow ridge. A number of other large Chanka Phase sites were also built behind it following the ridge line.

FIGURE 6.8. A large ditch has been cut across the ridge at the southern entrance of Achanchi (PAA 225).

contain sheer cliffs, and a deep ditch has been dug at the southern entrance to the site (Figure 6.8). It is not surprising that a defensive ditch was constructed on the site's southern side, since this slope provides the only easy access to the settlement. Other large Chanka Phase sites are also located along the same ridge to the northwest of Achanchi as it descends toward the Chumbao River (see Figure 6.1).

As noted above, a carbon sample taken from a looters' pit at Achanchi during the survey provided an uncalibrated AMS date of AD 1113 ± 32.[16] Three carbon samples collected during excavations at Achanchi, which were conducted by Kellett (2010), provided uncalibrated AMS dates of AD 1129 ± 36,[17] AD 1134 ± 36,[18] and AD 1219 ± 36.[19] While there are minor differences in the sizes and construction quality of different patios and individual structures, there were no discernible patterns at the site that suggest the existence of distinct elite and commoner social classes, as has been argued for large Wanka hill-top sites of the Mantaro Valley (D'Altroy 1992; D'Altroy and Hastorf 2001; DeMarrais 2001).

The other very large Chanka Phase site in the Andahuaylas region is Usma (PAA 57), which is located at 3,880 masl and is also estimated to be between 10 and 15 ha (Figure 6.9). Usma is one of the best-known sites in the region, since it dominates the southern rim of the valley and is visible from the city of Andahuaylas. Situated on a large, rounded ridgetop on the edge of an expansive puna grassland area, the site contains numerous circular structures, habitation terraces, small patios, and several looted chullpas. Carbon recovered at the site during the survey provided an uncalibrated AMS date of AD 1123 ± 30.[20] As observed at Achanchi, while some patio groups and circular houses differ slightly in size and quality of construction, there are no clear indications of elite structures or other evidence of ranked social groups within the site.

The site of Luisinayoc (PAA 220)[21] is also of considerable importance within the local

FIGURE 6.9. Usma (PAA 57) is the largest site on the southern side of the Andahuaylas Valley.

Drawn by Lucas C. Kellett

FIGURE 6.10. Map of Luisinayoc (PAA 220).

FIGURE 6.11. The site of Luisinayoc (PAA 220).

settlement system (Figures 6.10, 6.11). This Chanka Phase site sits at an elevation of 3,716 masl on a broad east-west-running ridge above and to the north of the town of Pacucha. The site is long, extending for more than two-thirds of a kilometer over two small knolls of the ridge, and is approximately 10 ha in size. The site is defined by a high density of diagnostic Chanka ceramics and poorly preserved architectural remains. The site offers a stunning view of Lake Pacucha (3,100 masl) and the surrounding valleys. The northern and southern slopes of the ridge are extremely steep, and a ditch (not shown on map) has been dug across the eastern end of the ridge, a moderate distance (ca. 400 m) from the site's eastern boundary. Unfortunately, the site is heavily disturbed by modern cultivation as well as by a road which runs most of its length. On close inspection, one can discern the foundations of numerous small habitation terraces, patios, enclosures, and circular structures, but there is no architec-tural evidence of social hierarchies present at the site. Furthermore, there is no evidence of formal internal divisions within the site, and the arrangement of the structures is haphazard. A carbon sample collected from the road-cut during the regional survey yielded an uncalibrated AMS date of AD 1227 ± 36.[22] Three additional carbon samples collected during excavations at Luisinayoc by Kellett (2010), reflect a slightly earlier occupation of the site. These samples provided uncalibrated AMS dates of AD 982 ± 36,[23] AD 1045 ± 36,[24] and AD 1052 ± 36.[25]

There are several other Chanka Phase sites of significant size and composition in the Andahuaylas region. For example, the large Chanka Phase site of Circapata (PAA 192)[26] is located at the far eastern end of a long, broad ridge and holds a striking overview of the Pincos River Valley (Figure 6.12). The Inca road from Andahuaylas to Curamba ran through an important mountain pass beside this site. Despite intensive cultivation

FIGURE 6.12. The large Chanka Phase site of Circapata (PAA 192) is located on the ridge in the center of this photograph.

FIGURE 6.13. The large site of Cerro Maraypata (PAA 850). This site has substantial Chanka as well as Inca remains. The site is included in the 1539 *Andahuaylas Encomienda Document* under the name Ccaccacha (the name of the modern village at the base of the ridge).

and the installation of an antenna, the site still contains numerous terraces and circular structures. There is also a large Chanka Phase site immediately east of the Inca site of Sondor. This site (PAA 199)[27] extends for several hundred meters, and the foundations of many poorly preserved terraces and circular structures can still be observed. Carbon collected at this site during the survey yielded an uncalibrated AMS date of AD 1080 ± 32.[28] Other important Chanka Phase settlements include Waywaka (PAA 72) beside Andahuaylas, as well as the sprawling ridge sites of Cerro Maraypata (PAA 850)[29] (Figure 6.13) and Cruzpata (PAA 285)[30] near Talavera. Carbon collected during the regional survey from soot-encrusted pottery at the last of these sites provided an uncalibrated AMS date of AD 934 ± 32.[31]

The moderate distribution of medium to large size Chanka Phase hilltop sites suggests that local populations were distributed across the landscape, with no distinct regional capital or established site hierarchy (Table 6.1). Nevertheless, population aggregation is documented by increases in average site size, with Chanka Phase sites having an average site size of 1.3 ha in comparison with Qasawirka Phase and Wari Phase average site sizes of 0.5 and 1.1 ha, respectively.

Settlement and Conflict in the Andahuaylas Region

Late Intermediate Period sites in the central and south central Andes are well known for having defensive works associated with them (Arkush 2006; Arkush and Stanish 2005). For example, one site in the Lake Titicaca region, Pukara Juli, is surrounded by five concentric fortification walls totaling more than 16 km in length (Stanish et al. 1997), and there are dozens of other fortified sites in the area (Arkush 2008). Likewise, many of the major Late Intermediate Period sites of the Jauja region are surrounded by substantial fortification walls. Despite this broad pattern, we have only mixed evidence of village defensive works within our survey region. As has been noted, the largest Chanka sites are located on ridgetops, which contain naturally steep slopes. While these sites can be considered as defensively positioned, many lack evidence of other obvious defensive features. In many cases, large walls are found at outer living terraces along site margins, but they may be simply built this way to accommodate for the steep topography (see Borgstede and Mathieu 2007).

There are only three sites in the Andahuaylas area that are currently documented as containing clear defensive works. Two of the sites, Luisinayoc and Achanchi, have been briefly described above. At both of these sites, ditches have been dug across the lower ends of the ridges and are located at site margins on moderate slopes, where access by intruders would have been easiest. The third site, PAA 893,[32] is a much smaller site and is located on the other side of the valley, but it too has a ditch running across its only area of flat access (Figures 6.14, 6.15). While several other sites have possible ditches or defensive walls which need to be further investigated, more common indicators of conflict, such as concentric walls, parapets, baffled doorways, as well as stores of sling-stones, are absent (Kellett 2010).

Figure 6.14. Site PAA 893 is located on the south side of the Andahuaylas Valley.

FIGURE 6.15. Ditch dug to protect the Chanka Phase site of PAA 893.

Although our interpretations are complicated by the poor preservation of Chanka Phase sites, especially in comparison with the Late Intermediate Period ruins in other areas such as Junín and the Titicaca Basin, it is clear that the level of public investment in defensive works in the Andahuaylas region does not match that reflected in many other areas of the Andean highlands. Finally, a note of caution: Despite defensive site positioning and the existence of some defensive works at Chanka Phase sites in Andahuaylas, such a defensive stance does not always indicate actual conflict (LeBlanc 1999). More likely, local populations were preoccupied with the threat of occasional raids, rather than actual pervasive endemic warfare.

SETTLEMENT AND AGRO-PASTORALISM IN THE ANDAHUAYLAS REGION

Based on the relatively light public investment in defensive works surrounding the Chanka Phase settlements, we currently believe that regional conflict was not the sole variable in determining the exact settlement locations for many of the Chanka villages in the Andahuaylas region (Kellett 2008; Parsons, Hastings, and Matos Mendieta 1997, 2000a, 2000b). In fact, during the course of his early research in Andahuaylas, Joel Grossman made the following comment on these large conspicuous Chanka hilltop sites:

> [T]he ridge-top locations of the pre-Inca sites of Andahuaylas must be considered to reflect a variety of pressures. Such pressures could include the economic priorities . . . as well as defense and protection from natural disaster, without the need to treat them as mutually exclusive. (Grossman 1983: 48)

In a similar vein, we argue that the establishment of hilltop settlements in the region was a multicausal response to concomitant shifts in the social, political, *and* economic landscape during the Late Intermediate Period.

Several studies suggest that the Peruvian and Bolivian Andes suffered a period of prolonged drought soon after the first millennium AD (Abbott et al. 1997, 2000; Binford et al. 1997; Chepstow-Lusty et al 2003; Thompson et al. 1985, 1986, 1995). This time of decreased rainfall is believed to have dramatically influenced the subsistence strategies of the Lake Titicaca region inhabitants, causing various groups to shift away from traditional systems of raised field agriculture toward a more mixed economy in which pastoralism played an increasingly important role (Graffam 1992; Stanish 2003). Frye and de la Vega (2005) have documented a particularly clear case among the Lupaqa, a large ethnic group that lived on the southern side of Lake Titicaca during the Late Intermediate Period. They write:

> Responses to the deterioration of the Tiwanaku state and climatic downturn that occurred in this period included the abandonment of Tiwanaku political centers and agricultural systems, a dispersal of the population from large centers across the landscape, competition over available resources, and increase economic focus on animal husbandry. We see the increased settlement density, and the fact that the largest and most architecturally complex fortified sites developed within the agro-pastoral zone, as an indication that animal husbandry played a critical role in the . . . [local] political economy. (Frye and de la Vega 2005: 183)

Agro-pastoralism is viewed as a highly successful subsistence strategy and continues to be used in many areas of the Andes today (e.g., Brush and Guillet 1985; Yamamoto 1985; Browman 1987). In the Andahuaylas region, the productivity of the lower-altitude maize zones, which were intensively exploited during the period of Wari influence, may have been reduced by decreased rainfall toward the end of the first millennium AD (Seltzer and Hastorf 1990). Around that same time, we also see the construction of new sites on remote ridgetops. Although a relatively low number of large agricultural terraces are found around the ridgetop sites, it is likely that tuber agriculture did take place near these settlements, utilizing a simple, low-labor strategy without terrace construction. Furthermore, the concentration of cor-

rals around many of these high-elevation sites appears to support the suggestion that pastoralism increased in importance. A mixed agro-pastoral economy would have served as an effective risk-reduction subsistence strategy in the face of widespread demographic, settlement, and environmental change during the Late Intermediate Period (Graffam 1992; Stanish 2003; Kellett 2008). We suggest that the selection of new ridgetop site locations at the ecotone between the upper limits of agriculture and the higher pastoral lands (ca. 3,700–4,000 masl) in the Andahuaylas region during the Late Intermediate Period reflects not only a reduction in regional security, but also a fundamental shift in regional subsistence systems in the face of changing climatic conditions.

OVERVIEW OF THE CHANKA PHASE

An analysis of our regional survey data indicates that there were significant shifts in the local subsistence-settlement patterns in the Andahuaylas region near the end of the first millennium AD. The abandonment of high-quality, lower-elevation agricultural land that had been farmed for millennia and the subsequent construction of new, defensibly positioned sites suggest that the Late Intermediate Period in the Andahuaylas region was a time of major flux, with some threat of local or regional conflict. The fact that at least three of the newly established sites were constructed with defensive ditches, and that similar settlement shifts have been noted elsewhere in the highlands during this period, strengthens this conclusion.

Our radiocarbon evidence documents that a radical shift in settlement location occurred across the Andahuaylas region within a remarkably short period of time. Valley-bottom sites with Wari pottery appear to have been occupied up to AD 1000, after which there is a sudden establishment of a host of new ridgetop sites. The period around AD 1000 correlates with the time that Wari influence is believed to have been in sharp decline (Williams 2001) and a series of prolonged droughts was just beginning (Thompson et al. 1985). Disentangling the relationships among these complex phenomena (settlement shifts, political decline, and climatic change) is difficult, but the concomitant occurrence of all three is difficult to ignore. The exact chronological relationships between the defensive structures (e.g., ditches and walls) at the Chanka sites and the construction dates of the ridgetop sites themselves also remain to be investigated. It is possible that these constructions did not occur simultaneously, and that the defensive works were later additions to the sites in response to fluctuating levels of conflict (see Arkush 2008). Such findings would have important implications for the historical reconstruction of the shifting settlement patterns and for understanding the social conditions during which the sites were occupied.

However, it is clear that the shift from lower valley sites to ridgetop sites required a change in the subsistence economy. We believe that, perhaps responding to a period of prolonged droughts, the establishment of new villages in proximity to larger expanses of puna grasslands reflects the increased importance that pastoralism held during this period. This is further supported by concentrations of corrals in and around several of these large hilltop sites. In short, it appears that an increased dependence on agropastoral subsistence was required for the successful survival of local populations in this high-elevation landscape during the Late Intermediate Period (Kellett 2008, 2010).

The shift from valley-bottom to ridgetop settlements may have also had other important implications for the organization of the regional society. The concentration of an unprecedented number of villagers in ridgetop settlements surely brought with it new directions in leadership. As Arkush (2006, 2008) argues for the Titicaca Basin, the increased intervisibility between Chanka ridgetop settlements in Andahuaylas may have contributed to the increasing development of local alliances for stronger defense in times of attack. However, as the communities became larger and yet more isolated on ridgetops, we can presume that they also became more autonomous than the more closely spaced and interconnected villages

on the valley floor of the preceding period. The fragmentation of the political and social landscape makes territorial expansion more difficult and the acquisition of land and other natural resources more complex (Beck 2003, 2006). The development of distant and widely separated villages would have also lent power to the individual village leaders, while at the same time it would have become increasingly difficult for any single village leader to grow influential enough to dominate other settlements in the region. The imposed separation and isolation of villages across the Andahuaylas area during the Late Intermediate Period would have worked against the development of a single regional authority and against the general forces of regional unification. As the local society reacted against political and environmental stress and relocated their settlements in higher and more remote locations, a cycle may have been started in which regional unification became increasingly more difficult, if not impossible.

In this respect, it is worth noting that the survey data also suggest that a complex settlement hierarchy did not develop in the Andahuaylas area during the Late Intermediate Period. There is no single, disproportionately large site in the Andahuaylas region indicative of a paramount village or capital for the Chanka. While Achanchi and Usma are the two largest Chanka sites, they are not qualitatively different from several other Chanka settlements in the region. The internal composition of the Late Intermediate Period village sites, defined by chaotic clusters of circular buildings, patios, and terraces, are all roughly similar. There is no evidence of large elite structures at any of the sites, and there is no evidence of large-scale public works (such as temple mounds, platforms, or sunken courts) at any site, beyond the construction of fortification ditches and several possible defensive walls. We also found no evidence of well-organized craft production during the Late Intermediate Period. Indeed, regional craft production, as reflected in ceramics, reached a nadir during this period. The local ceramics of the Chanka are poorly made, and there is little uniformity or standardization in designs, forms, or vessel shapes (see Appendix 8).

Rather than a centralized hierarchy, Chanka settlement patterns are suggestive of a dual social organization. The sites of Achanchi and Usma are located at approximately the same altitude (Achanchi 4,030 masl; Usma 3,886 masl), and they are roughly the same distance from the valley floor (Achanchi 10 km; Usma 7 km). They are also both about the same size (~12 ha), and each is the largest site within its respective side of the valley (see Figure 6.1). Furthermore, there is a series of six nearly equally sized (5–10 ha) villages spread across the region. This is just the kind of patterning one would expect from an Andean moiety system. We know that during the Inca and Colonial periods, the Chanka were divided into Hanan and Hurin divisions, each of which contained a number of kin groups (see Chapter 2). The archaeological survey findings suggest that the moiety system of the Chanka may have extended back into pre-Inca times, and we speculate that the sites of Achanchi and Usma represented the two most powerful settlements within this system of dual social organization.[33]

Based on the different locations of these two large settlements (Achanchi and Usma), it is possible that the two Chanka moieties engaged in slightly different forms of agro-pastoralism. For example, Achanchi is situated at the top of a very steep ridge which contains smaller tracts of puna grasslands. Yet, on either side of the ridge are two huge mountain slopes which range in elevation between 2,000 and 4,200 masl, and which to this day contain numerous ecological zones for the production of an extraordinarily diverse suite of agricultural crops (including bananas, maize, quinoa, potatoes). In contrast, the site of Usma is located on the southern rim of the Andahuaylas Valley. It was situated more distant from lower valley agricultural land than Achanchi, yet it is adjacent to an enormous expanse of high-elevation puna lands (3,800–4,500 masl). Given these differences in micro-resource availability, it is possible that the Chanka populations living in and around Achanchi, while still agro-pastoralists, may have focused more attention on agricultural production, while those occupying Usma, who also engaged in agro-pastoral production,

developed a higher commitment to camelid husbandry.

The overall settlement pattern of the Andahuaylas region during the Chanka Phase (or Late Intermediate Period) is in sharp contrast to that of the Cuzco Basin, where the sprawling, valley-bottom city of Cuzco was already emerging as an urbanized center with a series of large satellite communities surrounding it. There were also numerous public works constructed, including massive agricultural terraces, numerous storage units, and various elite structures, in the city of Cuzco and throughout the surrounding basin during this period. In other words, there is clear archaeological evidence in the Cuzco region of ethnic integration, class formation, and the development of a regional political hierarchy during the Late Intermediate Period (Bauer 2004; Bauer and Covey 2002; Covey 2006). Similar evidence is lacking from the Andahuaylas region during the same period.

Our fieldwork indicates that the processes of cultural development that occurred among the Chanka was distinctly different from what occurred in the Cuzco region among their so-called rivals. As such, the results of the research suggest that the Chanka may not have been as politically unified as generally assumed in the archaeological and historical literature. While the lack of elites, complex settlement hierarchies, and large public works does not necessarily preclude the existence of some level of regional cohesion, these findings do force us to reexamine and to question the historical accuracies of much of the information presented by the Spanish chroniclers concerning the Chanka.

By the end of the Late Intermediate Period in the Cuzco region, the Inca had formed a large cultural heartland and unified over a dozen formally independent regional groups. They had developed a clear state architectural style, built a large central capital city, and were in the process of transforming the landscape with immense terrace systems. While it is possible that at the same time autonomous polities could have briefly united or formed temporary confederations in the Apurimac, Ayacucho, and Huancavelica areas, our findings do not support the existence of a cohesive complex polity. This is to say, the current vision of a united central Andean area under the strong regional influence or control of the Chanka is not supported by the available archaeological data.

In this context, it is worth repeating that our findings for the Andahuaylas region are similar to those recently recovered in the Lake Titicaca region by Frye and de la Vega (2005) among the Lupaqa, and by Arkush (2006, 2008) among the Colla. The Lupaqa and the Colla are described in some chronicles as the two largest and most powerful ethnic groups of the Lake Titicaca region, and both are traditionally thought to have reached relatively high levels of social complexity. The Spanish chroniclers frequently refer to the leaders of these groups as "kings" and suggest that their regional powers matched those of the emergent rulers of Cuzco. The Lupaqa and the Colla, like the Chanka, are generally believed to have been on the verge of hegemonic expansion when their armies were defeated and their leaders captured by Inca forces. Yet, recent archaeological research in the Titicaca Basin supports a more nuanced picture of their cultural development. For example, regional survey results within the area of the Lupaqa indicate that they were not as centrally organized as generally believed. Frye and de la Vega write:

> Although there are differences in the size and number of structures at major fortified sites, within the Lupaqa territory as a whole no one site can be considered a political capital. Instead, as the systematic survey and reconnaissance data show, the pattern of small habitation sites located near fortified sites is one that is repeated throughout the Lupaqa territory. . . . At present there are no archaeological indicators to suggest the existence of a Lupaqa King, a Lupaqa capital, or a unified Lupaqa confederation. (Frye and de la Vega 2005: 183–184)

These findings are supported by those recovered by Arkush (2006, 2008) among the nearby Colla, where she reports a general lack of political

unity and widespread evidence of internal warfare. She proposes that the regional settlement movement from lower-altitude to hilltop sites in the Lake Titicaca region occurred near the beginning of the Late Intermediate Period, with a concomitant regional drought (ca. AD 1000) and the collapse of Tiwanaku political influence. Furthermore, Arkush suggests that intraregional warfare did not reach its climax until several centuries after the settlement shifts had occurred. Instead of experiencing a period of slow political unification following the chaotic end of the Middle Horizon (ca. AD 1000) as seen in the Cuzco region, the Lake Titicaca area may have witnessed a nearly continuous period of segmentation and conflict. Arkush writes:

> It is highly probable that drought and attendant resource stress played a significant part in the escalation of war in the late LIP. Resource stress could have fostered violent competition for limited arable land, and encourage raids on stored crops; it may have indirectly led to livestock rustling as people became more reliant on camelids, or perhaps it simply caused greater social friction between neighboring communities in hard times. Nevertheless, in the Titicaca basin, fort-building continued after the droughts eased, suggesting that warfare outlived this impetus and generated its own momentum. Good times did not result in peace any more than collapse resulted in widespread war. The causes of continued war are difficult to pinpoint securely, but it may have been power-hungry warlords, durable fortifications, and the cycles of revenge encouraged by segmentary organization that embroiled the Colla in periodic wars for the rest of the LIP and beyond. (Arkush 2008: 365)

Rather than being two rapidly developing polities (señoríos) that presumed to rival the growing regional power of the Inca, the Colla and Lupaqa were of modest complexity and appear to have been enmeshed in internal conflict and strife. More speculatively, their menacing stance toward Cuzco may have even been fashioned, or greatly exaggerated, after the fact by Inca narratives to justify the annexation of the Lake Titicaca region by the Incas.

While we have a more coarsely grained chronology in comparison with that of the Colla and Lupaqa, it is becoming increasingly clear that the presence of scattered, densely occupied but internally homogenous, defensively positioned ridgetop sites in the Andahuaylas region forces us to reexamine some of the basic assumptions concerning the Chanka and their neighboring groups that have been derived from readings of Spanish accounts. Currently we find no archaeological evidence to suggest that the Chanka were a highly stratified or uniquely powerful ethnic group at the time of the Inca expansion. The Late Intermediate Period settlement pattern recorded in the Andahuaylas region is similar to that found across many other areas of the central highlands and suggests that the Chanka were but one of numerous, relatively small polities occupying specific regions of the Andes during this time period. Powerful Chanka leaders, or a loose confederation of central Andean ethnic groups, may have briefly arisen near the end of this period with the legendary Chanka-Inca War, but they have left few material correlates to be identified.

NOTES

1 Parts of this chapter are presented in Bauer and Kellett (2010). They are reprinted here by permission from *Latin American Antiquity* (© Society for American Archaeology), volume 21, number 1.
2 Also see Meddens and Vivanco Pomacanchari (2005) for a review of work on the Late Intermediate Period sites in the central highlands.
3 The Upper Mantaro Archaeological Research Project has been able to divide the Late Intermediate Period into two distinct eras: Wanka I (AD 1000–1300) and Wanka II (AD 1300–1450). Unfortunately, we have not been able to provide such a refined study of settlement pattern shifts in the Andahuaylas region.
4 Also called the Urubamba River Valley.
5 Previous archaeological research in Andahuaylas focused on the earliest village sites, which are located in the lower valley areas (Grossman 1972a, 1983). This being the case, the largest and most impressive Chanka Phase sites, which are situated on high ridgetops, have gone largely undocumented, and the local ceramic style of this period remains poorly defined.
6 Sample AA 51450.
7 Sample AA 78332.
8 Samples AA 56651 and AA 56650.
9 Sample AA 56646.
10 Sample AA 56651.
11 Samples AA 80683–AA 80688.
12 Sample AA 80687.
13 Sample AA 80685.
14 18L 0680901, 8495774; 4,030 masl.
15 18L 0670781, 8483011; 3,886 masl.
16 Sample AA 56648.
17 Sample AA 80683.
18 Sample AA 80684.
19 Sample AA 80685.
20 Sample AA 56653.
21 18L 0678586, 8496149.
22 Sample AA 51456.
23 Sample AA 80687.
24 Sample AA 80688.
25 Sample AA 80686.
26 18L 0692023, 8495235; 3,558 masl.
27 18L 0687876, 8495120; 3,302 masl.
28 Sample AA 56645.
29 18L 0666309, 8485770; 3,612 masl.
30 18L 0668633, 8487046; 3,371 masl.
31 Sample AA 56646.
32 18L 0669469, 8482310; 3,875 masl.
33 For a similar discussion, see D'Altroy (1992) on the territorial divisions of the Wanka moieties in the Mantaro Valley.

CHAPTER 7

THE INCA OCCUPATION OF THE ANDAHUAYLAS REGION

On the last day of January 1571, while on route from Lima to Cuzco, the newly appointed viceroy, Francisco Toledo, spent the night at the *tambo* (way station) of Pincos and interviewed two local authorities said to represent the Chanka. The viceroy's secretary, Diego López de Herrera, recorded the interviews, while Gonzalo Gomez Ximenes functioned as the Quechua–Spanish translator (Levillier 1940: 51–53). The two Chanka leaders were Cristóbal Guaman Arcos and Pedro Asto, both of whom were thought to be about 80 years old.[1] The questions presented to the two leaders were both leading and formulaic; for example, the first question was, "Is it true that Topa Inca Yupanqui, son

of Pachacuti Inca Yupanqui, was the first to conquer these lands?"[2] Guaman Arcos was obliging to the Spaniards and simply answered, yes, "Topa Inca Yupanqui, son of Pachacuti Inca Yupanqui, was the first to conquer these lands."[3] Asto, however, provided a slightly more nuanced answer, indicating that while Topa Inca Yupanqui had *finished* the Inca conquest of the region, it had been his father, Pachacuti Inca Yupanqui, who had *started* the conquest.[4]

Several other Spanish authors who also conducted interviews with the indigenous leaders support Asto's carefully worded answer, which credits Pachacuti Inca Yupanqui as being the first Inca ruler to enter into the Andahuaylas region.[5] For example, Sarmiento de Gamboa (2007: 128 [1572: Ch. 35]) notes that Pachacuti Inca Yupanqui's first military foray reached 40 leagues to the west of Cuzco, which would have included the Andahuaylas region. Cieza de León (1976: 230 [1554: Pt. 2, Ch. 47]), who discussed the matter with local leaders while in the town of Andahuaylas itself, is more specific, indicating that Pachacuti Inca Yupanqui's first campaign took him as far as the Chanka and the Soras. Betanzos (1996: 166 [1557: Pt. 1, Ch. 91]) concurs, indicating that the Chanka and the Soras, as well as their western neighbor the Lucanas, all fell to Pachacuti Inca Yupanqui during a single early campaign. Betanzos (1996: 167 [1557: Pt. 1, Ch. 41]) also provides the intriguing observation that it was because of this expansion that the Chanka, Soras, and Lucanas were assigned the responsibility of maintaining Pachacuti Inca Yupanqui's mummy after his death.[6]

Following these independent sources, there appears to be some agreement that the Andahuaylas region was incorporated relatively early into the Inca Empire, perhaps during its initial period of imperial expansion under Pachacuti Inca Yupanqui. If this is the case, then the Chanka were ruled by four Inca kings (Pachacuti Inca Yupanqui, Topa Inca Yupanqui, Huayna Capac, and Huascar) before the arrival of the Europeans. By the time of Huascar's brief reign (ca. 1526–1532), the Andahuaylas region appears to have accepted Cuzco control, as the Chanka fought with Huascar in the civil war against his half-brother Atahualpa.[7] In this chapter, we discuss some of the changes that occurred in the Andahuaylas region as a result of its conquest and later successful incorporation into the Inca Empire. We begin by providing an overview of the state infrastructure established across this region, and then turn to the effects that the Inca conquest had on the local settlement patterns.

THE HUANCARAMA REGION: THE TAMBOS OF PINCOS AND COCHACAJAS AND THE LARGE CENTER OF CURAMBA

There are three well-known Inca sites immediately east of Andahuaylas near the town of Huan-carama: the tambo of Pincos, the tambo of Cochacajas, and the large administrative center of Curamba. These sites are located along the royal road of Chinchaysuyu which left Cuzco and ran to the northwestern provinces of the empire (Figure 7.1). The smallest site, the Pincos tambo, was located on the floodplain of the formidable Pincos River Valley, which separates the modern provinces of Andahuaylas and Huancarama (Figure 7.2).[8] The tambo is mentioned by Vaca de Castro (1908: 444 [1543]), Salazar (1867: 265 [1596]), the Anonymous Description of Peru (1972: 114 [1610]), and Guaman Poma de Ayala (1980: 1005 [1615: 1090 (1100)]), as well as in various other early colonial documents. It was at this tambo that Viceroy Toledo rested on his way to Cuzco and interviewed the local leaders (Levillier 1940: 51–52).

Another tambo was located approximately one day's walk east of Pincos at the summit of a mountain pass, just before a long descent to the Pachachaca River in the Abancay area. Called Cochacajas, the tambo was built beside a small lake. Pedro Pizarro (1921: 357 [1571: Ch. 22]) provides a good description of this tambo: "[Alonso de Alvarado] stopped in this place Cochacaxa, which is a high peak with a small flat place upon it, and on this flat place a lake, likewise small, is formed, which the Indians call Cocha and for this reason they call this place Cochacaxa. From this peak and from this lake a slope of almost a league goes down to the river of Abancay."[9] The tambo appears to have been burned in 1537 during a battle between Spanish forces for control over the central Andean road. Soon afterward, the Huan-carama *encomienda*, which included the Cochacajas tambo, was given to Pedro de Candia, a strong supporter of Francisco Pizarro. After Candia's death in 1542, the holdings were given to Capitan Pedro de Peranzures (Vaca de Castro 1908: 444 [1543]).[10]

The pass of Cochacajas is still a well-known location in the Huancarama region. The rectangular outline of the tambo and an adjacent small mound, possibly an *ushnu*, can be seen beside the small lake at the summit of the pass (Figure 7.3). The modern road, which crosses the pass just

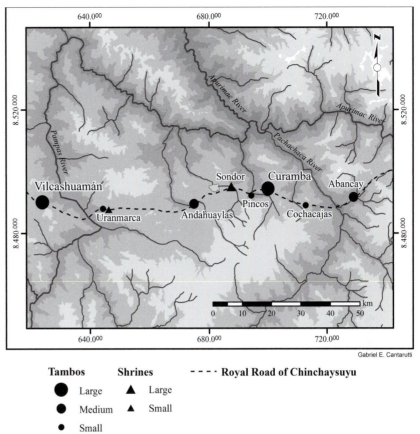

FIGURE 7.1. The Royal Road of Chinchaysuyu crosses the Andahuaylas region. There are several important Inca sites along this road.

FIGURE 7.2. The Pincos Valley divides the Huancarama and the Andahuaylas regions. (*Anonymous photograph ca. 1960.*)

FIGURE 7.3. The tambo of Cochacajas (*left*) and lake (*right*) with possible ushnu (*center*).

north of the old tambo, has exposed a substantial midden, suggesting that a large settlement was once associated with this Inca installation.

The Site of Curamba

In between the tambos of Pincos and Cochacajas, on a high ridge overlooking the Pincos River Valley, is the impressive site of Curamba (3,600 masl).[11] Despite the fact that this is the largest Inca site in the Department of Apurimac, it is poorly known outside of the region.[12] Curamba, which is located along the royal Inca road, is briefly mentioned by various early colonial writers,[13] and several nineteenth-century explorers visited the site while on their way to Cuzco. For example, both the French traveler Léonce Angrand (1972) and the American surveyor Lard-

ner Gibbon (1854) stopped at the site long enough to make sketches of the large ushnu (platform) in its plaza.[14] The British explorer Clements Markham, who traveled to Cuzco around the same time, also provides a brief description of the site's ushnu, which he misclassified as a fort:

Leaving the vale of Pincos, we had to skirt for two leagues along the sides of the mountains in the midst of magnificent scenery. There is a small plateau beyond, on which is situated the ancient fortress of Curamba. Though small it has some interest connected with Inca history, having been originally a stronghold of the Chancas. Curamba is a square fort of solid masonry in three terraces, one above the other, the wall of the outer terrace being thirty feet on each side. The upper terrace is approached by a ramp from the plain, with a slope sufficient to enable a mule to ride up to the summit. There are extensive ruins near the fort, the whole overgrown with bushes. The fort is now surmounted by a wooden cross. (Markham in Blanchard 1991: 80–81 [1852])

Some 25 years later the site was visited by Charles Wiener (1880), who drew a reasonably accurate map of the ruins. At the southern edge of the site, on a terraced hill, Wiener shows an area of "hornos de fundición" or smelting furnaces. Today, there are no longer any standing remains of these furnaces; however, the terraces show clear evidence of burning. As Lechtman (1976: 28) writes, "Walking the length of each terrace, one passes in rapid succession strip after strip of fire-reddened earth, each lying parallel to the next." Several writers suggest that the furnaces

were used for silver smelting (Olaechea 1901; von Hagen 1959), although Lechtman has cautioned that additional research is needed before such a conclusion can be reached with certainty. Nevertheless, these preliminary data suggest that Curamba may have functioned as an important center of metal production for the Inca Empire. More recently, Amorín Garibay and Alarcón Gutiérrez (1999) have written a brief description of the site and provide a map of its central sectors (Figure 7.4). Huaypar, Vetter, and Bravo (2007) have also analyzed burned soil samples from the furnaces and conclude that temperatures reached as high as 900°C.[15]

With more than 100 Inca structures, there is no doubt that Curamba was a major Inca installation within the Apurimac Department.[16] The site contains a large plaza area and an impressive terraced platform (ushnu) with a staircase (Figure 7.5).[17] The areas to the north and west of the plaza display dense configurations of buildings. The area to the south contains the furnaces and a

FIGURE 7.4. Curamba is the largest Inca site in the Department of Apurimac, yet it remains little known. This picture shows the central plaza and the ushnu (*right*).

FIGURE 7.5. There is a large, terraced ushnu with a staircase in the central plaza of Curamba.

series of possible storage buildings. Cieza de León (1976: 230 [1554: Pt. 2, Ch. 47]) suggests that the site may have also contained a Temple of the Sun.

The Shrine of Huancarama

Within any discussion of the Inca remains near Huancarama it should be noted that there are two unusual, but overlapping descriptions of an indigenous shrine in the region. The first account was written by the Jesuit priest Luis de Teruel, who spent time in the town of Huancarama preaching against idolatry.[18] Teruel's account was published by Joseph de Arriaga in his 1621 book, *The Extirpation of Idolatry in Peru*, and reads as follows:

> There is also an ancient huaca here, the name of which I forgot, that used to talk in the time of the Incas. There is a tradition about it that when Manco Cápac was passing through the town, he went to it to offer a sacrifice and it told him that it would not receive him because he was not the legitimate Inca, and it told him to leave the kingdom. At this Manco Cápac became very angry and had the huaca thrown down the hill. When they went to move the stone, a brightly colored parrot came out of it and flew up the hill. And although the Inca commanded the people of the town to follow it and throw stones at it, they could not hit it before it reached another stone, and this stone split open and shut the parrot up inside and then became whole again. And these two stones that the parrot came out of and went into were huge. Some years ago a virtuous Indian of this town, a member of our Society in Cuzco, wished to set up some crosses on the hill where the stones are; although the Indians tried to frighten him off, he went up with his crosses, and a great wind came up and a noise so loud that it sounded like talking. He was very frightened, and his hair, so he told us, stood on end. But invoking the name of Jesus, he concluded his devotions. Then the wind blew so hard that the crosses broke, and although they were set up again they broke a second time. He told me that that kind of gusts do not generally occur in that area.[19] (Teruel in Arriaga 1968: 76 [1621: Ch. 9])

The second description of the Huancarama shrine is recorded by Fernando Montesinos, who provides a transcription of an anonymous and excessively complex history of the Inca (Hyland 2007). The original author of the anonymous history had passed through the Huancarama region, and knowing of Teruel's report, had investigated the local shrine. Although the anonymous author suggests that it may have been a different king, Inca Roca, who encountered and destroyed the Huancarama shrine, he emphasizes the importance that it held in the region. The passage is as follows:

[Inga Roca] made preparations for a campaign against Vilcas. The king of Lima Tambo offered him free passage and soldiers; the king of Abancay did the same. The king of Guancarrama sent messengers to tell him not to pass through his land in order to do harm to the king of Vilcas, because he would not permit it . . . [saying] that his huaca (thus they call their idols) had told him that the Inga was not a true Lord, and that, until he knew it for certain, he was not obliged to keep his promise. . . . [And there] was a very bloody battle in which the king of Guancarrama was vanquished and killed, and the Inga took the idol which had given the reply and rolled it down the mountain. Today, there is a tradition there among the Indians that when they came to seize the stone a very gaily colored parrot came forth and went flying down the mountain till it entered a stone which the Indians afterwards greatly esteemed, and even today they *mochan* [make offerings] to it . . .

Inga Roca remained at the fortress, which he called [blank] and it is a league from Guancarrama. He finished it and perfected it, leaving there a garrison of soldiers; and he went on with his army. And, before arriving at Andaguáilas, he found many warriors who were holding against him the pass in a narrow part of the valley. Inca Roca had prepared for this beforehand, having been informed that the king of Andaguáilas was of the same mind as the king of Vilcas, on account of the reply which the idol of

Guancarrama gave.[20] (*The Quito Manuscript* in Montesinos 1920: 77–78 [ca. 1644])

While the precise historic validity of these passages should be questioned, the narratives contain some geographic clues about the ethnic distributions in this region. It seems that the area of Huancarama held a different ethnic group than those that occupied the Andahuaylas, Abancay, and Vilcashuamán areas.

These accounts of the Huancarama shrine also highlight the important role that rock outcrops held in Andean religious traditions at the time of contact. The site of Sondor, which is described below, contains just such an outcrop, and it undoubtedly represented one of the most important shrines (*huacas*) in the Department of Apurimac. We can speculate that Sondor may have even contained one or both of the sacred outcrops described in the Huancarama shrine accounts. However, systematic archaeological surveys need to be conducted in the Huancarama and Curamba regions before this can be stated with more certainty.

Sondor

Sondor is the largest Inca site in the Andahuaylas region (Figures 7.6, 7.7). It is composed of a series of distinct clusters of buildings and a magnificently terraced, conical hill called Muyumuyu. The ruins are spread across several knolls along a low, but undulating ridge that separates the Pacucha and Cotahuacho drainages. There are four distinct clusters of rectangular structures, each of which contains classic hallmarks of Inca architecture (Gasparini and Margolies 1980). These include buildings with trapezoidal doorways and niches arranged around small courtyards (called *canchas*). Large amounts of classic Inca ceramics have been recovered during recent excavations at the site, firmly dating its final occupation to Inca times (Amorín 1998; Amoríin et al. 1999; Pérez, Vivanco, and Amorín 2003).

Given the size of Sondor, it is surprising that there are no clear references to the site in the classic chronicles of Peru. One of the few possible Colonial Period references to the site can be found in the writings of Cieza de León, who

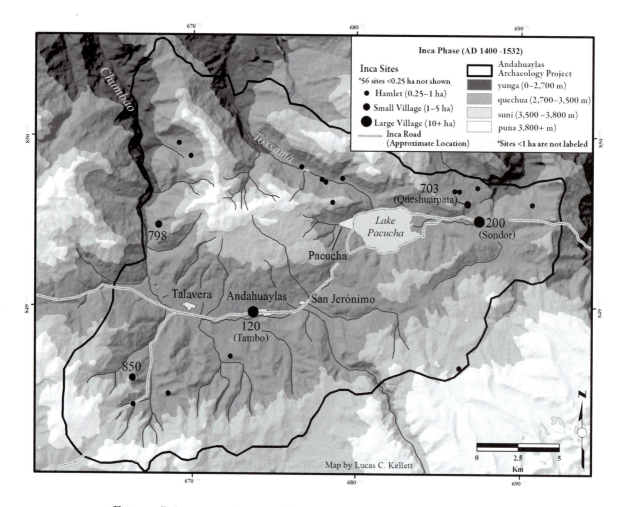

FIGURE 7.6. The Inca Phase settlement pattern in the Andahuaylas region.

notes, "In the center of the province [of the Chanka] there were great lodgings and store-houses for the rulers" (Cieza de León 1976: 132 [1553: Pt.1, Ch. 90]).[21] Another possible reference can be found in Santillán (1950: 59 [1563]), who mentions that the coastal shrine of Pachacamac had four children shrines, one of which was located in Andahuaylas. However, given the generalities of these statements, it is unclear if they are references to Sondor or to some other Inca facilities that may have once stood near the city of Andahuaylas or elsewhere in the province.[22] Various land documents recovered during the course of our project include references to the ridge of Sondor, the earliest of which dates to 1595, yet they too lack unambiguous references to the archaeological remains.[23]

The earliest definitive reference to the archaeological remains at Sondor is relatively late and comes from Charles Wiener (1880). His description is especially important, since it links the site of Sondor with one of the largest collections of Inca artifacts held outside of Peru: the Montez Collection at the Field Museum in Chicago. How a collection of artifacts from Sondor ended up in Chicago is an intriguing story. Until recently, the area of Sondor fell within the lands of the Cotahuacho Hacienda, the remains of which can still be seen a few kilometers north of the site. In 1877, while traveling from Lima to Cuzco, Wiener spent several days resting in the town of Andahuaylas. During this period, he decided to visit the Cotahuacho Hacienda, and while en route he passed by the ruins of Sondor.

FIGURE 7.7. The site of Sondor (view to the east). The constructions on the western part of the ridge (*center, cleared of vegetation*) date to Inca time (Site 200), while the narrow eastern part of the ridge (*upper left, with vegetation*) contains Chanka Phase remains (Site 199).

Wiener (1993: 294 [1880]) writes:

> Two leagues from Cotahuacho the trail leads to a pass dominated by two large cones, where there are the considerable remains of old fortifications. In same Cotahuacho the owner of the property, Don Emilio Montes, gave me the kindest welcome, and opening a big room had me enter a true museum of antiques, found by him in his surrounding lands. . . . While he showed me the thousands of pieces that comprised his Cotahuacho museum, he [also] told me that he had near twice as much in his house in Cuzco.[24] (translation by the authors)

At the time of Wiener's visit, the owner of Cotahuacho was a prominent citizen of Cuzco named Emilio Montez. Sr. Montez was an avid collector of antiquities and natural curiosities and

had amassed a large number of objects in Cuzco that he enjoyed showing to visitors (including Marcoy [1875] and Wiener [1880]). Apparently, Montez also kept a large number of objects in his hacienda at Cotahuacho which he had extracted from the nearby Inca site of Sondor. Wiener, who was himself an enthusiastic student of antiquities, spent time during his visit to Cotahuacho sketching various objects from Sondor (Figure 7.8). He published his drawings under the title "Objects found in the ruins of Cotahuacho."[25]

The following year, Montez's enormous collection was sent to Paris for display in the 1878 World's Fair (Exposition Universelle); however, it may have arrived too late to be of use. The collection was sent 15 years later to Chicago for the 1893 World's Fair (Columbian Exposition). Montez was in Chicago at the close of the fair, and on 9 September 1893, having an urgent need to return to Peru, he sold his collection to the

Loro de bronce
fundido
(Red, a la mitad)

Vizcacha de
bronce fundido
(Red, a los tercios)

Cincel de bronce.
(Red, al tercio)

Indio con zampoña
(brince fundido).
(Red, a la dos tercios)

Llama de basalto negro.
(Red, al cuarto)

Llama de mármol negro
(quemador de incienso).
(Red, a la quinta)

Llama en mármol
(quemador de incienso)
(Red, a la sexta)

Modelo de coluna
(granito gris).
(Red, a la cuarta)

Mortero de serpentina
verde.
(Red, a la décima)

Objetos encontrados en las ruinas de Cotahuacho

FIGURE 7.8. Objects from Sondor drawn by Charles Wiener (1993: 25 [1880]).

Columbian Museum of Chicago (the precursor to the Field Museum). The Montez collection totaled some 1,200 objects, including a wide variety of ceramic, metal, cloth, and stone artifacts, as well as some natural items (Bauer and Stanish 1990).[26] Most of the objects within the collection lack provenience information; however, because of Wiener's visit to Cotahuacho and his drawings, we now know that some of them were collected from the Chanka homeland, including the site of Sondor. The most notable of these is an enigmatic stone column, which is featured in the center of Wiener's drawing and which is easily matched with an identical item in the collection (Figure 7.9). There may also be matches in the Montez collection for two of the three stone llama figurines (*conopas*) presented in Wiener's drawing. However, because stone llama figurines are rather common Inca artifacts, and the Field Museum owns numerous examples, the identification is not as secure as

the unique stone column.[27] A review of the original inventory list for the Montez collection also found six metal items that are recorded as being from the site of "Kotawacho." The majority of these are small copper or silver pins (*tupus*), although one of the items was a small copper knife (*tumi*) with a llama-head handle (Figure 7.10).

For many decades following Wiener's visit, little new information was produced on the site, and descriptions of Sondor are still largely absent from the national and international literature on the Inca. This does not mean, however, that the site was locally unknown or not recognized for its antiquity. For example, there is a short reference to the ruins in Olaechea (1901: 6), and Pesce (1942: 10) briefly describes the site within his early inventory of archaeological sites in the Province of Andahuaylas.[28] They are also mentioned within the later, and much larger, inventory written by González Carré, Pozzi-Escot, and

FIGURE 7.9. A large stone column from the Montez collection at the Field Museum (cat. no. 2734). This object comes from the site of Sondor (Cotahuacho) and was drawn by Charles Wiener (1993 [1880]) while he was in the Andahuaylas region (see Figure 7.8).

FIGURE 7.10. A copper knife (tumi) with a llama-head handle from the Montez collection at the Field Museum (cat. no. 2260). The original inventory list for the collection indicates that this object is from the site of Sondor (Cotahuacho).

Vivanco (1988) as well as in local guidebooks (Quintana 1967; Barrio Contreras 1975; Tello Valdivia 2001) and memoirs (Quintanilla 1981), although by a number of different names.

Since the 1990s, with the end of the political turbulence of the region, interest in the site has grown. The first site map was produced by Truyenque Cáceres (1995). His work was soon fol-

lowed by a series of research and restoration projects directed by Ismael Pérez Calderón (Universidad Nacional de San Cristóbal de Huamanga) and supported by the Municipalidad de Pacucha and the local Tourism Board (Sub-Region Chanka). Excavations were conducted at the site by Amorín Garibay (1998). The site is also becoming better known nationally, as it is now the focus of the

Sondor Raymi festivities, in which thousands of local residents gather to celebrate their Chanka heritage (Figure 7.11).

During the course of our work in the Andahuaylas region, we divided the Sondor archaeological complex into two separate sites, since they appear to date to two different time periods (see Figure 7.7). Separate surface collections were made at each of these sites. The eastern part of the Sondor ridge contains a dense concentration of Chanka ceramics as well as the remains of numerous circular buildings and small terraces typical of the Chanka Phase. It was designated as PAA 199, and carbon collected from a looters' pit at this site during the course of our survey yielded an uncalibrated AMS date of AD 1080 ± 32.[29]

In contrast, the western side of the Sondor ridge (PAA 200) contains rectangular remains typical of the Inca (Figure 7.12). The previous archaeological excavations and restoration projects have all been conducted on the western side of the site, and they have yielded ample evidence that its rectangular buildings were occupied during Inca times. Of special note is a plaza area located between two small knolls (Figure 7.13). One side of the plaza contains a large terrace bordered by a raised wall with a series of large niches. Excavations on the terrace recovered the remains of 33 complete or partially complete sets of human remains, most of which were children or young adults. These individuals may well have been sacrificial victims (Pérez, Vivanco, and Amorín 2003).

FIGURE 7.11. Each year during the June solstice there is a large celebration of Chanka heritage at the archaeological site of Sondor (year 2004).

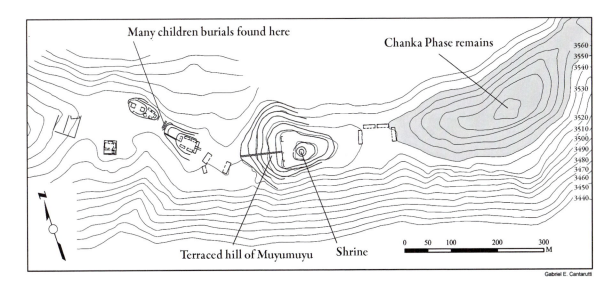

FIGURE 7.12. Map of the major Inca buildings at Sondor. The site extends across several knolls along an undulating ridge. The western half (PAA 200) of the site contains several clusters of Inca buildings and the terraced hill of Muyumuyu. The eastern half (PAA 199) contains the poorly preserved remains of a Chanka Phase village. (*Adapted from Pérez et al. 2003: 369.*)

FIGURE 7.13. The plaza area at Sondor *(lower right)*. A large number of human remains were recovered on the terrace in front of the niched wall.

The dominant feature of the site is the magnificent conical hill known as Muyumuyu (Figure 7.14). The slope of the hill has been enhanced with six large terraces. The hill also contains an impressive staircase which is accessed through a double jambed doorway at the base of the hill. At the top of staircase on the summit of the hill are two distinct outcrops, surrounded by a low wall (Figure 7.15). This wall clearly demarcates and encloses these stones within a sacred space at the site. These stones were certainly huacas during Inca times, and they recall *The Quito Manuscript*'s (in Montesinos 1920: 77–78 [1643]) and Teruel's (in Arriaga 1968: 76 [1621: Ch. 9]) descriptions of rock shrines in the nearby town of Huancarama.

The Inca propensity to incorporate preexisting shrines into their empire as it expanded across the Andes has been well documented. For example, the Wanka origin shrine of Wari Willka, which was a sacred location long before the Inca arrived in the region, continued to be worshiped under Inca rule (Shea 1969; Isbell 1997). Other sacred loci, including the Islands of the Sun and the Moon in Lake Titicaca and the coastal site of Pachacamac, were enlarged as the Inca took control of them (Bauer and Stanish 2001). We currently believe that the site of Sondor underwent similar transformations. It is clear that the eastern side of the site held a Chanka Phase village, which was constructed adjacent to an important local shrine. In contrast, the western side of the site was built after the Inca incorporated the Andahuaylas region into their territorial holdings. Given the general quality of the Inca buildings, the large amount of classic Inca pottery, and the recent identification of what are believed to be numerous sacrificial victims (many of whom

FIGURE 7.14. The sculpted hill of Muyumuyu at Sondor (PAA 200). The long stairway leads to the summit where there are two large outcrops (view to the east).

Figure 7.15. Two large outcrops mark the summit of Muyumuyu at Sondor (PAA 200). Like the stones mentioned in *The Quito Manuscript* and in Teruel's report, these rocks most certainly functioned as a shrine during Chanka and Inca times. View to the west, with Lake Pacucha appearing between the two rocks. (Note the low masonry wall at the foot of the outcrops).

were children), it appears that a pre-Inca shrine continued to hold regional importance during the Inca Period and that the Inca Empire was actively involved in maintaining it after their occupation of the Chanka homeland.

Adjacent to Sondor lies another well-preserved Inca site, Queshuarpata, which is located approximately 1 km to the north and just above the small community of Cotahuacho Alto. The site extends for 3.5 ha on a moderate slope and contains at least two plaza areas with rectangular enclosures (*canchas*) on several sides. One long (35 × 5 m) rectangular structure with multiple doorways, possibly a *kallanka*,[30] is located at the northwest corner of the site (Figures 7.16). In addition, three circular storage structures (*collcas*) can be found at the far northwest corner of the

site. Although partially destroyed by modern agriculture, a dense scatter of imperial Inca pottery can still be found among the enclosures and on the terraces. Since only surface collections and site mapping were completed at the site, further work needs to be completed to understand its relationship to Sondor. Nevertheless, we suspect that Queshuarpata held administrative functions related to the larger, and nearby, ceremonial complex of Sondor.

The Andahuaylas Tambo

During Inca times, a tambo and a small town, both of which were called Andahuaylas, were maintained on the floor of the Andahuaylas Valley near

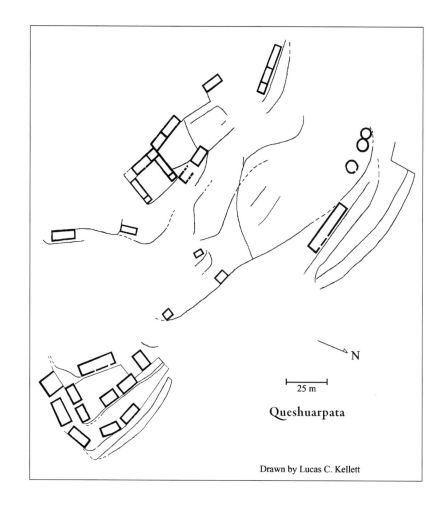

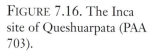 FIGURE 7.16. The Inca site of Queshuarpata (PAA 703).

Queshuarpata

Drawn by Lucas C. Kellett

the Chumbao River. Located approximately halfway between the large Inca centers of Curamba and Vilcashuamán, Andahuaylas was a major stopping point for travelers on the royal road of Chinchaysuyu. For example, Francisco Pizarro spent the night there on his famous journey from Cajamarca to Cuzco (Sancho 1917: 77–78 [1534]), as did most other highland travelers who crossed through this region. Although the urban growth of Andahuaylas has destroyed the remains of the Inca town and the tambo, historical research can be used to determine the former location of this important facility.

Andahuaylas and Vaca de Castro's List of Tambos

One of the best descriptions of the Andahuaylas tambo is provided by Cristóbal Vaca de Castro.

Only a few years after Diego Maldonado was awarded the encomienda of the Chanka, Vaca de Castro was sent to Peru by Charles V to restore order among rival Spaniards. While in Cuzco in 1543, Vaca de Castro recorded the distribution of tambos along the major Inca roads as well as the encomiendas through which they crossed. Among the members of the Cuzco town council who helped draft the report were Maldonado and Gabriel de Rojas, both of whom controlled large landholdings west of Cuzco and who knew the region of Andahuaylas well. While the exact boundaries of the encomiendas are not recorded, their relative positions along the Inca roads are noted, as are the relative locations of the various tambos. Moving east to west, the document indicates that there were Inca tambos in Abancay, Cochacajas, Curamba, Andahuaylas, Uranmarca, and Vilcashuamán (see Figure 7.1).[31]

Several other documents, consisting of seventeenth- and eighteenth-century wills and land sales, indicate that the tambo itself was located near the town's plaza and central church (see Figure 1.8).[32] Since these features of the community were established as part of Toledo's *reduccion* movement, evidence of the tambo has long since been destroyed. We were, nevertheless, still able to find a few sherds of Inca pottery within garden plots on the western edge of the city, suggesting that there was also a substantial settlement surrounding the tambo during the Inca period.

The Mitimaes of the Andahuaylas Region

After the conquest of a region, the Inca frequently transported portions of the indigenous population to other areas of the empire and brought colonists of differing ethnic backgrounds into the newly annexed territory. The transported populations were known as *mitimaes* (or colonists), and they were part of various pacification efforts undertaken by the Inca. While policies of forced population relocation are not rare among expansionist states, the extent to which the Inca carried out these practices is remarkable. Spanish documents reveal that thousands, if not tens of thousands, of individuals were relocated across the Andes after their homelands were annexed by the Inca.

During the time of Inca control of the Andahuaylas region, various members of the Chanka polity were sent to other areas of the empire as mitimaes. For example, a small group of Chanka, along with representatives from many other ethnic groups, were sent to Copacabana to help maintain the ritual complexes on the Islands of the Sun and the Moon (Ramos Gavilán 1988: 84 [1621]; Bauer and Stanish 2001; Stanish and Bauer 2004). Furthermore, documents dating to 1586 indicate that there were clusters of "Chankas from Andahuaylas" in the towns of Lircay and Julcamarca, both near the modern city of Ayacucho (Carabajal 1974 [1586]), and we presume that there were other settlements of transported Chanka elsewhere in the Inca Empire.

It is also clear that some non-Chanka mitimaes were brought into the Andahuaylas region

under the direction of the Inca. For example, our earliest document from the Andahuaylas region, dating to 1539, indicates that members of the Aymaraes, a group that inhabited the high grasslands to the southeast of Andahuaylas, were transported as mitimaes into the Andahuaylas region and established their own community. This document also indicates that members of the Quechua group from the area between Andahuaylas and Cuzco were resettled in a number of communities, including Vilcaporo, Totoro, Guarillane, and perhaps Pucuyo.[33] Another community, Omamarca, is also described as being inhabited by *orejones*, a term generally used to denote high-ranking individuals from the Cuzco region.[34] And there are other, more ambiguous cases. For example, the leaders of the towns of Caquesamarca, Guayaconi, and Chua are said to have been Inca, Chachapoya, and Yauyo, respectively, but it is not clear if the populace of those towns were outsiders. Another ambiguous case is the subtropical settlement of Cocas (see Figure 2.2), which is recorded as containing Yungas. Since "Yungas" is a general Andean term for lowlanders, it is not clear if these individuals were indigenous to that low-lying region or if they were outsiders who had been brought into the area by the Inca (AGI, Patronato 93, No. 11, Ramo 2).

Other archival documents indicate that an even greater range of ethnic groups was transported into the region by the Inca. For example, based on the *ayllu* names of various communities, it can be suggested that a large percentage of the population that lived around the towns of Ocobamba and Ongoy were removed by the Inca and that these two communities were resettled with a variety of people from the northern Andes. Documents dating as late as 1684 record the communities of Ocobamba and Ongoy as still being composed of ayllus with distinctly nonlocal names, including Jauja, Wanka, Quito Quichua, Yauyo, Huayllas, Huánuco, Huamachuco, Chachapoyas, and Otavalo, among others (ADC, Corregimiento de Andahuaylas, Leg. 1). Interestingly, these names represent many of the largest highland ethnic groups located between Andahuaylas and Ecuador that came under the control of the Inca during the time of Tupac Inca Yupanqui and his son Huayna Capac. The implication is that during the rule of these two Incas, various groups of the northern Andes were specifically selected to repopulate a section of the Chanka homeland.

Among the groups that suffered the most under the Inca policies of resettlement were the Chachapoyas. They were incorporated relatively late into the empire, as the Inca pushed the limits of their empire northward into Ecuador, and members of their population were then distributed across the empire. Schjellerup (1997: 66) has found evidence of Chachapoyas in 18 different locations across the Andes, and there are surely more to be identified. One of the locations where Chachapoyas were sent was the Andahuaylas region.

Our earliest documentation of Chachapoyas in the Chanka region comes from the 1539 encomienda document, which simply lists the leader of the town of Guayaconi as being a Chachapoya (AGI, Patronato 93, No. 11, Ramo 2; Julien 2002). However, other local documents provide a more detailed telling of their history. The Chachapoyas were brought to the Andahuaylas region during the rule of Huayna Capac and were settled in the region now known as Argama. After the Toledo reduction movement (ca. 1572), they, along with other groups of that region, were resettled into the town of San Jerónimo (Hyland 2002a). They were included within the upper moiety of San Jerónimo, only because they had been settled by the Inca on lands within this division (ADC, Corregimiento de Andahuaylas, Leg. 2, Autos seguidos por Diego Checmollo; AGN, Real Audiencia, Causas Criminales, Leg. 154, Cuaderno 579). Their special status under the Inca was recognized by the Spanish authorities, and they continued to be free from labor obligations to the crown well into the eighteenth century (Hyland and Amado González n.d.).

The Tucuyrico of the Chanka

It is widely noted by the classic chroniclers of Peru that the Inca appointed regional governors to oversee the state's interests in important provinces. These provincial lords were called *Tucuyricos*,

which is generally translated as "he who sees all,"[35] The name is derived from the various accounting tasks and inspections that these individuals carried out in their assigned provinces (2006 Cerrón-Palomino). For example, Cobo writes:

> In these provincial capitals there was in residence a *tocricuc* or representative of the Inca; this official had the power to administer justice and punish offenses in accordance with their seriousness. . . . He went out to visit his district at certain times; he had the tributes and royal revenues collected and placed them in the warehouses, replenished the supplies at the *tambos*, took a census of the children that were born each year and those who reached the age to pay tribute, and listed those who no longer had this obligation.[36] (Cobo 1979: 199–200 [1653: Bk. 12, Ch. 25])

Among the specific centers that Cobo lists as having Tucuyricos are Quito, La Tacunga, Tumitambo, Cajamarca, Hatun Jauja, Pachacama, Chincha, and Vilcashuamán. Damian de la Bandera (1965: 178 [1557]) provides very specific information on the Tucuyrico of Vilcashuamán, indicating that he controlled the regions surrounding this royal tambo, from Uranmarca in the east to Acos in the west.

Knowing the important role that Tucuyricos held within Inca rule, it is logical to ask if such a governor was assigned to oversee the Chanka of the Andahuaylas region. The answer to this question is complex. All the documents we have examined suggest that the Chanka were divided, like many polities of the Andes, into two groups, or moieties, and that the leaders of these two groups continued to hold influence over the Chanka well into colonial times. Furthermore, our regional survey of the Andahuaylas region has not found any site comparable to the Inca centers where Tucuyricos are known to have governed (for example, Hatun Jauja or Vilcashuamán). Nevertheless, the 1539 *Andahuaylas Encomienda Document* does indicate that there was a Tucuyrico living in the Chanka region. In the last entry detailing the names of the leaders and the towns included within the encomienda, we find this listing:

and another [leader] they say is [a] Tucuyrico who is called Urco Guaranga[37] (a nobleman), [who is] lord of the towns of Mayomarca and Chabibanba.[38]

It is important to note that the Andahuaylas Tucuyrico is not described as living within one of the central towns of the Chanka, but he is listed as overseeing the small communities of Mayomarca and Chabibanba (Julien 2002: 185). Other documents from the region lend clarity to why this was the case. The area of Mayomarca was located some distance from the Chanka homeland, between Huanta and Andahuaylas (Stern 1982: 31). It was a region of coca production, which in later colonial times would also produce a large quantity of placer gold. Disputes over the Mayomarca region and its coca fields continued for centuries, and the Chanka entered into colonial courts arguing that they had controlled the region during the time of Inca rule (AGN, Derecho Indígena, Leg. 3, Cuaderno 17). The fact that the *Andahuaylas Encomienda Document* records the presence of a Tucuyrico still functioning in the region in 1539 suggests that the Inca were very interested in the region's coca production and had established a special overseer to supervise its tribute collections for Cuzco.

OVERVIEW OF THE INCA PERIOD SETTLEMENT PATTERN IN THE ANDAHUAYLAS REGION

Given the relative importance that the Chanka were believed to have held in the development of the Inca state, when we began our project in the Andahuaylas region we expected to find at least one very large Inca occupation (30+ ha) that served to administer this bellicose ethnic group. We also expected to find a dramatic shift in the local settlement pattern, with the general population moving from a limited number of large ridgetop sites in the Chanka Phase to numerous smaller settlements on the valley floor during the Inca Period. These types of regional changes had been well documented among various other ethnic groups, including those of the Jauja region, an

area that was conquered by the Inca soon after they established control of the Andahuaylas region. Hastorf and D'Altroy provide a concise summary of the overall impact of the Inca among the Wanka:

> The populace largely moved out of the high-elevation, fortified, Wanka II settlements down to more dispersed, smaller settlements under Inca rule. This resettlement was coupled with the construction of major state facilities, most notable, the provincial center of Hatun Xauxa and the largest concentration of storage buildings known in the empire. One result of the move by the native people was a shift from environmental zones most suited to a tuber farming pastoral mix into areas conducive to cultivating all highland crops. In the process, the Xauxa became more accessible as they vacated their defensive citadels for many smaller, more open villages. (Hastorf and D'Altroy 2001: 5–6).

We also expected, given the hostile relationships believed to have existed between the Chanka and the Inca, that pronounced changes would have occurred within the Andahuaylas region as a result of its incorporation into the Inca Empire, as had been documented in the Jauja region. Our survey results suggest, however, that the Inca incorporation of the Andahuaylas region did not bring as much of a radical reorganization of Chanka society as was originally postulated, and the shifts that did occur appear to have been of a slightly different nature than those recorded in other areas. We know that the Inca built the large site of Curamba in the Huancarama region to the east of the Andahuaylas Valley, and they established the formidable site of Vilcashuamán much farther to the west, but Inca investments in the Andahuaylas region appear to have been on a far more moderate scale. As discussed above, only two sites in the survey zone had intact Inca architecture: Sondor and the relatively small, nearby site of Queshuarpata. A third site, the tambo of Andahuaylas, most likely also had formal Inca architecture; however, it has been destroyed by urban development. Although the exact size of the

Andahuaylas tambo is difficult to estimate, there is no reason to believe that it was anything more than a moderately sized installation with an adjacent village.[39]

Although Inca investments in the Andahuaylas region were only moderate, it is important to note that the Inca occupation of the Andahuaylas region did bring with it shifts in the local settlement pattern. As seen in the Jauja region and elsewhere in the Andes, during Inca times a series of new sites were established in the lower elevations of the region (Table 7.1). Unlike the large, ridgetop settlements of the Chanka Phase, the Inca sites are small and are scattered across the maize-producing sectors. Yet the small number of Inca sites and the paucity of lower valley terrace complexes during the Inca Phase within the Andahuaylas Valley suggest that there was a low level of investment (for example, large terraces) in maize agriculture by the empire. This contrasts with other areas of the empire, such as the Cuzco (Bauer 2004; Covey 2006) and Colca (Wernke 2006) regions, where large investments in intensive agriculture were undertaken. Furthermore, although our site-size resolution is not as fine as we would have liked, and there are still remaining

TABLE 7.1
Elevations and sizes of sites with Inca ceramics in the Andahuaylas region

ECOLOGICAL ZONES	HOUSE-HOLD < 0.25 HA	HAMLET 0.25–1 HA	SMALL VILLAGE 1–5 HA	MEDIUM VILLAGE 5–10 HA	LARGE VILLAGE > 10 HA	TOTAL
Yunga (0–2,700 masl)	1	0	0	0	0	1
Quechua (2,700–3,500 masl)	47	14	2	0	2	65
Suni (3,500–3,800 masl)	5	1	1	0	0	7
Puna (3,800+ masl)	3	0	0	0	0	3
Total	56	15	3	0	2	76

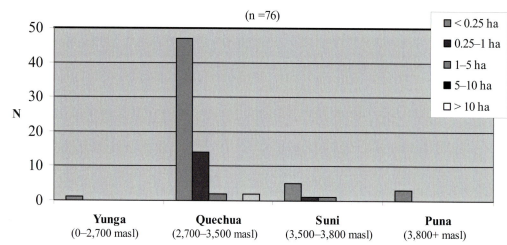

Inca Phase Settlement Distribution

issues with the site chronologies, it appears that the total area of Inca Period occupations is significantly less than that during the Chanka Phase. This suggests to us that the region may have suffered a population decline during Inca rule.[40]

We also note that during Inca times, the ridgetop sites were no longer supporting the large populations that they held during the Chanka Period. Nevertheless, the presence of a very small number of Inca sherds at some of these sites indicates that they were not completely abandoned during Inca rule.[41] The impression that the Inca created a lower population level and a more dispersed settlement pattern in the Andahuaylas region is supported by a brief statement by Juan Arias Maldonado, who indicates that the region of the Chanka was lightly populated when his father received the Andahuaylas encomienda, and that natives had to be resettled from more remote *puna* settlements into the central valley (AGN, Derecho Indígena, Leg. 3, Cuaderno 17).

NOTES

1   Pedro Asto is listed as the leader of the Hurin Chanka, while Cristóbal Guaman Arcos is reported to be the Lord of Andahuaylas. Since the names of these two men do not match those of known Chanka leaders, we presume that they were the Hanan and Hurin leaders of the Pincos Valley and that their titles as the lords of the Chanka were an exaggeration.

2   ". . . ques verdad que topa ynga yupangui hijo de pachacuti ynga yupanqui fue el que conquisto estos reynos . . . ?" (Levillier 1940: 51).

3   ". . . topa ynga yupangui hijo de Pachacuti Inca Yupangui fue el que conquista estos reynos" (Levillier 1940: 53).

4   "... pachacuti ynga yupangui fue el que coneço a conquistar estos rreynos e después los acabo de conquistar topa ynga Yupanqui su hijo . . . " (Levillier 1940: 52).

5   Also see Polo de Ondegardo (1990: 86 [1571]). It should be noted, however, that a few writers suggest that the Andahuaylas region first came under Inca rule much earlier. For example, Callapiña, Supno, and other Quipucamayocs (1974: 31 [1542/1608]) state that the Inca arrived in Andahuaylas in the time of Mayta Capac, the fourth Inca, while Garcilaso de la Vega (1966: 218 [1609: Pt. 1, Bk. 4, Ch. 15]) indicates that the Chanka were first contacted during the reign of Inca Roca, the sixth Inca. Cobo (1979: 125 [1653:

Bk. 12, Ch. 9]) and Vázquez de Espinosa (1948: 533 [1628]) also place the first contact between the two groups during the time of Inca Roca. However, both of these authors took their information from Garcilaso de la Vega. The indigenous writer Guaman Poma de Ayala places the Inca-Chanka contact one generation later, during the rule of Yahuar Huacac. According to Guaman Poma de Ayala, the westward expansion of the Inca was overseen by a captain of Yahuar Huacac, named Inca Maytac, who not only conquered the Chanka, but a host of other ethnic groups as well. To illustrate his point, Guaman Poma de Ayala (1980: 134 [1615: 155 (157)]) includes a drawing of Inca Maytac and his troops attacking an unnamed fort. Other detailed descriptions of early contact between the Chanka and the Inca can be found in *The Quito Manuscript* (2007 [1644]) recorded by Fernando de Montesinos. This chronicle is, however, fraught with difficulties because of its bewildering list of Inca kings. The anonymous author of the *Quito Manuscript* (2007: 113, 114, 141, 142) provides various descriptions of conflicts said to have occurred between the Chanka and the Inca, some of which took place near Cuzco while others occurred near Andahuaylas. To this rather eclectic list of accounts, which suggests pre-Pachacuti contacts between the Chanka and the Inca, we can add the *Acta de Uranmarca* (see Appendix 4). Although the Uranmarca document does not state which Inca ruler was involved in the initial incorporation of the region, it places this event before the time traditionally associated with the reign of Pachacuti Inca Yupanqui.

The lack of conformity, in both the timing and the nature of Chanka-Inca contact, provided in these accounts makes it difficult to support the proposition that the Inca held an early, dominant role in the affairs of Andahuaylas. To this observation we can also add the fact that during our archaeological survey of the Andahuaylas region and in our many visits to Chanka Phase sites, we found no evidence of early Inca (Killke) pottery (Bauer 1999, 2002). This is not to say that the two cultures existed in absolute isolation during the Chanka Phase. Both groups would have certainly been aware, at least in general terms, of the social and political changes that were occurring within each other's separate regions. They and other central Andean groups may have also been linked by, or included within, the same trade networks of exotic or highly valued items, such as obsidian or seashells. For example, Cieza de León (1976: 201 [1554: Pt. 2, Ch. 34]) suggests that contact was first established during the time of Capac Yupanqui, during which representatives of the two groups exchanged gifts. However, claims of an early Inca occupation of the Andahuaylas region seem at this time not to be well supported.

6   These authors also suggest that the pacification of the Andahuaylas region took many years (for example,

Sarmiento de Gamboa 2007: 147 [1572: Ch. 44]; Betanzos 1996: 85 [1557: Pt. 1, Ch. 18]; Cieza de León 1976: 117–118 [1554: Pt. 2, Ch. 19]). For more detailed reviews of sources and dates of Inca expansionism, see Rowe (1946), Pärssinen (1992), and D'Altroy (2002).

7   At the time of the Spanish invasion, the Inca Empire was in the midst of a dynastic war between two half-brothers: Atahualpa and Huascar. Atahualpa was winning the war as his army slowly pushed southward into Huascar-controlled territory and toward the imperial city of Cuzco. The Chanka had allied themselves with Huascar and were drawn directly into the war as Atahualpa's army took Vilcashuamán. With aid from the Chanka, Huascar's men tried to stop Atahualpa's army from crossing the Pampas River, but they were defeated on a plain called Choquepampa, near the modern village of Soras. Huascar's army was then forced to pull back even farther toward Cuzco while Atahualpa's troops occupied Andahuaylas (Betanzos 1996: 210–211, 217–221 [1557: Pt. 2, Chs. 8, 11–13]; Cobo 1979: 166 [1654: Bk. 12, Ch. 18]). Then, after winning a major battle near the pass of Vilcacunga on the western edge of the Inca heartland, Atahualpa's army marched on Cuzco. The principal leader of the Chanka at that time was a man named Huasco, who served with Huascar's forces (Betanzos 1996: 239 [1557: Pt. 2, Ch. 18]). Huasco survived the fraternal conflict and may have been interviewed by Cieza de León in 1547.

8   The former Pincos Hacienda, then an agrarian cooperative, was one of the first landholdings attacked by the Sendero Luminoso as it became active in the Apurimac Department in 1982. See Skar (1981) for additional information on the Pincos Valley.

9   "…paró en este asiento de Cochacaxa, que es un cerro alto, y en èl se haze una llanada pequeña; aquí en esta llanada se haze una laguna asimismo pequeña, y por esto llaman a este asiento Cochacaxa. De aquí, de este cerro y de esta laguna, baxa una questa auaxo hasta el rrío Auancay, de casi una legua" (Pizarro 1986: 164 [1571: Ch. 22]).

10 Other references to the tambo of Cochacajas can be found in Garcilaso de la Vega (1966 [1609]), Pizarro (1921 [1571]), Santa Cruz Pachacuti Yamqui Salcamaygua (1950 [ca. 1613]), Vázquez de Espinosa (1948 [1629]), Cieza de León (1996 [1554]), Anonymous Description of Peru (1972 [1610]), and Middendorf (1974 [1895]).

11 In 1572 the repartimiento of Curamba held 506 tribute payers, 165 elders, and 720 youths (Toledo 1975: 207 [1570–1575]).

12 Toledo (1975: 207 [1570–1575]) indicates that Curamba was also known as Cataguacho. The small town below Sondor has almost the same name, Cotahuacho.

13 Sancho (1917 [1534]); Vaca de Castro (1908: 444 [1543]); Cieza de León (1995 [1553], 1996 [1554]); Betanzos (1996 [1559]); Pizarro (1921 [1571]); Sarmiento (2007 [1572]); Garcilaso de la Vega (1966 [1609]); Santa Cruz Pachacuti Yamqui Salcamaygua (1950 [ca. 1613]); Cabello de Balboa (1951 [1586]).

14 Other late nineteenth-century visitors to the site include Antonio Raimondi (1876–1879) and Ernest Middendorf (1974 [1895]). The latter provides the following description of the site:

> To the right of the trail the ruined buildings of an ancient town can be seen, [and] to the right on the edge of the summit are the remains of a small isolated temple, with two terraces and a staircase. [A la izquierda del camino se ven restos de muros de una antigua población, a la derecha, en el borde de la ladera, las ruinas de un pequeño templo aislado, con dos terrazas y una escalera.] (Middendorf 1974: 3: 421 [1895])

15 This temperature is sufficient for the preparation of silver-copper alloys.

16 Sarmiento de Gamboa (2007: 147 [1572: Ch. 44]) describes Topa Inca Yupanqui as attacking the fort of Curamba. This may suggest that a reconquest of the region was necessary following the death of Pachacuti Inca Yupanqui.

17 The ushnu was rebuilt by the Institute of Culture in the late 1990s.

18 Luis de Teruel was the author of several important reports, including the now-lost account called *Contra idolatrium*, on indigenous religious practices; he traveled with Joseph de Arriaga and Hernando de Avendaño during some of their campaigns against idolatry (Duviols 1983).

19 "Hay aquí una huaca antigua muy famosa cuyo nombre se me ha olvidado, la cual en tiempo de los ingas hablaba. Y es tradición entre ellos que pasando por este pueblo Mancocapac, le fue a hacer sacrificio, y ella le dijo que no quería recibillo porque no era Inga legítimo, y que le había de quitar el reino. De lo cual, enojado Macocapac, hizo arrojarla por el cerro abajo. Cuando fueron a menear la piedra salió de ella un papagayo muy pintado, y fue por el cerro adelante volando. Y aunque mandó el Inga que con piedras, y ayllos, o libis le siguiesen, no le alcanzaron; antes, llegando a una gran piedra, se abrió y le encerró en sí, y se volvió a juntar como antes estaba. Y estas dos piedras de donde salió y entró el papagayo son muy temidas. Quiso algunos años ha un indio muy virtuoso de este pueblo y de nuestra cofradía del Cuzco poner una cruces en estos cerros donde están estas piedras, y aunque los indios le ponían mucho miedo, subió allí con sus cruces, y se levantó tan gran viento y con tan gran ruido, que parecía que hablaba. Tuvo gran pavor, y los cabellos (como él me dijo) se le erizaron; pero con todo, repitiendo e invocando el nombre de Jesús, concluyó con su devoción. El aire arreció de manera que las cruces se quebraron, y aunque otra vez se renovaron y pusieron, se volvieron a quebrar, y dijo-

me él mismo que no suele haber allí aquellos airazos" (Teruel in Arriaga 1999: 89 [1621]).

20 "Dispuso [Inga Roca] jornada para Vilcas; el rey de Limatamlo le ofrezió pasase y gente; lo mismo hiço el de Avancay, y el de Guancarrama le imbió mensaxeros que no pasase por su tierra a hazer mal al de Vilcas, porque no lo consintirían; . . . respondió que su guaca, así llaman a su ídolo, les auía dicho que no era verdadero Señor; que hasí, hasta sauer lo çierto, no estaua obligado a cumplir lo prometido. . . . [Y] ubo una vatalla muy sangrieta, en que quedó vençido y muerto el de Guancarrama, y el Inga coxió el ídolo que hauía dado la rrespuesta y lo echó a rrodar por el çerro avaxo; y ay hoy tradiçión entre estos indios, que quando llegaron amenaçar la piedra, salió della con papagayo muy pintado, y se fue volando el çerro avaxo y se entró en una piedra, que después estimaron los indios en mucho, y aún el día de oy la mochan. . . .

"Detúbose Inga Rroca en el puesto de la fortaleça, que llamó [blank] y está una legua de Guancarrama, alauándola y perfiçionándola, y dexando en ella guarniçión de soldados, passó adelante con su exérçito; y antes de llegar a Andaguailas, halló mucha gente que le impedía el passo en la hangahora de una quebrada. Hauíase preuenido ante el Inga Rroca, porque, teniendo noticia de que el rey de Andaguaylas estaua del mismo pareçer que el de Vilcas . . ." (*The Quito Manuscript* 2007: 136 [ca. 1644]).

21 "En el comedio de la prouincia auía grandes aposentos y depósitos para los señores" (Cieza de León 1996: 254–255 [1553: Pt. 1, Ch. 90]).

22 As detailed elsewhere, the descriptions of the Huancarama shrine (*The Quito Manuscript*, in Montesinos 1920: 77–78 [1643]; Teruel in Arriaga 1968: 76 [1621: Ch. 9]) may refer to Sondor.

23 BN, Ms. B-405 (1669/1596); ADC, Notarial de Andahuaylas del siglo XIX, Protocolo 4.

24 "A una legua de Cotahuacho el sendero lleva a un abra dominada por dos grandes conos donde hay vestigios de considerables fortificaciones antiguas. En Cotahuacho mismo el propietario de la finca, don Emilio Montes, me dispensó la más amable acogida, y abriendo una habitación grande me hizo entrar en un verdadero museo de antigüedades, encontradas por él en las inmediaciones de su propiedad. . . . Me dijo mientras me mostraba las mil piezas que comprendía su museo de Cotahuacho que tenía cerca del doble en su casa del Cuzco." (Wiener 1992: 294–295 [1880]).

25 While in Cuzco, Wiener (1880) also drew many other objects owned by Montez.

26 For additional information concerning the Montez collection, see Bauer and Stanish (1990).

27 Artifacts 3415 and 3419 of the Montez collection.

28 "Ruinas bastante conservadas, con apariencia de fortalezas, en el cuello que sepárate la laguna de Pacucha del vale de Kotahuacho" (Pesce 1942: 10).

29 Sample AA 56645.

30 *Kallanka* were large structures used for ceremonial gatherings.

31 The entry for the Andahuaylas tambo reads as follows:

Y del dicho Pueblo de Curamba se tiene de ir al Pueblo y Tambo de Andaguaylas y Oponguanche o Chuchicocha o Vilar puraychita, que son Pueblos de Diego Maldonado con todo lo a el sugeto y los Indios de Diego de Silva [de Guzman] y de Cespedes y de Origuela, o de Andres Enamorado. Y del Pueblo y Tambo de Andaguaylas se tiene de ir al Tambo de Vramarca . . . que son del repartimiento que solia ser del Padre Sosa y de Gabriel (de Rojas) . . . (Vaca de Castro 1908: 444 [1543]).

32 Among the best local documents recording the presence of a tambo in Andahuaylas is a 1796 will by Juliana Rojas. Although this is a relatively late will, it does record land controlled by Rojas's family for more than a century. In the will, Rojas states she has a large parcel of land called "Tambo" which is located in the city of Andahuaylas where the trail leaves for the town of Talavera (ADC, Notariales de Andahuaylas del siglo XVIII, Leg. 3, Escritura publica de José Gabriel Pacheco [1700–1820]). Another, much earlier will, dating to 1659 and belonging to Alvaro Gil de Aragon, states that he purchased a plot of land called "Old Tambo" near the Andahuaylas church (ADC, Notariales de Andahuaylas del siglo XVII, Escritura publica de Pedro Julio de Ojeda [1659–1663]).

33 During Toledo's reduccion movement, several Quechua were relocated into the town of San Jerónimo (BN, Ms. B405 [1669/1596]).

34 *Orejon* is a slightly ambiguous term since it refers to individuals with ear plugs. Two other communities, Alcaracay and Chua, are said to have had leaders who were orejones.

35 Damian de la Bandera (1965: 178 [1557]) writes, "In each province there was a governor and they were a captain of the Inca, which was called *tucuyrico*, which is to say, 'he who sees all'." ["Sobre cada provincia había un gobernador y éste era un capitán del Inga, al cual llamaban *tucuyrico*, que quiere decir, todo lo mira. . . ."] Sarmiento (2007: 127–128 [1572: Ch. 35]) writes, "In each province he appointed one person, superior to all the other leaders he had appointed in the towns, to act as general or governor of that province. These are called *tucurico* in the language of this land, which means 'he who sees and understands all'." ["Poniendo por sus provincias uno superior á todos los demás, que en los pueblos singularmente ponía, por general ó gobernador de los de aquella provincial, al cual en la lengua desta tierra llaman *tucuyrico*, que quiere decir 'el que todo los vee y entiende'."]. In the same spirit, González Holguín (1989: 344 [1608]) writes, "The supervisor who was in charge of a town or a people." ["Ttocricuk: La guarda el que tiene a cargo el pueblo

o gente."] For additional information, also see Santillán (1950: 48–49, 51 [1563]) and Discurso (1906: 152 [ca. 1570]). See Schreiber (1993) for a possible identification of the Tucuyrico's building within the Andamarca Lucanas.

36 "En estos pueblos cabeceras de provincias tenía asistencia el *tocricuc* o delegado del Inca; el cual tenía poder de administrar justicia y castigar los delitos conforme a su gravedad . . . Salía a visitar el distrito a sus tiempos; hacía recoger los tributos y rentas reales y ponerlos en los depósitos, bastecer los *tambos* y empadronar los que nacían al año y los que entraban en edad de tributar, y alistar los que salían desta obligación" (Cobo 1964: 114–115 [1653: Bk. 12, Ch. 25]).

37 A man named Urco Guaranca can also be found in the account of the Chanka-Inca War by Betanzos (1996: 22 [1559: Bk. 6]) .

38 "e otro que se dize tucuyrico que se llama Horcoguaranga (es orejon), senores del Pueblo Mayomarca y Chabibanba" (Julien 2002: 194).

39 Such a pattern of indirect rule with few Inca installations has been noted elsewhere in the central Andes, such as the Carahuarazo Valley, Ayacucho (Schreiber 1987, 1992). See also Malpass (1993) for a discussion of differing levels of imperial investments and political control in provincial areas of the Inca Empire.

40 Several writers, including Sarmiento de Gamboa (2007: 131–134 [1572: Ch. 38]) and Cobo (1979: 137 [1653: Bk. 12, Ch. 12]), describe a legendary migration of Chanka warriors from the Andahuaylas region into low-lying areas of the Andes toward the end of Pachacuti Inca Yupanqui's rule. Until more evidence is collected from the Andahuaylas region and the lowlands, we hesitate to draw links between what we see as a possible population decline in the Andahuaylas region during the Inca Period and these vague suggestions of prehispanic population movements.

41 Excavations by Kellett (2010) at two of the largest Chanka Period sites in the region, Achanchi and Luisinayoc, yielded a total of some 22,440 sherds, of which only 15 were classified as Inca.

CHAPTER 8

OVERVIEW OF THE CHANKA

The Chanka are long thought to be one of the most important ethnic groups of the prehistoric Andes. A momentous battle is said to have taken place between the Chanka and the Inca on the edge of Cuzco, a battle that marked the start of Inca imperial expansion and determined the course of late Andean cultural history. The Inca are believed to have emerged as the victors of that battle, and the Chanka were sorely defeated. As a result of this conflict, Pachacuti Inca Yupanqui was crowned king and began an aggressive campaign of expansion that continued for three generations, resulting in the development of the largest empire in the Americas. Although there has been much scholarship on the rapid rise and spread of Inca hegemony, the role that the Chanka played in the history of the Andes has gone largely unexamined.

OVERVIEW OF OUR RESEARCH IN THE ANDAHAUYLAS REGION

In this study we have examined the long-term development of the Chanka in their homeland of Andahuaylas. More specifically, we present the results of an archaeological survey that was conducted in the Andahuaylas area from 2002 to 2004. The goal of the field research was to document the distribution of archaeological remains across the region. The project also involved intensive work in various archives in Andahuaylas, Cuzco, Lima, and

Seville. Together, the archaeological and historical data integrate to provide a better understanding of how the area was first occupied and what events occurred there during prehistoric and early colonial times.[1]

One of the most important contributions of our archaeological and historical work has been the establishment of Andahuaylas as the long-term homeland of the Chanka. It has long been suggested that the Chanka were originally from the Ayacucho region and that they only expanded toward Andahuaylas relatively late in prehistory. This traditional view was first established by Markham (1871), Arca Parró (1923), and Navarro del Águila (1939), and it has been continued by many contemporary scholars of the central Andes. The previous theories that suggest that a Chanka migration took place are generally based on Colonial Period accounts that describe the mythical ancestors of the Chanka as having first appeared outside of the Andahuaylas region and then having traveled into the region to settle. We believe that modern researchers have misread these passages, assuming that they record an actual migration of people rather than mythical events. There is currently no archaeological evidence to support the migration theories, yet the misreading of Chanka origin myths as fact-based histories has become deeply ingrained in the scholarly literature.

Through our archaeological research in the Andahuaylas region, we can begin to construct the full prehistory of the region rather than rely on the mythical explanations offered within the Spanish chronicles. Our 300 km² archaeological survey of the Andahuaylas region has provided new data on the size and location of some 600 prehistoric settlements. We have also helped to develop a regional ceramic chronology supported by a series of radiocarbon dates. Furthermore, this research, combined with the results of a limited number of earlier projects from the region, enable us to begin developing a broad outline of the major events that occurred in the Andahuaylas region before the Spanish invasion.

Our survey suggests that, like many areas of the Andean highlands, the Andahuaylas region was first occupied by hunters and gatherers sometime after the end of the last glaciation. By the third millennium BC, groups of individuals had begun a gradual shift from a reliance on wild food resources to an increased use of domesticated plants and animals. Perhaps the most remarkable record of these early inhabitants of the Andahuaylas Valley is the large number of petroglyphs that are concentrated east of the town of San Jerónimo (Appendix 2). By 1500 BC, several villages and a series of scattered hamlets had developed in the lower elevations of the area. These communities continued and others were established as the valley bottom and lower slopes of the region witnessed increased cultivation and population growth over the following centuries.

Our research results also suggest that the Andahuaylas region came under the influence, if not direct control, of the Wari state during its period of cultural expansion (AD 600–1000). While no Wari administrative center has been identified in the Andahuaylas area, imported Wari ceramics have been recovered at a wide range of sites. The area of Andahuaylas would have been of interest to the Wari, not only for its great agricultural potential, but also because the region lies midway between the capital city of Wari in Ayacucho and the second largest Wari site in the Andes, Pikillacta of the Cuzco region.

There was a significant change in the regional settlement pattern of the Andahuaylas area, sometime after the dissolution of the Wari state (ca. AD 1000). The lower elevations of the region, which had been densely occupied since the time of the first villages, were abandoned; and a smaller number of much larger settlements were established on ridgetops. Some of these new settlements contained defensive ditches; most, however, did not. This same pattern of valley-bottom abandonment and ridgetop occupation has been noted in many other areas of the Andes during the Late Intermediate Period (AD 1000–1400), and it is widely believed to reflect growing levels of political competition and conflict, perhaps exacerbated by a period of climate change. Our survey results suggest that the Chanka may have been integrated into a regional moiety system during the Late

Intemediate Period, but contrary to many current models, there is no evidence of a large-scale centralization of power, prestige, or wealth among the Chanka during this era.

While traditional theories suggest that Chanka expansion into the Cuzco region provided the catalyst for Inca state development, we believe that another scenario is also possible. The Chanka-Inca conflict may not have been caused by the territorial expansion of an organized Andahuaylas polity, but instead it may have been a reaction against the growing centralization of political power in the Inca heartland. Frye and de la Vega (2005: 184) suggest that similar processes occurred in the Lake Titicaca region among the Lupaqa. They write, "Despite the appearance of large fortified sites across the Lupaqa landscape, the complexity attributed to the Lupaqa in several ethnohistorical documents appears to be due more to the effects of Inca imperial expansion into the region than to internal political development." In other words, the territorial and ethnic unification of the Cuzco region may have stimulated brief periods of social and political centralization in the groups located on its peripheries, such as the Lupaqa to the southeast and the Chanka to the west. Nevertheless, these short-lived confederations proved to be politically fragile when faced with the larger and better-organized forces of the Inca, who had been undergoing a process of heartland development for several centuries (Bauer 1992, 2004; Covey 2006).

Historical sources suggest that the Inca entered into the Andahuaylas region almost 100 years before the arrival of the Spaniards, and the Inca were keen to preserve a narrative of the expansion that glorified the achievements of their noble ancestors and justified their own wars of conquest. Inca imperial ideology included a process of memorializing the Chanka-Inca War, which built up the Chanka into more formidable enemies than they probably had been. Yet, we also know that the process of Inca incorporation was highly successful, since at the time of European contact, the Chanka had been transformed from traditional rivals into strong supporters of the Inca Empire. Current research has shown that the

Inca used a variety of different mechanisms to incorporate conquered ethnic groups into their empire. For example, regional archaeological surveys of the Upper Mantaro Valley document that the Inca conquest of the Wankas brought dramatic changes to the social and economic organization of the region (D'Altroy and Hastorf 2001). Major shifts in the regional settlement systems occurred as the inhabitants of the area were forced to abandon their fortified hilltop sites and were relocated into new settlements. These new sites were much smaller than the previous occupations of the area and were located in lower parts of the valley. As the Inca state consolidated its control over the Upper Mantaro area, it built a series of installations which included the large center of Hatun Jauja, an extensive road network, numerous storage complexes, and a series of smaller settlements. These facilities represent an intensive intrusion into the preexisting social and political organization of the region and appear to have been built exclusively to meet the administrative and military needs of the empire in the region (D'Altroy and Hastorf 2001).

The expansion of the Inca into the Andahuaylas region brought with it similar, although not identical, changes. One of the most important roads of the Inca Empire, the Royal Road of Chinchaysuyu, ran through the Andahuaylas region. This road linked Cuzco with Vilcashuamán and eventually reached the distant areas of Ecuador. Like all important Inca highways, this major artery included a well-maintained road and bridges to cross the largest rivers (Hyslop 1984: Bauer 2006). The major Inca installations of the Andahuaylas region included the large center of Curamba, the important shrine site of Sondor, and a series of tambos (or way stations) spaced along the royal road. We have also documented a series of small Inca Period sites scattered in the lower elevations of the region, and there appears to have been a large village located where the modern town of Andahuaylas is now situated. The recovery of small numbers of Inca sherds at the ridgetop sites suggests that some of these settlements may not have been completely abandoned at the end of the Chanka Phase and that some residual populations may have continued to inhabit these sites during Inca times. Overall, however, there appears to have been a population decline in the region between the period of Chanka control and the end of the Inca occupation. This decline may have been particularly brought about by Inca policies of forced resettlement or outward migration.

CLOSING STATEMENT

When we began this project, our goal was to produce a seamless narrative of the rise and fall of the Chanka as an important ethnic group of the south central Andes. We wanted to present a broad, compassionate vision of the prehistory and early history of the Andahuaylas region. We were especially intrigued with the idea that the Chanka had experienced a number of significant political shifts through time. They came under the control of the Wari state (AD 600–1000), after which they experienced a period of independent development (AD 1000–1400). The Chanka were then defeated and occupied by the Inca (AD 1400–1532), and subsequently they came under the domination of Spain (AD 1532+). When we began our research, we wanted to know how the local political leadership of the Chanka developed, reacted, and changed when confronted with these different challenges. Yet, as we conducted our work and lived in the town of Andahuaylas, we were also touched by the remarkable pride that the modern inhabitants have in their past. In Andahuaylas, the name "Chanka" is proudly displayed across a wide variety of businesses and public places. Although their descent from a group widely believed to have contested the Inca for regional rule serves as a point of pride for many citizens of Andahuaylas, most also confided to us that they knew little about the history of the Chanka. We were frequently asked, "Where did they live?" and "What were they really like?" In this work, we have tried to answer some of the questions that served as the initial impetus for the project as well as some of those that were asked of us during the fieldwork. Far from being the seamless narrative and detailed retelling of the Chanka past we had anticipated, we find we have only just begun to develop an outline of early times in Andahuaylas. We hope, however, that this work will serve as a staging for others and will stimulate additional research so that the history of the Chanka will be better understood.

NOTE

[1] The archival research, which will be presented in a separate volume, reveals that Spanish colonialism had a radical effect on the Chanka. Although it is widely held that a strongly functioning local elite able to extract tribute from the indigenous population was essential to the Spanish colonial system, the power of the Chanka leaders declined markedly under Spanish rule. A variety of factors eroded the authority of the ruling Chanka families, including a diminishing population, the rise of a new native leadership under the auspices of the Catholic Church, and the effects of massive clerical corruption (Hyland and Amado González n.d.).

APPENDIX 1

INVENTORY AND PROVENIENCE OF RADIOCARBON SAMPLES FROM THE ANDAHUAYLAS REGION

Sample #	Type	Site	Diagnostic Ceramics	δ 13C	Radio-carbon Age	Calendar Date	%	Calibrated Date*
Dates from the Andahuaylas Archaeological Project (2002–2004), directed by Brian S. Bauer								
AA 51456	AMS charcoal	PAA 220-1 Luisinayoc	LIP Chanka	-22.7	723 ± 36 BP	AD 1227 ± 36	68.2%	AD 1284 (57.0%) AD 1314 AD 1358 (43.0%) AD 1380
							95.4%	AD 1273 (54.3%) AD 1327 AD 1339 (45.7%) AD 1390
AA 56651	AMS charcoal	Uranmarca 42 Ancasijllapata	LIP	-22.63	826 ± 30 BP	AD 1124 ± 30	68.2%	AD 1228 (100%) AD 1269
							95.4%	AD 1210 (100%) AD 1283
AA 56653	AMS charcoal	PAA 57 Usma	LIP Chanka	-23.57	827 ± 30 BP	AD 1123 ±30	68.2%	AD 1227 (100%) AD 1269
							95.4%	AD 1209 (100%) AD 1283
AA 56648	AMS charcoal	PAA 225 Achanchi	LIP Chanka	-22.04	837 ± 32 BP	AD 1113 ± 32	68.2%	AD 1222 (100%) AD 1267
							95.4%	AD 1189 (2.5%) AD 1197 AD 1201 (97.5%) AD 1280
AA 56650	AMS charcoal	Uranmarca 39 (Achuarazo)	LIP	-23.37	853 ± 32 BP	AD 1097 ± 32	68.2%	AD 1213 (100%) AD 1266
							95.4%	AD 1180 (100%) AD 1276
A 56645	AMS charcoal	PAA 199 Sondor	LIP Chanka	-23.31	870 ± 32 BP	AD 1080 ± 32	68.2%	AD 1184 (80.7%) AD 1231 AD 1248 (19.3%) AD 1262
							95.4%	AD 1162 (100%) AD 1271
AA 56647	AMS charcoal	PAA 280	LIP Chanka	-21.57	885 ± 32 BP	AD 1065 ± 32	68.2%	AD 1163 (6.1%) AD 1169 AD 1175 (93.9%) AD 1227
							95.4%	AD 1055 (0.2%) AD 1056 AD 1151 (99.8%) AD 1270

Sam-ple #	Type	Site	Diagnostic Ceramics	δ 13C	Radio-carbon Age	Calendar Date	%	Calibrated Date*
AA 56654	AMS charcoal	PAA 134	LIP Chanka	-22.99	918 ± 31 BP	AD 1032 ± 31	68.2%	AD 1153 (100%) AD 1213
							95.4%	AD 1046 (16.3%) AD 1085 AD 1110 (0.9%) AD 1118 AD 1130 (82.8%) AD 1227
AA 56646	AMS charcoal	PAA 285 Chanka	LIP	-20.95	1014 ± 32 BP	AD 934 ± 32	68.2%	AD 1027 (28.5%) AD 1047 AD 1083 (71.5%) AD 1138
							95.4%	AD 1018 (100%) AD 1154
AA 56649	AMS charcoal	PAA 600	None Petroglyph	-21.67	1339 ± 30 BP	AD 611 ± 30	68.2%	AD 678 (58.3%) AD 722 AD 740 (41.7%) AD 770
							95.4%	AD 659 (97.9%) AD 781 AD 792 (2.1%) AD 807
AA 51451	AMS charcoal	PAA 206-2 Anccopaccha	Qasawirka Wari	-24.2	1140 ± 120 BP	AD 810 ± 120	68.2%	AD 778 (99.7%) AD 1041 AD 1095 (0.3%) AD 1096
							95.4%	AD 684 (99.3%) AD 1164 AD 1167 (0.7%) AD 1176
AA 51450	AMS charcoal	PAA 206-1 Anccopaccha	Qasawirka Wari	-19.3	1312 ± 55 BP	AD 638 ± 55	68.2%	AD 676 (82.2%) AD 782 AD 789 (13.4%) AD 811 AD 847 (4.3%) AD 855
							95.4%	AD 661 (100%) AD 888
AA 51453	AMS charcoal	PAA 140B-1	Qasawirka	-17.7	1363 ± 42 BP	AD 587 ± 42	68.2%	AD 662 (69.2%) AD 716 AD 744 (30.8%) AD 768
							95.4%	AD 644 (97.0%) AD 782 AD 789 (2.6%) AD 812 AD 847 (0.4%) AD 853

Sam-ple #	Type	Site	Diagnostic Ceramics	δ 13C	Radio-carbon Age	Calendar Date	%	Calibrated Date*
AA 51457	AMS charcoal	PAA 140B-4	Qasawirka	-18.8	1436 ± 41 BP	AD 514 ± 41	68.2%	AD 618 (100%) AD 673
							95.4%	AD 579 (96.4%) AD 709 AD 747 (3.6%) AD 765
AA 51455	AMS-charcoal	PAA 140B-3	Qasawirka	-18.2	1464 ± 39 BP	AD 486 ± 39	68.2%	AD 609 (100%) AD 658
							95.4%	AD 565 (100%) AD 675
AA 51454	AMS charcoal	PAA 140B-2	Qasawirka	-19.2	1512 ± 48 BP	AD 438 ± 48	68.2%	AD 570 (100%) AD 645
							95.4%	AD 441 (1.2%) AD 454 AD 458 (2.9%) AD 485 AD 532 (95.9%) AD 664
AA 51452	AMS charcoal	PAA 158-1	Qasawirka	-18.4	2262 ± 77 BP	312 ± 77 BC	68.2%	380 BC (100 %) 195 BC
							95.4%	399 BC (97.1%) 84 BC 80 BC (2.9%) 54 BC
AA 56640	AMS charcoal	PAA 269	Chacamarca	-22.97	2494 ± 33 BP	544 ± 33 BC	68.2%	731 BC (21.1%) 691 BC 660 BC (4.5%) 651 BC 544 BC (74.5%) 412 BC
							95.4%	753 BC (22.1%) 685 BC 668 BC (12.0%) 610 BC 597 BC (65.9%) 405 BC
AA 56642	AMS charcoal	PAA 307	Chacamarca	-22.29	2539 ± 41 BP	589 ± 41 BC	68.2%	760 BC (27.4%) 701 BC 696 BC (6.3%) 682 BC 671 BC (66.3%) 538 BC
							95.4%	773 BC (90.6%) 481 BC 468 BC (9.4%) 415 BC

Sample #	Type	Site	Diagnostic Ceramics	δ 13C	Radio-carbon Age	Calendar Date	%	Calibrated Date*
AA 56652	AMS charcoal	PAA 179	Chacamarca	-24.63	2735 ± 44 BP	785 ± 44 BC	68.2%	894 BC (26.8%) 870 BC 850 BC (73.2%) 801 BC
							95.4%	927 BC (100%) 786 BC

Published Dates from Grossman (1985:58)[1]

Sample #	Type	Site	Diagnostic Ceramics	δ 13C	Radio-carbon Age	Calendar Date	%	Calibrated Date*
UCLA 1808D	Conventional charcoal	PAA 72 Waywaka	Muyu Moqo A	NA	2200 ± 430 BP	250 ± 430 BC	68.2%	763 BC (7.0%) AD 680 673 BC (93.0%) AD 251
							95.4%	1263 BC (99.9%) 689 BC AD 752 (0.1%) AD 760
UCLA 1808F	Conventional charcoal	PAA 72 Waywaka	Muyu Moqo B	NA	2660 ± 250 BP	710 ± 250 BC	68.2%	1014 BC (100%) 400 BC
							95.4%	1395 BC (99.9%) 164 BC 128 BC (0.1%) 121 BC
UCLA 1808I	Conventional charcoal	PAA 72 Waywaka	Muyu Moqo B	NA	3240 ± 210 BP	1290 ± 210 BC	68.2%	1735 BC (3.1%) 1713 BC 1694 BC (95.6%) 1193 BC 1142 BC (1.3%) 1132 BC
							95.4%	1951 BC (100%) 907 BC
UCLA 1808A	Conventional charcoal	PAA 72 Waywaka	Muyu Moqo A	NA	440 ± 110 BP	1490 ± 110 BC	68.2%	1870 BC (7.4%) 1845 BC 1811 BC (2.0%) 1803 BC 1776 BC (90.6%) 1528 BC
							95.4%	1950 BC (100%) 1143 BC
UCLA 1808J	Conventional charcoal	PAA 72 Waywaka	Muyu Moqo A	NA	3185 ± 160 BP	1235 ± 160 BC	68.2%	1607 BC (7.0%) 1570 BC 1561 BC (2.4%) 1546 BC 1541 BC (88.8%) 1193 BC 1142 BC (1.8%) 1132 BC
							95.4%	1750 BC (99.1%) 970 BC 961 BC (0.9%) 932 BC

Sample #	Type	Site	Diagnostic Ceramics	δ 13C	Radio-carbon Age	Calendar Date	%	Calibrated Date*
UCLA 1808E	Conventional charcoal	PAA 72 Waywaka	Muyu Moqo A	NA	3550 ± 100 BP	1600 ± 100 BC	68.2%	1947 BC (100%) 1688 BC
							95.4%	2128 BC (2.2%) 2089 BC 2045 BC (94.7%) 1602 BC 1590 BC (3.1%) 1533 BC

Dates from the Chanka Settlement Project (2005–2006), directed by Lucas C. Kellett

Sample #	Type	Site	Diagnostic Ceramics	δ 13C	Radio-carbon Age	Calendar Date	%	Calibrated Date*
AA 78331	AMS charcoal	Anccopaccha (1-A-V-2)	Qasawirka Wari	-26.2	1175 ± 38 BP	AD 775 ± 38	68.2%	AD 893 (100%) AD 975
							95.4%	AD 782 (1.3%) AD 790 AD 810 (98.7 %) AD 993
AA 78332	AMS carbonized maize	Anccopaccha (1-A-II-3)	Qasawirka Wari	-9.6	1095 ± 38 BP	AD 855 ± 38	68.2%	AD 909 (1.6%) AD 910 AD 974 (98.4%) AD 1028
							95.4%	AD 894 (97.8%) AD 1044 AD 1088 (2.2%) AD 1104
AA 78333	AMS charcoal	Anccopaccha (1-A-I-4)	Qasawirka Wari	-24.3	1123 ± 37 BP	AD 827 ± 37	68.2%	AD 900 (21.6%) AD 918 AD 962 (78.4%) AD 1018
							95.4%	AD 893 (100%) AD 1024
AA 80683	AMS carbonized maize	Achanchi (2-E-E-2)	LIP Chanka	-8.2	821 ± 36 BP	AD 1129 ± 36	68.2%	AD 1227 (100%) AD 1272
							95.4%	AD 1190 (0.5%) AD 1192 AD 1202 (99.5%) AD 1289
AA 80684	AMS carbonized maize	Achanchi (2-A-II-4)	LIP Chanka	-8.1	816 ± 36 BP	AD 1134 ± 36	68.2%	AD 1228 (100%) AD 1274
							95.4%	AD 1204 (100%) AD 1292
AA 80685	AMS carbonized maize	Achanchi (3-A-I-4)	LIP Chanka	-9.2	731 ± 43 BP	AD 1219 ± 43	68.2%	AD 1279 (60.5%) AD 1315 AD 1357 (39.5%) AD 1381
							95.4%	AD 1235 (1%) AD 1242 AD 1265 (99%) AD 1392

Sample #	Type	Site	Diagnostic Ceramics	δ 13C	Radio-carbon Age	Calendar Date	%	Calibrated Date*
AA 80686	AMS carbon-ized maize	Luisinayoc (2-A-I-2)	LIP Chanka	-8.3	898 ± 36 BP	AD 1052 ± 36	68.2%	AD 1158 (100%) AD 1221
							95.4%	AD 1049 (8.2%) AD 1080 AD 1144 (91.8%) AD 1268
AA 80687	AMS carbon-ized maize	Luisinayoc (2-B-I-4)	LIP Chanka	-9.0	968 ± 36 BP	AD 982 ± 36	68.2%	AD 1045 (47.5%) AD 1088 AD 1105 (52.5%) AD 1159
							95.4%	AD 1029 (99.6%) AD 1189 AD 1198 (0.4%) AD 1201
AA 80688	AMS carbon-ized maize	Luisinayoc (2-C-I-5)	LIP Chanka	-9.3	905 ± 36 BP	AD 1045 ± 36	68.2%	AD 1155 (100%) AD 1219
							95.4%	AD 1047 (11.6%) AD 1083 AD 1137 (88.4%) AD 1267

* Calibrated dates were generated by Calib 5.1 beta, courtesy of the University of Washington (Stuiver and Reimer 1993). Dates were calibrated using software using southern hemisphere data (ShCal04 calibration curve) (McCormac et al. 2004).

[1] These dates have been recalibrated using Calib 5.1 beta and therefore are slightly different from Grossman's (1985: 58) calibrated dates.

APPENDIX 2

THE PETROGLYPHS OF ANDAHUAYLAS

Our archaeological research documented that the Andahuaylas region contains an unusually high concentration of rock art (Figure A2.1).[1] Petroglyphs—designs carved or pecked on rock outcrops or on isolated boulders—are relatively rare features of the central highlands. While theoretically they can date to any period, a fact that is emphasized by the occasional portrayal of post-European contact elements (such as horses or Christian crosses), the majority of the petroglyphs found in the highlands are presumed to date to preceramic or early ceramic times (Hostnig 2003). Although examples of rock art are exhilarating to find, they tend to be underreported because they are so difficult to date and interpret (Figure A2.2).

Building on the regional research of Hostnig (1988, 1990), we recorded a cluster of approximately 40 individual figures at a single site near the town of Talavera and more than 750 figures distributed across several sites east of San Jerónimo. In all cases, the rock art is represented by designs pecked into the surface of the rock, rather than pictographs. By far the greatest number of carvings show camelids, although other animals, including deer, were also noted. Most of the camelids, which number over 600 examples, are stylized figures. Some, however, are clearly males (Figure A2.3), while others are lactating females and nursing young (Figure A2.4). Some camelids are depicted mating (Figure A2.5), and a few are shown held by humans (Figure A2.6). Geometric elements, including horizontal lines, vertical lines, spirals, and circles, were also widespread. Some anthropomorphic beings and faces were identified, and there is one possible depiction of a solar eclipse. Brief descriptions of the petroglyph sites identified during the survey are provided below.

The best-known petroglyph site in the Andahuaylas area is called Huayllao (PAA 226).[2] It is approximately 2 km south of Talavera on the western slope of a small river valley. The site consists of a single outcrop with two panels of well-preserved petroglyphs. There are approximately 40 designs, including numerous spirals and circles as well as a human figure, a few camelids, and several unidentified figures. Unfortunately, the site has been somewhat defaced with modern etchings and painted graffiti (Figure A2.7).

The area east of San Jerónimo contains a series of incised streams along which various clusters of petroglyphs can be found (Figures A2.8,

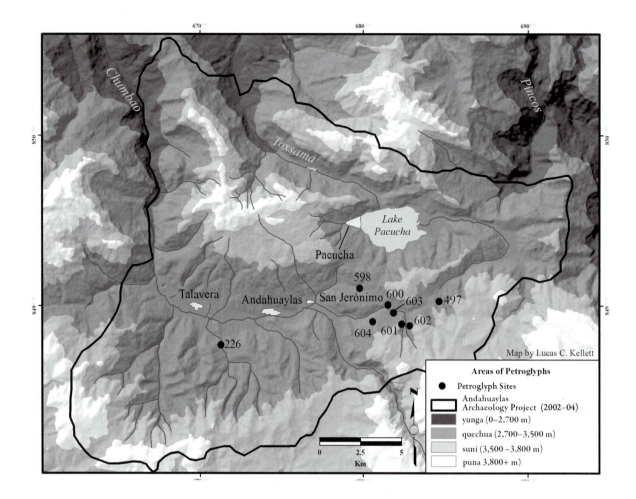

FIGURE A2.1. Distribution of rock art in the Andahuaylas region.

FIGURE A2.2. A large panel of petroglyphs at Llamachayoc (PAA 601).

FIGURE A2.3. A small panel with male camelids at Llamachayoc (PAA 601).

FIGURE A2.4. A large panel of petroglyphs at Llamachayoc (PAA 601). Note the mother and calf in the center.

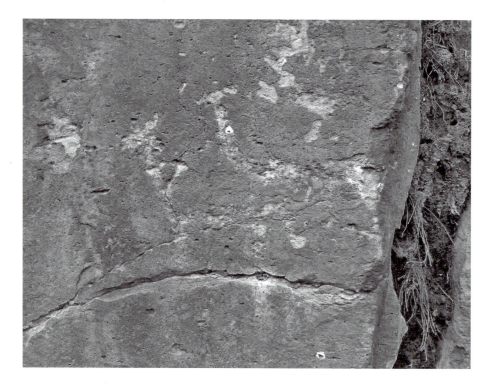

FIGURE A2.5. Mating camelids at Llamachayoc (PAA 601).

FIGURE A2.6.
A petroglyph showing a human and a camelid at Pacambamba (PAA 602).

FIGURE A2.7. The best-known petroglyph site in the Andahuaylas area is called Huayllao (PAA 226).

FIGURE A2.8. Caqa Corral (PAA 497) is a ravine that contains various clusters of petroglyphs.

FIGURE A2.9. In the Andahuaylas region, most petroglyphs are found on the upper cliffs of the ravines (PAA 497, Caqa Corral).

A2.9). The largest density of petroglyphs is located in and around the Llamachayoc ravine (PAA 601). Within an area of the ravine less than 1 km long, we documented 15 separate sectors of carvings with a total of approximately 360 individual figures. While most of the carvings are of camelids (several of which are depicted with humans), there are also a few isolated human figures, several geometric elements, as well as a Christian cross.

A few kilometers west of Llamachayoc, near the community of Champacocha, is a ravine called Caqa Corral (PAA 497).[3] The area contains four separate sectors of carvings with approximately 110 individual figures. Although most of the figures are of camelids, there are humans with camelids, various geometric figures, and several unusually large anthropomorphic beings (Figure A2.10).

Another group of petroglyphs is located in the Pacambamba ravine (PAA 602) immediately to the east of Llamachoyoc.[4] The area contains 10 separate sectors of carvings, with a total of approximately 75 individual figures. Most of the figures are of camelids, several of which are

shown with humans. However, a face, two Christian crosses, and various geometric elements were also recorded.

Near the junction of the Pacambamba and Llamachoyoc ravines and continuing down the Uchurana River, there is another zone of scattered petroglyphs carved into the cliff face (PAA 603). The area contains four separate sectors of figures, with a total of approximately 25 individual camelids. Farther down the valley there is another small cluster of petroglyphs (PAA 598) that contains two separate sectors of carvings, totaling approximately 15 camelids. And there is yet another small cluster of petroglyphs carved in the cliffs south of the Uchurana River (PAA 604). That site contains only two sectors of carvings but holds more than 100 individual figures, most of which are camelids, although a few deer, three humans riding horses, and several geometric figures were also recorded.[5]

By far the most intriguing set of rock carvings in the Andahuaylas region is located within the petroglyph-rich region east of San Jerónimo. The site, PAA 600, is situated within the Uchurana

FIGURE A2.10. A petroglyph panel with several large anthropomorphic beings at
Caqa Corral (PAA 497).

River Valley between sites PAA 604 and PAA 603, along a small exposed cliff. The site contains three sectors of carvings, with a total of some 90 individual figures. Unlike the other petroglyph concentrations in the immediate region, which are dominated by carved camelids, this site does not contain a single camelid. Instead, it displays a dense concentration of geometric designs, faces, humans, and anthropomorphic beings (Figure A2.11).

The most interesting carving at PAA 600 may show a rayed image of the sun which is located in a well-protected rock overhang. The possible body of the sun, shown as a circle, measures 8 cm in diameter, while the rays that extend from it average 15 cm in length (Figure A2.12). This petroglyph is of special importance, since immediately to the right of the possible sun, but within the area of the rays, is a second circle of equal size. We suggest that the second circle may represent the moon which is about to pass in front of the sun. If this is the case, then this is one of the few depictions of a solar eclipse found in rock art in the Andes.

As noted above, dating petroglyphs is a difficult task, since they typically are not associated with any datable material. In addition, we did not locate any archaeological sites adjacent to the petroglyphs that could provide diagnostic lithics or ceramics or material for radiocarbon dating. While it is generally assumed that most petroglyphs, especially those that depict camelids, predate the establishment of large-scale agricultural communities in the Andes, the fact that rock art continued to be produced in the Andahuaylas area in historic times is documented by the occasional Christian cross and horseback riders. Nevertheless, we were particularly interested in site PAA 600, because the different artistic style and the unusual repertoire of images at this site suggest that these rock carvings may have been made by different people than those who created the camelid depictions that dominate the other petroglyph sites of the region. Unfortunately, the style of the petroglyphs seen at PAA 600 does not match that of any known artistic tradition of the central highlands, and there are no temporal clues within the images (such as horseback riders) to help us date the carvings. Furthermore, the fact that a solar eclipse may have been recorded at this site does not alone provide concrete infor-

FIGURE A2.11. One of many faces carved into the cliff at site PAA 600.

FIGURE A2.12. A petroglyph at site PAA 600 may show the moon
passing in front of the sun.

mation for dating the carving, since there were many occasions during prehistory when an impressive eclipse (either complete or annular) was visible from the Andahuaylas region.[6]

In an attempt to date the site, we collected carbon from smoke soot on the ceiling of one of the various small rock overhangs at the site, approximately 10 m from the solar petroglyph. The carbon provided a radiocarbon date of 1339 ± 30 BP.[7] The resulting calibration indicates that there is a 95.4% chance that the carbon was deposited between AD 659 and AD 807. With this date, it is worth mentioning that notable solar eclipses were visible from the Andahuaylas region on 22 April 711 and 7 December 717.[8] The correlation between these celestial events and the eclipse recorded in the petroglyph is, however, speculative at best, since the dated carbon was not directly associated with the carving. Furthermore, while our archaeological survey indicates that the Andahuaylas region was under the influence of the Wari culture during the eighth century AD, the style of the carvings at the site does not conform with the classic artistic canons of this major highland culture. Whatever the exact date, the fact that this event was re-corded on a rock cliff, and that the surface of the pecking is now covered with a natural patina, indicates that the event witnessed was one of great antiquity.

NOTES

[1] Henry Gamonal Quillilli led the effort to document the Andahuaylas petroglyphs in 2001 (Hostnig 2003: 32, 34). This work was continued by Kimberly Klock and Miriam Aráoz Silva in 2002.

[2] This area is also known as Hualalache, after the nearby village.

[3] This area is also called Chinchillpay and Culispuquio.

[4] This area is also called Lyanmayo.

[5] The large number of figures at this small site results from the fact that a single cliff face contains some 80 designs.

[6] A small fraction of the earth's surface experiences a total solar eclipse only once every few centuries. However, if annular eclipses and partial eclipses in which a substantial fraction of the sun is occulted are considered, solar eclipses are experienced in most spots on the earth every few decades (Bauer and Dearborn 1995: 142–146).

[7] Sample AA 56649.

[8] See http://sunearth.gsfc.nasa.gov/eclipse/eclipse.html for dates and other information on solar and lunar eclipses.

APPENDIX 3

THE ARCHAEOLOGY OF URANMARCA

Carlo Socualaya Dávila and Brian S. Bauer

The village of Uranmarca is located on the eastern slope of the Pampas River Valley, between the Inca center of Vilcashuamán and the town of Andahuaylas, along the most important Inca road of the central highlands (see Figures 1.5, 7.1).[1] Long before and after Inca rule in the region, the inhabitants of Uranmarca helped to maintain a bridge across the river and provided lodging to travelers. While the people of Uranmarca have traditionally identified themselves as a distinct social group, largely defined by their relative isolation in a rugged region, their lives have been heavily influenced by the various states and empires that have held control of the central Andes. In this study, we examine the cultural transformations that occurred in the Uranmarca area between the Wari (AD 600–1000) and Inca (AD 1400–1532) imperial expansions. The history of the small community of Uranmarca is significant for several reasons. First, like all communities, Uranmarca has its own particular history, which is worthy of investigation. Second, it provides insights into how a region on the edge of the Chanka homeland witnessed and experienced the cultural changes that swept through the Andes during the last millennium before European contact. Third, according to Garcilaso de la Vega (1966: 218–220 [1609: Pt. 1, Bk. 4, Ch. 15]), the Uanmarcas were part of the Chanka Confederation. Finally, there are unusually well-preserved archaeological ruins in the region, and valuable historical documents have been conserved by community leaders. These remains serve as an effective tool with which to examine the history of Uranmarca, at a level of detail not possible for many other villages in the Department of Apurimac (Socualaya Dávila 2005).

INTRODUCTION TO URANMARCA

The community of Uranmarca, located at an altitude of 3,100 masl, rests on a steep west-facing valley slope, perched high above the Pampas River (2,200 masl).[2] In less than 10 aerial km, the lands of the community rise steeply from the banks of this large river, encompassing first the fruit-bearing *yunga* zone, then the maize-dominated *quechua*

139

agricultural zone, and finally the high rolling *puna* grasslands (4,100 + masl) which are used for herding. As such, community members have direct access to a wide range of natural resources distributed across distinct elevational zones within a single day's walk. Our archaeological survey of the region found that all of the environmental zones have been occupied in the past, but as in the Andahuaylas region, there have been clear settlement shifts over time.

Various Spanish chroniclers mention the presence of a *tambo* and bridge at Uranmarca (for example, Sancho 1917: 117 [1534]; Garcilaso de la Vega 1966: 219 [1609: Pt. 1, Bk. 5, Ch. 15]). One of the earliest accounts comes from Cristóbal Vaca de Castro's description of tambos located along the Inca royal roads (Vaca de Castro 1908: 444 [1543]).[3] Another early report is provided by Cieza de León, who noted the remains of the tambo while traveling between Vilcashuamán and Andahauaylas: "Returning to the main road, one arrives at the lodgings of Uranmarca, which is a settlement of *mitimaes*, for the natives were nearly all killed during the [dynastic] war of the Incas."[4] An anonymous writer of the early 1600s also describes traveling the route between Vilcashuamán and Andahuaylas, and passing through the Uranmarca area:

> Many villages lie in this district from which one descends a long gradient to the Ura[n]-marca River, one of the biggest tributaries of the Marañón. It is forded in summer and crossed by a suspension bridge in winter. Sugarcane brakes thickly line this river, from which one climbs up to the Ura[n]marca tambo. The trail then passes several Indian communities and dairy farms, and Andaguailas the Great, as the valley is called in Peru, is reached after passing a small native hamlet. (Anonymous Description of Peru 1972: 115 [ca. 1600])

A more detailed account that mentions Uranmarca was recorded by Luis de Teruel, a Jesuit priest involved in the extirpation of idolatry in the Andes. Arriaga provides a transcription of a letter written by Teruel in which this zealous priest describes his brief time in Uranmarca:

> In Ura[n]marca another good old man told me that when someone dies, they bury him in new clothes and offer him food, and every year the offering is renewed. He told us also that they keep the bodies of their pagan ancestors in caves and ancient tombs and make sacrifices to them as they begin to work the ground for sowing while they make chicha [corn beer] on the farms. If a fire sparks, they say the souls of their ancestors are thirsty and hungry, and they throw corn and chicha and potatoes and other foods into the fire for them to eat and drink. They also sacrifice in the same way when they are ill. We were only there one afternoon and the following night, and so I was not able to get any more information out of the old men about the huacas, except that such and such a one, which he named, used to be worshiped but is not worshiped anymore. This is a common answer to all the towns I have visited. We preached against this practice during the afternoon, and on the following morning, which was a Sunday, we confessed a few persons. We could not accommodate them all, although they asked for it, as we did not wish to lose a day.[5] (Teruel in Arriaga 1968: 75–76 [1621])

Teruel was in Uranmarca sometime around 1615, while traveling between Lima and Cuzco. Like most travelers, he reached the tambo in the afternoon, spent the night there, and then continued on his journey the next day. This rest stop and river crossing must have been particularly well known, since Uranmarca is marked on various seventeenth- and eighteenth-century maps, and it is listed as an official "tambo" along the central highland road by Guaman Poma de Ayala (1980: 1005 [1615: 1090 (1100)]).[6] In contrast, except for the village and regional shrine of Cocharcas, located approximately two hours by foot from Uranmarca, the area is now little visited by outsiders.[7]

THE URANMARCA BRIDGE

During Inca times, there were several suspension bridges that crossed the Pampas River, connecting what are now the departments of Apurimac and Ayacucho. The continued importance of these bridges, and their adjacent tambos, during the Colonial Period is highlighted by a long-lasting dispute between the surrounding communities (Hyland 2002b). One of the bridges connected the large Inca center of Vilcashuamán (Department of Ayacucho) with Andahuaylas (Department of Apurimac). This bridge was located near the town of Uranmarca, and it is described as one of the largest bridges in the Andes. Like many other bridges along the major mountain roads, the Uranmarca Bridge was replaced annually. It also had to be rebuilt during times of regional conflict, since bridges were frequently burned to hinder the movements of troops. The repair and rebuilding of bridges was generally the responsibility of the communities that lived in the surrounding areas (Bauer 2006).

One of the earliest descriptions of the Uranmarca Bridge comes from Pedro Sancho, who described the Spanish and native forces under Manco Inca arriving at the bridge site as they chased Quisquis (a general of the defeated Inca Atahualpa) northward from Cuzco toward Jauja in 1534. When they arrived at the Uranmarca crossing, they found that the bridge had been burned by Quisquis and needed to be rebuilt. Sancho writes:

And the river being swollen and furious, and the bridge burned, it was necessary for them to stop and build it anew, for, without it, it would have been impossible to cross the river, either in those boats, which are called *balsas*, or by swimming or in any other way. Twenty days the camp was here in order to mend the bridge, for the officers [*maestros*] had much to do, because the water was high and kept breaking down the osier ropes that were put in place. And if the cacique had not had so great a number of men to build the bridge and to cross over by it and pull over the osiers, it would not have been possible to build it. But having twenty-four thousand warriors, and by crossing [the stream] again and again to attempt [to set the ropes in place] making use of cords and *balsas*, at last they succeeded in placing the osier ropes

and when they had been passed across [the river] the bridge was built in a very short space of time. [It was] so good and well built that another like it is not to be found in that land, for it is three hundred and seventy-odd feet long, and broad enough to allow two horses to cross at once without any risk.[8] (Sancho 1917: 117–118 [1534: Ch. 13])

Pedro Cieza de León traveled the same road as a Spanish cavalryman approximately 15 years later. The Uranmarca Bridge was so remarkable that he recorded a specific description of it:

From here (Vilcashuamán) the highway proceeds to Uranmarca, seven leagues toward Cuzco. . . . From one side of the river to the other there are two high rows of stone piles, stout and deeply buried, on which to lay the bridge, which is made of twisted withers, like well ropes for drawing up water with a pulley. The bridges made in this way are so strong that horses can gallop over them as though they were crossing the bridge of Alcántara or Córdoba. This bridge when I crossed it was seventy-six feet long.[9] (Cieza de León 1976: 129 [1553: Pt. 1, Ch. 89])

Guaman Poma de Ayala also mentions the Uranmarca Bridge. In his description of the tambos of the Inca Empire, Guaman Poma de Ayala (1980: 1090 [1615: 1100]) notes that the Uranmarca Bridge was one of the largest in the kingdom and that it crossed the Guambo Grande River (this is the name that Guaman Poma de Ayala used for the Pampas River).[10] Elsewhere Guaman Poma de Ayala (1980: 328 [1615: 356 (358)]) includes a drawing of the bridge and a bridge inspector. The inspector's large ear spools indicate that he is a man of considerable importance in the empire. Behind the inspector, a traveler with a large load can be seen crossing the bridge. The bridge rests on large stone foundations, and Guaman Poma de Ayala clearly depicts the braided bridge cables (Figure A3.1).

During the course of our work in the Andahuaylas region, Socualaya Dávila (2005) documented an area called Incachaka (Inca bridge) along the Pampas River downslope from Uranmarca.

FIGURE A3.1. Guaman Poma de Ayala (1980: 328 [1615: 356 (358)]) provides a drawing of the bridge near Uranmarca, which connected Andahuaylas with Vilcashuamán. The caption reads: "Gobernador de los puentes deste reyno chaca suioioc Acos Inga, Guambo chaca" (Supervisor of the bridges of this kingdom, Acos Inca, Guambo Bridge). Beneath the drawing is written, "uedor de puentes" (overseer of bridges). *Courtesy of Det Kongelige Bibliotek.*

On the Vilcashuamán side of the river are the remains of a late nineteenth-century construction that once supported a suspension bridge. A similar structure once stood on the Uranmarca side, but it was destroyed in a flood several decades ago. While this is certainly a possible site for the Inca bridge, Victor von Hagen (1959) suggests it was located farther upstream near the community of Pariabamba. We were unable to confirm or deny the existance of a bridge site at this other mentioned location.

THE URANMARCA SURVEY

Our interest in the Uranmarca region began during the initial phase of the Andahuaylas Archaeological Project. During a 2000 visit to Andahuaylas, Bauer was told that there were Inca ruins in the Uranmarca area. More importantly, that year he met with Arturo Gutiérrez Velasco (1999), a historian of the Andahuaylas region, to discuss the *Acta de Uranmarca*, a document owned by the village of Uranmarca. Gutiérrez Velasco had been shown a copy of the document by Dr. Romulo Tello Valdivia, a physician of Andahuaylas, who had been in Uranmarca several decades earlier.[11] When we visited Uranmarca in June 2002, we were overwhelmed by the openness of the community members to outsiders and their eagerness to help us study the history of their town. Carlo Socualaya Dávila (2005) returned to Uranmarca in September and October of that year to direct an archaeological survey, which formed the basis for his *licenciatura*.[12] In 2003, community officials gave us full access to the municipal archives, and we found their copy of the *Acta de Uranmarca* (see Appendix 4) as well as various other documents of historical importance. The information presented below is based on the archaeological survey work conducted in the region by Socualaya Dávila (2005) as well as our analysis of those documents.[13]

Survey Methods

The archaeological survey of the Uranmarca region covered an area of approximately 75 km². This included the territory currently held by the community; as we would later discover, this area is remarkably similar to that described as being controlled by Uranmarca within the *Acta de Uranmarca*. The survey procedures followed those already described for our work in the Andahuaylas region. In actuality, the survey conditions in Uranmarca were far more difficult because of the steep topography and lack of transportation and because the survey was conducted at the start of the rainy season. It should also be noted that the surface ceramics of the Uranmarca region are generally of poor quality. Most of the recovered sherds were from plain domestic vessels and could not be placed within our regional ceramic chronology. As a result, the sites described in this section have been dated by a relatively small number of diagnostic sherds.

The Qasawirka Phase Settlement Pattern (300 BC–AD 1000)

The Qasawirka settlement pattern in the Uranmarca region was defined by the distribution of sites with Qasawirka and Qasawirka-related

ceramics.[14] These, as noted in Chapter 4, are characterized by a dark red slip. In all, nine sites were found in the Uranmarca region with this ceramic style (Figure A3.2). By far the largest Qasawirka site in the region is Juchuy Muyumuyu[15] (PAA-U-30). Located at 2,573 masl, the site is positioned on a large knoll on a steeply descending ridge covered by dense vegetation. Artifacts can be found in ample quantities eroding down its slope, and although the size of the site is difficult to determine, we estimate that it covered more than 10 ha during this period. A road cut through the site has exposed various burials and middens. There are also the remains of terraces and scattered walls across the surface of the site.

The second largest Qasawirka site in the region is near the modern settlement of Uranmarca at 3,191 masl. Although modern debris and disturbance complicate the site-size estimate, we suggest that this site reached a maximum of 6 to 8 ha. The other seven Qasawirka sites were considerably smaller, measuring 1 ha or less. Overall, the settlement pattern reflects a concentration of sites within a rather narrow elevation band between 2,600 and 3,200 masl, a bit lower than those of the Andahuaylas region.

The dramatic differences in site sizes in the region during this phase suggest that there was a large village at Juchuy Muyumuyu, a second smaller village near modern-day Uranmarca, and various other hamlets and homesteads scattered across the mid-elevations of the region. Even though Uranmarca lies on a major prehistoric road connecting the departments of Apurimac and Ayacucho, we found no examples of Wari ceramics in our surface collections. Although additional research in the region may yield some evidence of imported Ayacucho pottery, it seems clear that the Wari state did not establish a major presence nor make substantial investments in the Uranmarca region. In other words, while the inhabitants of the region certainly would have been aware of the great political and economic changes that were occurring in the central Andes at that time, their lives may not have been significantly impacted by the expanding Wari state.

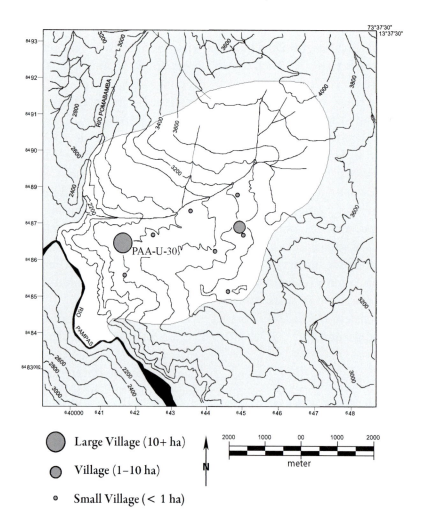

FIGURE A3.2. The Qasawirka Phase (300 BC–1000 AD) settlement
pattern in the Uranmarca area.

The Chanka Phase Settlement Pattern (AD 1000–1400)

The Late Intermediate Period, here called the Chanka Phase, is widely thought to be a time of regional conflict following the collapse of the Wari state. In the Andahuaylas region, where there is evidence of close links with the Ayacucho region, we have documented a significant shift in the regional settlement system around AD 1000. The data suggest that much of the population abandoned their traditional valley-bottom sites and established new and larger settlements at higher elevations (3,500+ masl).

A similar shift occurred in the Uranmarca area. Almost all of the Qasawirka Phase sites were aban-

doned, including the principal village of Juchuy Muyumuyu, and we identified 18 new sites dating to the Chanka Phase. These sites are clustered between 3,000 and 4,000 masl in areas that are now dominated by quinoa and tuber cultivation as well as herding. They range in size from numerous small scatters of ceramics to a single site more than 12 ha in size with well-preserved architecture (Figure A3.3).

The most impressive Chanka Phase site in the Uranmarca region is Ancasijillapata (PAA-U-42). Not only was this the largest site, but it also had the densest amount of ceramics. Located on a ridge summit at 3,576 masl, approximately 1,000 m higher than the largest village of the previous Qasawirka Phase, Ancasijillapata contains broad areas of poorly preserved circular struc-

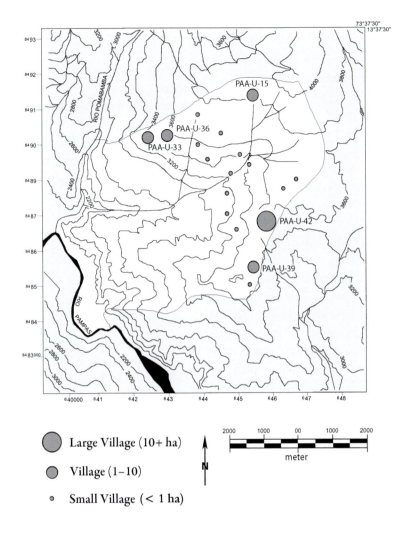

Large Village (10+ ha)

Village (1–10)

Small Village (< 1 ha)

FIGURE A3.3. The Chanka Phase (AD 1000–1400) settlement pattern in the Uranmarca area.

tures and habitation terraces. Soot concentrations on ceramics collected at the site provided an uncalibrated date of AD 1124 ± 30.[16] A short walk down the same ridge is the site of Achuarazo (PAA-U-39), which also contains circular structures. Carbon found encrusted on ceramics collected at the site yielded an uncalibrated date of AD 1097 ± 32.[17]

Evidence of large-scale herding practices comes from the site of Achupachayoc (PAA-U-15). Located at nearly 4,000 masl, this site contains numerous circular structures as well as corrals. Other sites larger than 1 ha include Capari (PAA-U-36) and Parjarumi (PAA-U-33). Both of these sites are located on a ridge that defines the northern limits of the research region.

The Inca Occupation of the Uranmarca Region

As the Inca expanded beyond their traditional homeland in the Cuzco Valley, they incorporated various entities into their state. Garcilaso de la Vega suggests that the Inca first encountered the people of Uranmarca during the reign of Inca Roca (the sixth Inca) and that those of Uranmarca fiercely resisted Cuzco domination. Guaman Poma de Ayala (1980: 1090 [1615: 1100]) places contact between the two groups a generation later, during the rule of Yahuar Huacac. Most other writers, however, suggest that the Andahuaylas region and its various groups were defeated during the reign of Pachacuti Inca Yupanqui, but they also imply that raids may have taken place into the region before this time.

By the time of the Spanish invasion, Uranmarca had become a crucial point along the royal Inca road of Chinchaysuyu. The Inca constructed a ceremonial platform (now called Muyumuyu), a tambo, a bridge over the Pampas River, and various other installations in the region. These installations are worth discussing before presenting a brief summary of the Inca settlement pattern.

Muyumuyu

Muyumuyu is the most impressive Inca site in the Uranmarca region (PAA-U-28).[18] Located just outside of the modern village, the site contains a large rectangular area, now largely destroyed by the village school, and a distinct platform (*ushnu*) formed with four conical terraces (Figure A3.4).[19] A small road leads to the platform, and a stairway extends to its summit where there is a small rectangular structure. The summit of Muyumuyu offers an expansive view of the region, including the Pampas River far below.[20] This combination of features (a conical mound, a central stairway, and a plaza at the base of the mound) can also be seen at the Inca site of Sondor near Andahuaylas.

Tambo Viejo and Mayabamba Pampa

A short walk uphill from the town of Uranmarca leads to several large fields and a small but distinct knoll (Figure A3.5). This area is known as Tambo Viejo (Old Tambo), and the nearby fields contain numerous ceramic fragments (PAA-U-4). Although no structures can be seen at the site, there is little doubt that this is the location of the Uranmarca way station as described by Cieza de León and others. Farther up the slope along the same trail is the site of Mayabamba Pampa, where there are the poorly preserved remains of several circular structures and other scattered wall foundations. Both of these sites are described in the *Acta de Uranmanca*:

> Another work to the northeast, that is, 600 rods distant from the plaza, is found a small, little hill called Tambo, on which ascends some steps, and likewise in the site called Mayabambapampa there is an Inca barrack

with ten rooms, in a rectangular form, next to the royal Inca road. . . .[21]

Incaracay

A large rectangular structure known as Incaracay (Inca Ruin [PAA-U-40]) is located southeast of Uranmarca, on a ridge called Ahuaraso. Although the structure is poorly preserved and overgrown, several trapezoidal niches can been seen in its interior walls. An Inca road that descends down to the Pampas River runs near these ruins. Like the other major Inca remains of the area, this complex is described within the *Acta de Uranmarca* (Appendix 4).[22]

Incachaca

The Pampas River is west of Uranmarca. As noted above, at a large bend in the river there is a well-known structure called Incachaca (Inca Bridge) that appears to date to the nineteenth century. Only the Ayacucho side of the bridge remains, as the Apurimac side was destroyed by a flood several decades ago. Although no remains of Inca stonework can be seen at the site, we believe that this marked the site of one of three bridges that once crossed this general stretch of the Pampas River. A second bridge spanned the river approximately 8 km upstream near the village of Pariatambo, and a third, connecting the town of Ocros (Ayacucho) with Chincheros and Uripa (Apurimac), crossed the river some 25 km downstream (Bauer 2006). During early colonial times, members of Uranmarca and Chincheros entered into a bitter debate to see which community would control the primary river crossing of the region and the revenue that came from the many travelers on the road (Hyland 2002b).

The Regional Distribution of Inca sites

The archaeological survey of the Uranmarca region identified 23 sites with Inca ceramics and/or stonework (Figure A3.6). Unlike the occupations of previous periods, none of these sites was larger than 10 ha, and the majority of them were smaller than 1 ha. These sites represent a scattering of homesteads, hamlets, and small villages across the

FIGURE A3.4. Muyumuyu (PAA-U-28) with its rectangular plaza.

FIGURE A3.5. The site of Tambo Viejo (PAA-U-4) contains a small knoll and several large fields.

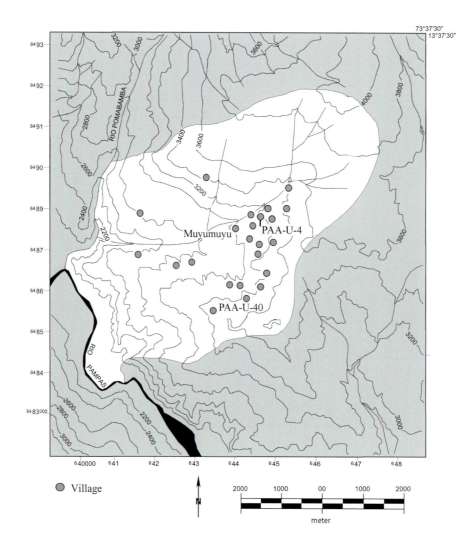

FIGURE A3.6. The Inca Phase (ca. AD 1438–1532) settlement pattern in the Uranmarca area.
Note the numerous small Inca sites.

region, as well as various small, special-purpose (civic-ceremonial or administrative) sites, such as Muyumuyu and Tambo Viejo. While most of the Inca sites are located within the best maize-producing zone of the region, between 3,000 and 3,500 masl, several can be found at lower elevations toward the Pampas River. Because the total occupation area of these sites is much smaller than that recorded for the Chanka Phase, we believe that the region may have experienced some population decline during Inca times, and we speculate that some of the Chanka sites may have continued to be occupied after the Inca expanded into the area. A similar pattern of population decline and the establishment of a series of smaller new settlements in lower elevations has been recorded in the Andahuaylas region.

OVERVIEW OF URANMARCA'S HISTORY

Archaeological research in the Uranmarca region has helped to define the general contours of the region's prehistory. During the Qasawirka Phase (300 BC–AD 1000), the region contained a sizable population that was heavily concentrated in a single village. Although there may have been a river crossing at this time near Uranmarca, the area appears to have been generally isolated from the cultural influences of the Wari as they expanded from their homeland in the Ayacucho region. At this time, greater Wari influence may have been felt in the Chincheros region, north of Uranmarca, which is on the most direct route from the Ayacucho Basin to the Andahuaylas Valley. However, this speculation remains to be tested through archaeological research.

Like many other areas of the central Andes, Uranmarca underwent a marked restructuring between the fall of the Wari and the rise of the Inca. Around AD 1000, at the start of the Chanka Phase (AD 1000–1400), the largest sites of the region were abandoned, and the majority of the population shifted to a series of newly constructed settlements along the highest ridges. Although none of these new sites contain clear evidence of defensive works, their locations on ridges provide some natural protection and offer clear views of the surrounding landscape. Given the presence of high-altitude corrals, the importance of herding appears to have increased during this period, but a series of scattered hamlets and homesteads were also maintained in the grain-producing zones.

The Uranmarca region appears to have been transformed and experienced an increase in regional stature during Inca times. With the development of a series of large centers along the Inca road of the central highlands, including Curamba, Sondor, and Vilcashuamán, the area of Uranmarca and its bridge over the Pampas River grew in regional importance. The armies of the Inca traveled along the road system, and local officials built a series of small installations, including way stations for the travelers to stay in. At the height of its power during the rule of Huayna Capac, the last Inca to govern a united empire, Uranmarca may have controlled various other villages in the northwestern parts of the Department of Apurimac, including those of Chincheros, Uripa, Ocobamba, and Ccasccabamba. During this same period, Uranmarca itself appears to have been under the control of an Inca provincial lord located in Vilcashuamán, rather than the Chanka of Andahuaylas (Bandera 1965: 178 [1557]). Then

during colonial times, as the role of Vilcashuamán declined in the regional economy and that of the city of Huamanga grew, the area of Uranmarca became less important, and the major river crossing shifted downriver nearer to the modern town of Chincheros. Today, despite the strong influence of modernization and the global economy, the small town of Uranmarca still retains great pride in the fact that it served as a tambo during Inca times and offers an excellent example of an Andean community that has worked hard to maintain its culture, history, and identity through the millennium.

NOTES

1 Uranmarca is approximately 10 hours by foot from Andahuaylas and 14 hours from Vilcashuamán. In the early Colonial Period, the boundary between the Bishopric of Huamanga (Villa de San Juan de la Frontera) and Cuzco was drawn between Uranmarca and Andahuaylas (Vaca de Castro 1908: 444 [1543]; Bandera 1965: 176, 178 [1557]).

2 The village is located at 18L 0644145, 8387995.

3 "Y del pueblo y tambo de Andaguaylas se tiene de ir al Tambo de Vramarca en el qual han de server los Indios del Pueblo Huriba o Tambo o baybamba Vingui, o Callo o Chachapoyao Caceviro o Inga que son del repartimiento que solía ser del Padre Sosa y de Gabriel de (Rojas) tal el qual dicho tambo es el primero de la Jurisdiccion de la Villa de S. Juan de la Frontera y ansi miso had de servir en el los Indios de Bolcan o de Andillca" (Vaca de Castro 1908: 444 [1543]).

4 "Y boluiendo al camino principal, se allega a los aposentos de Uramarca, que es la población de mitimaes: porque los naturales con las guerras de los Ingas murieron los mas dellos" (Cieza de León 1995: 253–254 [1553: Pt. 1, Ch. 89]).

5 ". . . y de otro buen viejo en Uramarca, el cual me contó lo que hacen cuando alguno muere, cómo lo entierran con ropa nueva y le ofrecen comida, y cada año renuevan la misma ofrenda. Y lo que hacen con los cuerpos de sus progenitores gentiles, que guardan en sus cuevas y entierros antiguos. A éstos sacrifican cuando empiezan a labrar la tierra para sembrar, echando chicha en las chácaras. Si el fuego chispea dicen que las almas de sus antepasados padecen sed y hambre, y echan en el fuego maíz y chicha, papas y otras cosas de comida para que coman y beban. Y a este modo les sacrifican en las enfermedades. No estuvimos allí más que una tarde y la noche siguiente, y así no pude sacar al viejo más noticias de huacas, sino que tal y tal que él me nombraba, eran adoradas antiguamente, pero que

ya no. Respuesta común de cuantos pueblos he visto. Predigámosles contra esto aquella tarde, y el día siguiente, por al mañana, que fue domingo, confesamos algunos, y por no perder jornada no lo hicieron todos, aunque lo pedían" (Teruel in Arriaga 1999: 88 [1621]).

6   Vázquez de Espinosa (1948: 508 [1628]) also provides a brief description of the bridge of Uranmarca.

7   The Uranmarca region holds the shrine of the Virgin of Cocharcas. The shrine was established in 1598 by local resident Sebastián Quimichi, honoring of healing powers which he experienced at the shrine of Copacabana on the shores of Lake Titicaca. The development of this shrine as one of the largest and most important pilgrimage centers of the Colonial Period greatly influences the internal politics of the region (Sabine Hyland, pers. com.).

8   "Y por estar el rió crecido y furioso, y el puente quemado, hubieron de detenerse para hacerlo de nuevo, porque sin él era imposible pasarlo, ni con sus barcos que llaman balsas, ni á nado, ni de otra manera. Veinte días estuvo aquí el campo para reponer el puente, pues los maestros tuvieron mucho que hacer, porque la agua estaba crecida y desbarataba las crisnejas que se ponían: y si el cacique no tuviera aquí tanto número de gente para hacer este puente y para él pasar y tirar de las crisnejas, no se habría podido hacer; pero habiendo veinticinco mil hombres de guerra y volviendo á probar una vez y otra, valiéndose de cuerdas y de balsas, al cabo pasaron las crisnejas, y pasadas hicieron luego en breve espacio el puente; tan bueno y tan bien hecho, que otro semejante y tan grande no se halla en aquella tierra, que es de trescientos sesenta y tantos pies de largo, y de ancho podían pasar dos caballos á un tiempo sin riesgo alguno" (Sancho 1898: 383–384 [1534: Ch. 13]).

9   "De aquí prosigue el camino real hasta Uramarca, que está siete leguas más adelante hazia el Cuzco. . . De vna parte y de otra del río están hechos dos grandes y muy crescidos padrones de piedra, sacados con cimientos muy hondos y fuertes, para poner la puente que es hecho de maromas de rama a manera de las sogas que tienen las anorias para sacar agua con la rueda. Y éstas después de hechas son tan fuertes, que pueden passar los cauallos a rienda suelta, como si fuessen por la puente de Alcántara, o de Córdoua. Tenía de largo esta puente quando yo la passé ciento y sessenta y seys passos" (Cieza de León 1995: 253 [1553: Pt. 1, Ch. 89]).

10   He also suggests that the Uranmarca Bridge was constructed during the time of Yahuar Huacac, the seventh king of Cuzco.

11   We met with Dr. Tello in 2000, and he generously shared with us his notes on the *Acta de Uranmarca* as well as his knowledge of the community.

12   Other members of the research team included Miriam Aráoz Silva and Henry Gamonal. Their work was greatly aided by the community who provided housing for the project. We offer special thanks to Alejandro Pastor, Edgar Florentino Garibay Orozco, Alejandro Ayma, Víctor Centeno, Jorge Alarcón, and Jorge Balboa Ortecho.

13   A copy of Carlo Socualaya Dávila's thesis was presented to the community on 12 November 2005.

14   Within our collections we also identified a small number of Qasawirka Polychromes.

15   Little Muyumuyu.

16   Sample AA 56651.

17   Sample AA 56650.

18   The earliest published reference we have to Muyumuyu is in Pesce (1942). He notes that there are two small ruins near the plaza of Uranmarca.

19   *Muyu* means "round" in Quechua.

20   The *Acta de Uranmarca* suggests that Muyumuyu was built by the first Inca regent of the region:

> The representative Cusi Ccoyllur governed eighty years; during his time he constructed the Inca fortress called Muyo, and next to the said fortress a rectangular field and in the lower part there were some walkways and a narrow road. All of the work [was done] with walls of well aligned stones; the said fortress is found to the west of the town, almost next to the Sondor River. (*Acta de Uranmarca*; see Appendix 4)

> El Mandatario Cusi Ccoyllur gobernó ochenta años; durante su período construyó la fortaleza llamada Muyo, y junto a dicha fortaleza una pampa cuadrangular y era parte baja unos andenes y un callejón, toda la obra es con paredes de piedras bien alineadas. Dicha fortaleza se encuentra al Oeste de la población casi junto al Río Sondor. (*Acta de Uranmanca*)

21   "Otra obra al Noreste o sea los seiscientas varas de distancia de la plaza se encuentra un pequeño cerrito llamado Tambo; en ella sube unas gradas y igualmente en el sitio llamado Mayabambapampa hay un cuartel incaico de diez cuartos en forma rectangular junto al camino real incaico" (*Acta de Uranmanca*).

22   "On top of the hill called Ahuaray, and two leagues distant to the southeast of the town, is located the construction of Incaraccay. . . ." ["En la punta del cerro llamado Ahuaray y que es dos leguas de distancia hacia Sureste de la población se halla la obra de Incaraccay" (*Acta de Uranmarca*)].

APPENDIX 4

THE ACTA DE URANMARCA

Sabine Hyland, Brian S. Bauer, and Carlo Socualaya Dávila

Information on the history of the Uranmarca region is contained within various local documents. Of special interest is the *Acta de Uranmarca* (Act of Uranmarca), a two-page document held in the municipal archive of Uranmarca. The importance of this document was first identified by Dr. Romulo Tello Valdivia several decades ago, and it was first published by Arturo Gutiérrez Velasco (1999). In 2001, during one of our visits to the community, we were able to transcribe and make a copy of the document.

The document is written in a late nineteenth-century or early twentieth-century script but recounts a much earlier event. Certain aspects of the text, such as the presence of modernized spellings in parentheses, would not be found in a sixteenth-century document. We currently do not know whether this document is based on an original sixteenth-century text to which modernisms have been added, or whether it is a forgery dating to the post-independence period.[1] Whatever the case, it does offer rare insights into local beliefs surrounding the Inca occupation of the area.

The *Acta de Uranmarca* tells of an unusual event which is said to have occurred on 22 June 1558. According to the account, on that day a Spanish priest from Lima, named Juan Pedro de Balboa,[2] and his "companions" gathered with village leaders to witness the 340th anniversary of the founding of the village. During this assembly, the principal village leader, Cusipacha, displayed 340 small stones, stating that each one represented a year in the town's history and then proceeded to tell the names of the four leaders who had governed the region since its foundation.

It is intriguing that the document suggests that small stones were involved in recording the passing of years since the founding of the town. Although the Inca are best known for using a system of knots on strings, called *quipos* (or *khipu*), to record important numbers, we also know that they used strings as well as other objects as mnemonic devises to help recall past events and important information. One of the best passages recording the use of small stones as a mnemonic device is provided by Acosta:

Apart from these string quipus they have others composed of pebbles, from which they accurately learn the words that they want to commit to memory. And it is something to see quite old men learning the Our Father with a circle made of pebbles, and with another circle the Ave Maria, and with another the Creed, and to know which stone represents "who was conceived by the Holy Ghost" and which "suffered under Pontius Pilate"; and you have only to see them correct themselves when they make an error, and the whole correction consists of looking at their pebbles. All I would need to forget everything I have learned by heart would be a circle of those pebbles.[3] (Acosta 2002: 343–344 [1590: Bk. 6, Ch 8])

Thus while not common, it does seem likely that Andean peoples did use stones as both a mnemonic device as well as charged religious objects which were kept for generations.

According to Cusipacha's reading of the Uranmarca stones, the town was founded by the first Inca regent, named Inca Apu Curaca[4] Cusi Ccoyllur, on 22 June 1218. In describing the territorial holdings of the town, Cusipacha mentions various toponyms that are still used; in fact, the area of the community seems little changed since the recording of the document. Cusipacha also notes that the first ruler built a number of installations in the area, including the sites of Muyu-[muyu], Tambo [Viejo], Mayabamba Pampa, and Inca Raccay on the valley slopes, the site of Incawasi on the floodplain, as well as the bridge over the Pampas River (Figure A4.1). These sites, like the boundary toponyms, are still known, and all were found to contain Inca pottery or stonework during our archaeological survey of the region (Figure A4.2). In the reference to the bridge site, the document notes that this is where Francisco Pizarro's troops passed. Perhaps this is a reference to the original journey of Pizarro from Cajamarca to Cuzco in 1533. The platform of

Figure A4.1. The platform of Muyumuyu is said to have been built by the first Inca regent of Uranmarca.

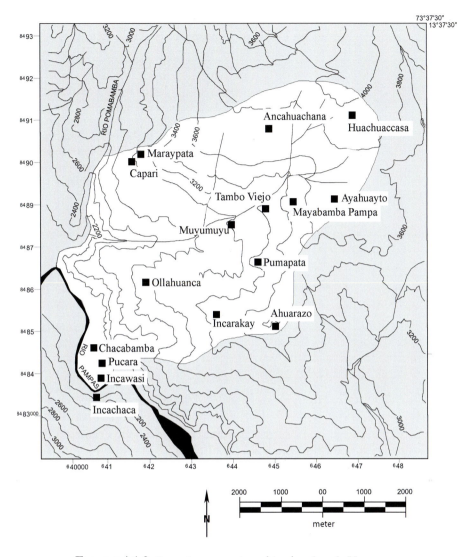

FIGURE A4.2. Locations mentioned in the *Acta de Uranmarca*.

Muyumuyu is said to have been build by the first Inca regent of Uranmarca.

After defining the boundaries of the community, and the major Inca works within it, Cusipacha records a four-generation-long dynastic line of men who ruled the region (Table A4.1). Cusipacha indicates that the first Inca regent (Cusi Ccoyllur) ruled for 80 years and that he was followed by his son Ccori Ccoyllur, who ruled for 70 years. This regent governed a relatively large number of towns, including Uranmarca, Uripa, Ocobamba, Cayara, and Ccascabamba. Ccori

Ccoyllur was followed by Ccondor Ccoyllur, who ruled for 78 years, and by Inca Mascaypacha, who ruled for 80 years. It is also stated that Cusipacha was the current regent (in 1558), and he had governed for 32 years. Accordingly, it appears that he took power in 1526, on the eve of the dynastic war between Huascar and Atahualpa.

The ceremony ended with Cusi Ccoyllur asking Pedro de Balboa for protection in the name of the then ruling Spanish viceroy, Hurtado de Mendoza.[5] Balboa then signed the document and his companions signed for the four native witnesses.

TABLE A4.1
The Lords of Uranmarca

NAME	LENGTH OF RULE	POSSIBLE DATES	NOTES
Inca Apu Curaca Cusi Ccoyllur	80 years	1218–1298	Founds the town of Uranmarca 22 June 1218; builds Muyumuyu, a tambo, a barrack, the bridge over the Pampas River, and various other installations. Governed Uranmarca
Ccori Ccoyllur	70 years	1298–1368	Governed Uramarca, Uripa, Ocobamba, and Cayara
Inca Ccondor Ccoyllur	78 years	1368–1446	Governed Uramarca, Uripa, Ocobamba, and Cayara, and Cascabamba
Apu Inca Mascaypacha	80 years	1446–1526	Governed Uramarca, Uripa, Ocobamba, and Cayara, and Cascabamba?
Inca Cusipacha	32 years	1426–1558	Records the *Acta de Uranmarca*, 22 June 1558

TRANSCRIPTION OF THE ACTA DE URANMARCA

En el Reyno de Uranmarca, a los veintidos días del mes de junio de mil quinientos cincuentiocho por ante el Sr. Reverendo Padre Juan de Balboa por orden de predicadores eclesiastico de la ciudad de los Reyes se hicieron presentes los indios notables con la finalidad de celebrar los trescientos cuarenta años de vida existencia del Reyno Uranmarca; en esta reunion tubo las palabras de los indios notables acerca de la fundación de este pueblo y igualmente el Sr. Reverendo tuvo la palabra del dicho acto y a continuación el Inca Cusipacha declaró por la que ha sido fundado este pueblo quien se presentó las trescientos cuarenta piedritas pequeñas y redondas en ella se contaban cada año que pasaban la vida de este pueblo de esta manera se comprueba de que el pueblo Incaico era fundado el veintidos de junio de mil docientos dieciocho por mandatario Inca Apu Curaca Cusi Ccoyllur. El pueblo Incaico se encuentra en centro y pampa donde se fundó el pueblo rodeado por los cerros de Ollahuanca, Achuarazo hacia lado derecho, los cerros Ayahuayto y Huachuaccasa en la parte altura y los cerros Ancahuachana, Maraypata y Ccapari en la

parte izquierdo y hacia parte baja son unas faldeadas quebradas llegar el Río Bambas que puso el nombre Pampas por Francisco Pizarro.

El Río Sondor que nace de las alturas llamado los sitios Ccullccayputo, Ancahuaycco, Jornadapuquio y Lambramapuquio uniendo en una sola y baja hacia abajo pasando a quinientas varas de distancia de la población; dicho río se desemboca al Río Pampas; el pueblo tiene clima cálido en la parte quebrada, clima temprado en la población, y clima frígido en la parte altura. Este pueblo se encuentra al Oeste del Reyno Ccandabaylas (actual Andahuaylas) además el Reyno de Uranmarca se halla al margen derecha del Río Bambas (actual Pampas). El Mandatario Cusi Ccoyllur gobernó ochenta años; durante su período construyó la fortaleza incaica llamada Muyo, y junto a dicha fortaleza una pampa cuadrangular y era parte baja unos andenes y un callejón, toda la obra es con paredes de piedras bien alineadas. Dicha fortaleza se encuentra al Oeste de la población casi junto al Río Sondor. Otra obra al Noreste o sea los seiscientas varas de distancia de la plaza se encuentra un pequeño cerrito llamado Tambo; en ella sube unas gradas y igualmente en el sitio llamado Mayabambapampa hay un cuartel incaico de diez cuartos en forma rectangular junto al camino real incaico, que viene de Vilcashuaman a Uranmarca, y después otro camino se dirige hacia Ccoscco; otra obra llamada Incahuasi también junto al camino incaico. Dicha obra se halla al Este de la población de cinco leguas de distancia.

En la punta del cerro llamado Ahuaray y que es dos leguas de distancia hacia Sureste de la población se halla la obra de Incaraccay; otra obra llamada Incahuasi en el sector de Chacapampa (actual Chacabamba) cerca de doscientas varas de distancia del Río Pampas al margen derecho y ultimo la obra llamada Pucara, el Puente sobre el Río Pampas por construído por los Incas o sea donde pasaron las tropes del Capitán General Francisco Pizarro.

El Inca Cusi Ccoyllur se dejó de mandatario por encontrarse de edad abanzada y dejando a su reemplazo al hijo Ccori Ccoyllur, quien gobernó a los pueblos de Uranmarca, Uripa, Occobamba, Ccayara hacia al Norte, y al Ccascabamba hacia al Sureste del pueblo Uranmarca y gobernó setenta años. Este Apu Curaca dejó su cargo a su hijo Inca Ccondor Ccoyllur, quien ejerció su cargo durante setentiocho años a los pueblos Occobamba, Uripa, Ccayara, Uranmarca, Ccasccabamba, y otros vecinos. El Inca Mascaypacha gobernó en reemplazo de Ccondor Ccoyllur; el Apu Curaca Mascaypacha ejerció el cargo durante ochenta años y después transfirió el cargo al Inca Cusipacha, actual mandatario que viene ejerciendo el cargo los treintidos años, quien acaba de relatar todos los sucesos del pueblo.

Los indios notables y el Inca Cusipacha surgió rogandole al Sr. Reverendo Padre Fray Pedro de Balboa quien para que de toda clase de amparo en nombre del señor Virrey Andrés Hurtado de Mendoza, Marquéz de Cañete; con esto se concluyó el acto.

Al final del presente acto de ceremonia, firmó el Padre Reverendo y compañeros que fueron presentes, en el nombre de los indios notables presentes.

Juan Pedro de Balboa
firma por
Cusipacha
José Francisco Ytuyate
Justo Yzo
Antonio Yzo
Hermenigildo R.

ENGLISH TRANSLATION OF THE ACTA DE URANMARCA

By Sabine Hyland

In the Kingdom of Uranmarca, on the 22nd day of the month of June, 1558, in front of the Lord and Reverend Father Juan de Balboa, of the order of preachers, ecclesiastic of the City of the Kings, the leading Indians were made present for the purpose of celebrating the 340 years of life [and] existence of the Uranmarca kingdom. In this gathering [were heard] the words of the leading Indians about the foundation of this town, and, likewise, the words of the Reverend Lord about the said act. And in continuation, the Inca Cusipacha declared how this town has been founded; the 340 small, round stones were presented in which were counted every year that had passed in the life of this town. In this way it was verified that the Inca town was founded on the 22nd of June, 1218, by the representative Inca Apu Curaca Cusi Ccoyllur. The Inca town is found in the center field where the town was founded, surrounded by the hills of Ollahuanca [and] Achuarazo to the right, the hills of Ayahuayto and Huchuaccasa in the high area, and the hills of Ancahuachana, Maraypata, and Ccapari to the left, and toward the lower area there are some broken slopes that reach the Bambas River, that Francisco Pizarro called by the name Pampas. The Sondor River, which originates in the heights called the sites of Ccullccayputo, Ancahuaycco, Jornadapuquio, and Lambramapuquio, unites in one single [river] and descends toward below, passing within fifty rods of the population. The said river flows into the Pampas River. The town has a warm climate in the rugged area, a temperate climate in the populated area, and a frigid climate in the high region. This town is found to the west of the Ccandabaylas[6] Kingdom; moreover, the Kingdom of Uranmarca is located on the right bank of the Bambas [currently Pampas] River. The representative Cusi Ccoyllur governed eighty years; during his time he constructed the Inca fortress called Muyo, and next to the said fortress a rectangular field and in the lower part there were some walkways and a narrow road. All of the work [was done] with walls of well-aligned stones; the said fortress is found to the west of the town, almost next to the Sondor River. Another work to the northeast, that is, 600 rods distant from the plaza, is found a small, little hill called Tambo, on which ascends some steps, and likewise in the site called Mayabambapampa there is an Inca barrack with ten rooms, in a rectangular form, next to the royal Inca road that leads to Vilcashuamán from Uranmarca, and afterward another road goes toward Ccoscco; another work called Incahuasi [is] also next to the Inca road; the said work is found five leagues distant to the east of the population.

On top of the hill called Ahuaray, and two leagues distant to the southeast of the town, is located the construction of Incaraccay; another work called Incahuasi [is] in the sector of Chacapampa (currently Chacabamba), nearly 200 rods distant from the Pampas River on the right bank. And finally the work called Pucara, the bridge across the Pampas River, constructed by the Incas, that is, where Captain General Francisco Pizarro's troops passed.

The Inca Cusi Ccoyllur left his office because he found himself at an advanced age, and leaving as his replacement his son Ccori Ccoyllur, who governed the towns of Uranmarca, Uripa, Occobamba, [and] Ccayara to the north, and Ccascabamba to the southeast of the town Uranmarca; and he governed 70 years. This Apu Curaca left his position to his son Inca Ccondor Ccoyllur, who carried out his duties for 78 years in the towns of Occobamba, Uripa, Ccayara, Uranmarca, Ccasccabamba, and other nearby [communities]. Inca Mascaypacha governed as the replacement for Ccondor Ccoyllur; Apu Curaca Mascaypacha carried out his duties for 80 years and then transferred his position to Inca Cusipacha, the current representative, who comes [having] carried out his duties for 32 years [and] who just finished relating all of the events of the town.

The leading Indians and Inca Cusipacha arose, begging the Lord Reverend Father Friar Pedro de Balboa for all kinds of protection in the name of the Lord Viceroy Andrés Hurtado de Mendoza, Marquis of Cañete. With this the act was concluded.

At the end of the present ceremony, the Reverend Father signed, and his companions who were present [signed] in the name of the leading Indians who were present.

Juan Pedro de Balboa

Signs for

Cusipacha
José Francisco Ytuyate
Justo Yzo
Antonio Yzo
Hermenigildo R.

NOTES

1   In the Andes and elsewhere, it is not unusual for documents to be transcribed anew when the original paper is in poor condition. However, it is also common for documents to be forged for use in various legal proceedings. Likewise, pseudo-indigenous works occasionally were created as literary texts in the post-independence period.

2   The Balboa mentioned in the text might possibly have been Juan de Balboa, a canon in the Lima cathedral and a skilled linguist. He is known to have authored at least one book, now lost, on the beliefs of the Incas. However, the Father Balboa mentioned in the *Acta* appears to have been a Dominican, given that he is referred to as "por orden de predicadores." The Juan de Balboa who was a famous linguist in the sixteenth century was a secular priest, not a religious.

3   "Fuera de estos quipos de hilo, tienen otros de pedrezuelas, por donde puntualmente aprenden las palabras que quieren tomar de memoria. Y es cosa de ver a viejos ya caducos con una rueda hecha de pedrezuelas, aprender el Padre Nuestro, y con otra el Ave María, y con otra el Credo, y saber cuál piedra es que fué concebido de Espíritu Santo, y cuál que padeció debajo del poder de Poncio Pilato, y no hay más que verlos enmendar cuando yerran, y toda la enmienda consiste en mirar sus pedrezuelas, que a mí para hacerme olvidar cuanto sé de coro, me bastará una rueda de aquellas" (Acosta 2002: 402–403 [1590: Bk. 6, Ch. 8]).

4   *Inca Apu Curaca* are honorific titles which can be roughly translated as King, Lord, and Chief, respectively.

5   Viceroy Hurtado de Mendoza was the third viceroy of Peru and was the first to govern for a relatively long period (1556–1561).

6   Andahuaylas.

APPENDIX 5

MUYU MOQO CERAMICS

This ceramic style was first noted by Rowe (1956: 143) during his brief fieldwork in Andahuaylas, and it was later more fully defined by Grossman (1972a) based on his excavations at the site of Waywaka (Figure A5.1).

WARE

Muyu Moqo ceramics contain a medium-fine paste with differing densities of aplastics that vary greatly in size from 1.0 to 3.0 mm. The ware can contain minute gold mica and is medium soft in hardness. Firing colors include light to dark gray and light to dark brown.

VESSEL FORMS

Because no complete vessels were recovered during the survey project, it is difficult to discuss the specific vessel forms found in our collection. Nevertheless, from the available fragments, it appears that there is a wide range of vessel forms within our samples, with globular, neckless vessels being especially common.[1] For example, numerous fragments of medium to large neckless ollas, which have a short, distinctly flaring rim with a flattened lip, were recovered. This form may come decorated with a raised horizontal band (5–10 mm thick), with a row of blunt horizontal punctations 20–30 mm below the lip (Figure A5.2).[2] Another common form is a medium-size globular *olla*, with only a slightly flaring rim and a flattened lip. This form can come decorated with a broad, slightly raised, flattened clay band extending 20–30 mm below the lip.[3] The lower margin of this band demonstrates a horizontal row of blunt punctations. A third common form seen in our collections is a large, globular, slightly incurving, neckless olla with a flattened lip (Figures A5.3–A5.6).

During our surface collection we also found fragments of figurines, made on roughly rectangular clay slabs (Figure A5.7).[4] Similar figurines have been recovered in the Cuzco Valley as well as to the south in the Province of Paruro (Bauer 1999: 138; Dwyer 1972).

157

DESIGN ELEMENTS, COLOR, AND SURFACE TREATMENT

The exteriors of Muyu Moqo ceramics are typically burnished (see Figure A5.1). Most commonly, the burnishing bands run horizontally across the body of the vessel. The effects of burnishing vary, with vessel exteriors exhibiting a low to medium luster. The burnished vessels can also exhibit small, blunt punctations or slashes on flattened lips as well as punctations on the vessels' exteriors (Figure A5.2). In the case of the latter, the exterior punctations are often framed by lightly incised (< 3 mm deep) horizontal bands or pendant triangles, which are found just below vessel lips.

FIGURE A5.1. The exteriors of Muyu Moqo ceramics are generally burnished.

FIGURE A5.2. Sherd from a Muyu Moqo vessel with a raised horizontal band containing blunt punctations.

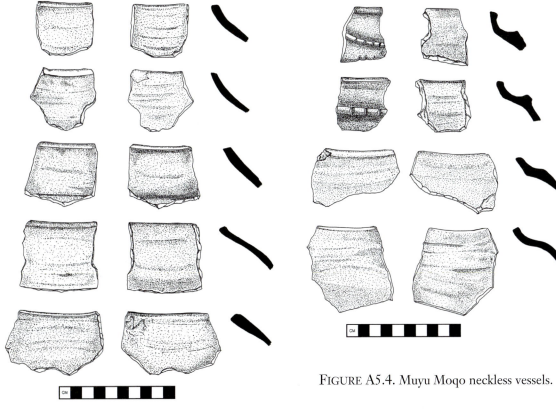

FIGURE A5.3. Muyu Moqo neckless vessels.

FIGURE A5.4. Muyu Moqo neckless vessels.

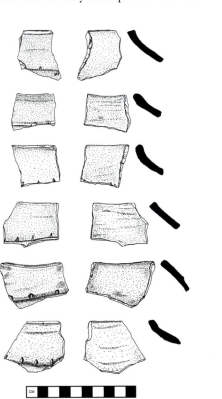

FIGURE A5.5. Muyu Moqo neckless vessels.

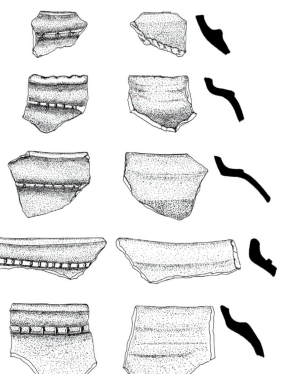

FIGURE A5.6. Muyu Moqo neckless vessels.

NOTES

1   For a detailed discussion of Muyu Moqo vessel types, see Grossman (1972a; 1983).
2   Also see Grossman (1972a: pl. XLIII).
3   Also see Grossman (1972a: pl. XLI).
4   Also see Grossman (1972a: pl. LXVI).

FIGURE A5.7. Muyu Moqo figurine fragment.

APPENDIX 6

CHACAMARCA CERAMICS

During our ceramic analysis, a thin pottery style was noted that occasionally contained incised and/or small appliqué designs (Figure A6.1). Termed "Chacamarca" by the project, these fragments represent a new style for the region. Due to the eroded condition and generally small sherd size, an in-depth discussion of form and decoration is impossible. Despite these limitations, enough samples exist to develop a general description.

WARE

Chacamarca ceramics contain a coarse fabric with white quartz aplastics ranging in size from 0.01 to 0.30 mm. The ceramic is medium to soft in hardness, and firing colors include gray, light brown, and light brick red.

FORM

The eroded nature of the collected Chacamarca ceramics precludes a discussion of vessel form.

Nevertheless, it is clear that these vessels were small to medium in size and globular in form. Furthermore, all of the vessels contained thin walls (0.3–0.8 cm).

DESIGN ELEMENTS, COLOR, AND SURFACE TREATMENT

Chacamarca ceramics exhibit a range of small, shallow (< 2.0 mm) incisions on the vessel exteriors and rims in the form of thin (1.0–4.0 mm) horizontal, vertical, or oblique lines. Commonly, these incised lines occur on the vessel body and can be parallel or serve as framing lines for areas of small (2.0–5.0 mm wide), evenly spaced circular or irregularly shaped punctations. In addition, the Chacamarca ceramics exhibit small, raised appliqué bumps, lines, or thin braids, which may have small punctations as well. A few pieces reveal very light burnishing on vessel exteriors as well.

161

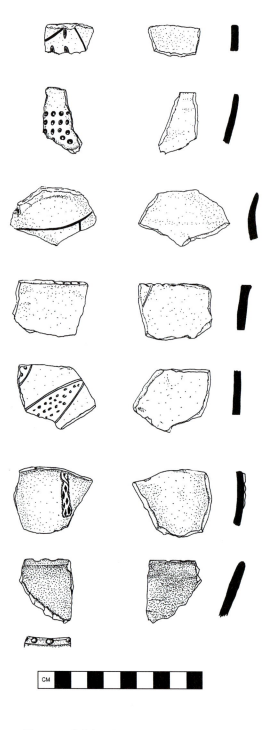

FIGURE A6.1. Chacamarca ceramics.

APPENDIX 7

QASAWIRKA CERAMICS

Qasawirka ceramics represent the most commonly recovered ceramic style in the Andahuaylas region. This general class of pottery is quickly identified by the dark red paint that covers most specimens. It was first identified by Rowe (1956: 143); however, a much more detailed description was later developed by Grossman (1972a) based on information he gained from his excavations at the site of Waywaka as well as during his exploratory work in the Andahuaylas Valley. Here we present our observations on this interesting, Andahuaylas-based ceramic style.

WARE

Qasawirka ceramics are distinguished by a coarse fabric containing high amounts of aplastics, notably quartz. The quartz likely comes from the numerous deposits of eroding granite in the valley. Other aplastics may include small quantities of black and gold mica and possibly ground limestone. Despite the often heavily eroded condition of Qasawirka ceramics, their large, white quartz grains (0.1–5.0 mm) serve as a useful indicator when no paint is present on the ceramics. The ware is medium soft in hardness and fires to light brown, orange, gray, and even brick red. The smaller, finer vessel forms tend to have dark gray to black unoxidized firing cores.

VESSELS FORMS, SURFACE TREATMENT, AND COLOR

Qasawirka ceramics are defined by a medium to thick red paint over part or all of the exterior of the vessel. The paint is most likely derived from hematite nodules which are common in the region. This style is also associated with fully painted (red) zoomorphic and anthropomorphic figurines as well as a roughly burnished brown ware. The burnishing on the Qasawirka vessels is not, however, as clear or as well executed as on the Muyu Moqo vessels. This pottery style comes in a variety of forms, each with variable, yet distinct red painting and/or incisions, burnishing or appliqué. Decoration will be discussed according

163

to each general form. These include (1) bowls, (2) neckless storage jars, (3) necked storage jars, (4) fine Qasawirka bowls, and (5) figurines.

Bowls (Figures A7.1–A7.3)

Qasawirka bowls come in various shapes and sizes. There are large shallow bowls with flat, flaring rims. These vessels generally exhibit red paint only on the upward-facing rim, and their paired handles are mounted on the rim. There are also finer shallow bowls with thin walls (2–8 mm thick) and tapering lips. These bowls often have small, opposing appliqué handles. The finer shallow bowls often have a red painted band, which extends down 20–30 mm on both the vessel interior and exterior. We also found various fragments of deep, rounded bowls which have a variety of rim forms, most commonly short and flaring, while more rarely they are flat or tapering. Burnishing is present on all bowl forms.

Neckless Storage Jars (Figures A7.4–A7.7)

The neckless storage jars come in various sizes but with consistent formal features. Most fragments have the thick, bulky rims, which include a wide

variety of forms, among them flat, triangular, rounded, or fold-over. Rim orientation varies from horizontal to bent toward the vessel interior. A small number may have incurving terminations. The neckless storage vessels have a wall thickness ranging from 5 to 12.5 mm. The neckless storage jars bear decorations very similar to those on other Qasawirka vessels, with red painted bands covering the thick, bulky rims and often extending down on the exterior between 30 and 50 mm.

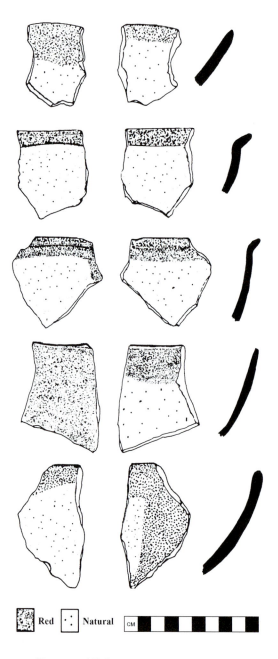

FIGURE A7.1. Qasawirka bowls

FIGURE A7.2. Qasawirka bowls.

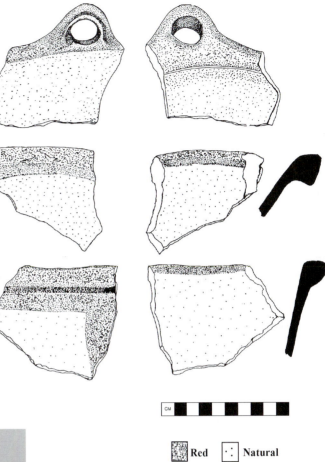

FIGURE A7.3. Qasawirka large plates and bowls.

FIGURE A7.4. Qasawirka neckless storage jars.

FIGURE A7.5. Qasawirka neckless storage jars.

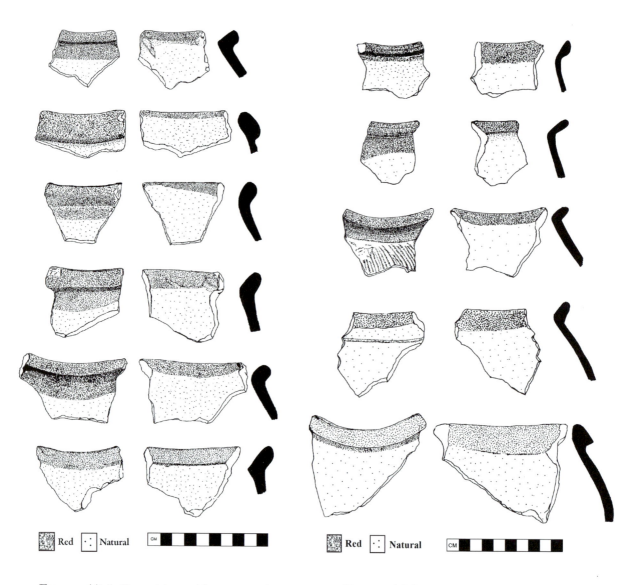

FIGURE A7.6. Qasawirka neckless storage jars.

FIGURE A7.7. Qasawirka neckless storage jars.

Necked Storage Jars (Figures A7.8–A7.12)

The final general vessel form of Qasawirka ceramics is the necked storage vessel. This vessel type is generally characterized by straight to slightly flaring necks. Neck heights range from 20 to 100 mm in length, and vessel walls range between 5 and 10 mm. The most common rim forms are triangular in cross section, although rounded rims have also been noted. The handles are frequently not located on opposite sides of the vessel, but are instead situated slightly offset on one side of the body (see Figure 4.1).

The necked storage jars in the valley are commonly decorated with a dark red paint uniformly covering the vessel exterior. Larger versions of these necked vessels often have a horizontal band of large, circular, blunt punctations (10–20 mm in diameter) delineating the vessel neck and body. Smaller versions of this form exhibit an incised line, instead of punctations, to mark the juncture of vessel neck and body. Below this incised line is often a horizontal band of narrow dashes on the upper part of the vessel body. Underneath the red paint of these vessels, horizontal burnishing lines often occur only on the neck region, while bur-

FIGURE A7.8. Qasawirka necked storage jar.

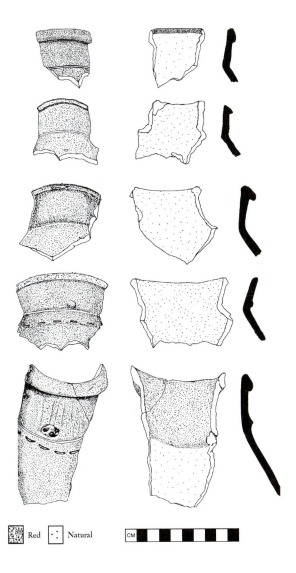

FIGURE A7.10. Qasawirka necked storage jars.

FIGURE A7.9. Qasawirka necked
storage jars with faces.

nishing lines become vertical on the vessel body. Some small appliqué bumps may be present on these incised necks.

In addition, some necked storage jars contain appliqué faces along straight to slightly incurved necks. These small, well-made faces include small, horizontally slit mouths and eyes, as well as small punctated ears and prominent noses with two nostrils. Most often these faces sit just below triangular rims, making the rims look like the brim of a hat. Horizontally incised lines frequently frame these small faces, and red or cream vertical stripes (5–20 mm in diameter) may extend over the face.

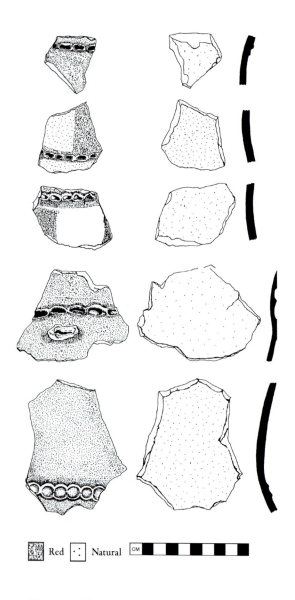

Red   Natural   CM

FIGURE A7.11. Qasawirka necked storage jars
with large body punctations.

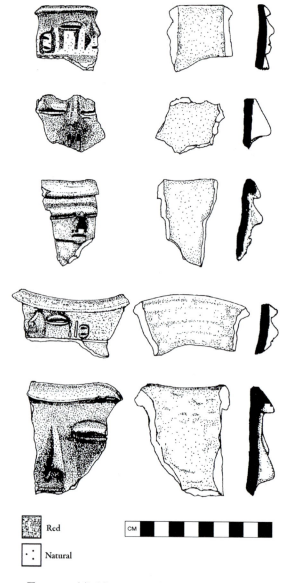

Red

Natural

CM

FIGURE A7.12. Qasawirka necked storage jars
with faces.

Fine Qasawirka Bowls (Figures A7.13–A7.14)

Within our collections we also found a large number of remarkably fine bowl fragments which we felt, based on their distinctive form and production uniformity, deserved a separate classification. Grossman (1983: 60) reached a similar conclusion: "The Qasawirka style differs markedly from the Muyu Moqo style in that apparent separation of its entire range of forms and decorative motifs into two major categories, plain, apparent-ly utilitarian shapes; and generally smaller, thin walled, slip decorated fancy forms."

Fine Qasawirka bowls are easily identifiable among the fancy forms. These bowls have very thin (< 5 mm), straight-sided walls, fine tapering rim terminations, and flat bottoms. Very small projecting handles are located on opposing sides, normally at the juncture of the vessel base and vertical walls. More rarely, the handles are located in opposing positions on the vessel rim. Bowl diameters can vary between 10 and 15 cm, and bowl depths vary between 50 and 70 mm. The

FIGURE A7.13. A fine Qasawirka bowl. Note the thin walls of the vessel and the two small handles near the base.

interior and exterior are almost always painted red, and very fine, thin-lined burnishing is often apparent underneath the paint.

FIGURINES

The Qasawirka collections can contain highly distinctive figurines. Unlike the solid, rectangular, slab figurines of the Muyu Moqo Phase, Qasawirka figurines tend to be elongated, hollow, and oval in form. They are frequently covered in a dark red slip and heavily burnished. The legs and arms are often poorly rendered. Their faces are depicted in slightly more detail and include slashes for the eyes and mouth, and well-formed noses. Grossman (1983: 117, fig. 70) includes a fine intact example, and our surface collections have yielded various broken specimens.

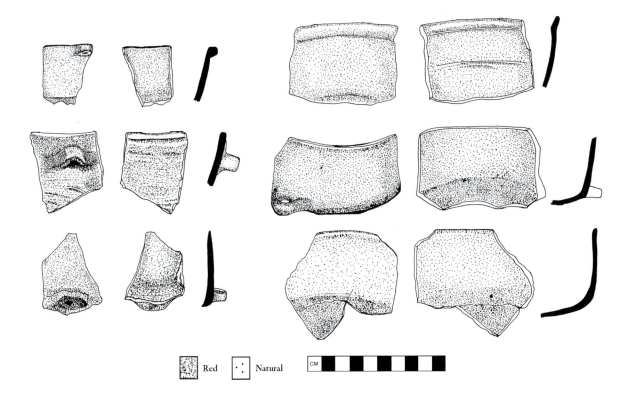

FIGURE A7.14. Fine Qasawirka bowls.

QASAWIRKA POLYCHROME CERAMICS

During the Andahuaylas Archaeological Project, crew members frequently recovered fragments of a finely made polychrome ceramic style at Qasawirka sites. Represented mainly by well-polished small vessels, examples of this style display three main colors: cream, dark red, and black. We have chosen to call this distinctive style Qasawirka Polychrome.[1]

Ware

Qasawirka Polychromes have a fine to medium coarse fabric with small (0.1–3 mm) white quartz grains serving as aplastics. In addition, there exist a small percentage (< 15%) of black inclusions, black mica, and possibly some ground dark volcanics (andesite, basalt). The thinnest fragments contain a dark gray to black firing core from incomplete oxidation. Aside from these dark firing cores, this ware fires from light brick red to a dull orange and is low to medium in hardness.

Forms, Surface Treatment, and Design Elements

The Qasawirka Polychrome sherds recovered are small. Nevertheless, we collected a number of rim sherds indicating that Qasawirka Polychromes come in at least three general vessel forms: (1) shallow bowls, (2) incurving bowls, and (3) small jars (Figure A7.15).

Shallow Bowls
The shallow bowls have a broad, round bowl form, which likely does not extend deeper than 12 cm. Of note is the opposing pair of decorated handles with circular holes mounted on a flat, wide rim. We recovered both a small and a large example of this shallow bowl with the exact same

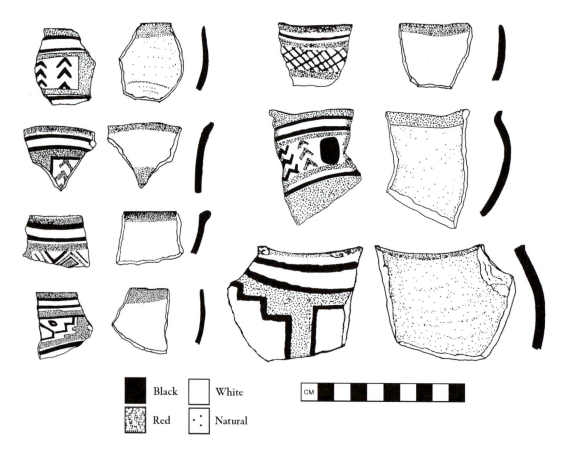

Black   White

Red   Natural

CM

FIGURE A7.15. Qasawirka polychromes.

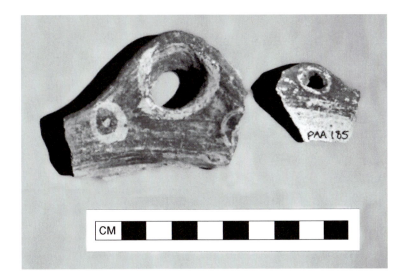

FIGURE A7.16. Qasawirka Polychrome shallow bowls.

FIGURE A7.17. Qasawirka Polychrome small incurving bowls.

decoration: a series of cream circles painted on the rim (Figure A7.16). Similar shallow bowls have been noted among the general Qasawirka vessels.

Small Incurving Bowls

The second vessel class of Qasawirka Polychromes is a small bowl form with incurving rims. The incurving bowls are no deeper than 10 cm and have relatively thin walls (3–6 mm thick). Nearly all recovered rims of these small bowls have fine, rounded lips. A few examples show a very thin, flattened rim angled toward the interior of the vessel. These small bowls also bear very small opposing handles, which extend vertically off the lip (Figure A7.17).

Small Jars

Qasawirka Polychromes also come in small jars with short vertical or flaring necks. Many of these jars may have been globular or teardrop-shaped in form. The exterior of the jars have a cream paint as a base, upon which are placed horizontal red and black lines, which may frame various red or black geometric designs. The rims generally contain a thin red band.

NOTE

[1] Grossman (1983: 61) also notes the presence of polychromes within his Qasawirka collections.

APPENDIX 8

CHANKA CERAMICS

Ceramics of the Chanka Phase are easily identified by their light-colored paste and a watery orange or black wash used on the vessels' exterior and interior surfaces. The paint used for vessel decoration is watery and has dull colors. Typically, these ceramics bear sloppy decorations with poorly executed line and design work. In contrast to the earliest ceramics styles of the Andahuaylas region, these vessels are almost never burnished.

While the Chanka Phase ceramics are clearly different in wear, form, and design from those of the Wari Phase, there are clear connections between the two ceramic styles. Most notably, the Chanka occupants of the Andahuaylas area continued to use red lines on the rims of drinking vessels, as well as casually framed wavy line designs on shallow bowls (Figure A8.1). Other features, such as the dense use of geometric designs, especially cross-hatching, show clear temporal links with other Late Intermediate Period styles, such as Killke of the Cuzco region (Bauer 1999)

WARE

Chanka ceramics generally contain a medium coarse fabric with small aplastics ranging from 1 to 3 mm in thickness, normally consisting of fine quartz and, to a lesser degree, dark volcanic inclusions (such as basalt and andesite). Samples of these ceramics are generally fully oxidized, with fired paste colors including orange, pink, and light gray. The ware is a medium hardness.

FORMS AND DECORATION

Chanka ceramics exhibit wide variations in forms and decoration. Although many of the stylistic characteristics of vessels are indicative of Wari stylistic influence, the orange-black wash, watery paint, coarser paste, and generally poor quality of artistry are reflective of the Chanka Phase. While working with the surface collections, we defined five general classes of decorated vessel forms,

FIGURE A8.1. Chanka Phase bowls. These decorations are reminiscent of earlier Wari-style pottery.

including (1) bowls, (2) incurving bowls, (3) small jars, (4) storage jars, and (5) drinking vessels. Each is briefly discussed below.

Bowls (Figures A8.1–A8.5)

These vessels commonly have rounded rims and vessel walls that measure between 4.0 and 7.0 mm thick. They often have a black and/or orange wash on both sides of the vessel, on top of which can be painted black, cream, or red lines. Commonly, the bowls exhibit various small, vertical tick marks (in black or red) at the rim extending down no more than 20 mm on the vessel interior. Occasionally, these tick marks are painted on a white or cream background. Some examples contain parallel black lines extending down into the center of the bowl, framing red wavy lines. More rarely, these bowls display larger sections of red or white slip, which serve as a base for line designs. Some examples have a thin, horizontal white band of paint on the rim.

Incurving Bowls (Figure A8.6)

The small incurving bowls commonly have rounded rims with vessel walls not exceeding 8 mm in thickness. They are frequently decorated with a light orange wash or, more rarely, with black or cream, on both vessel interior and exterior. The interiors of these bowls can be undecorated (except for the washes) or display a collection of sloppy red or black designs. In addition, a thin (< 10 mm wide) red or black band of paint may occur on the rim of the vessel. Bowl exteriors

exhibit variable decorations with red, black, and white lines (3–15 mm wide). At times, thicker red or black lines may frame other thinner lines, dots, or other figures.

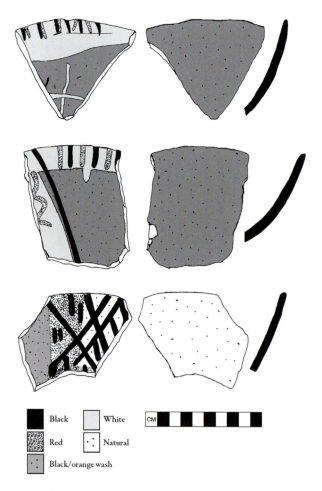

Black
Red
Black/orange wash
White
Natural

FIGURE A8.2. Chanka Phase bowls. These decorations are reminiscent of earlier Wari-style pottery.

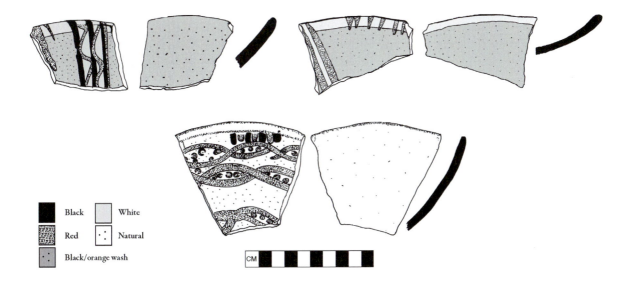

Black White

Red Natural

Black/orange wash

CM

FIGURE A8.3. Chanka Phase bowls. These decorations are reminiscent of earlier Wari-style pottery.

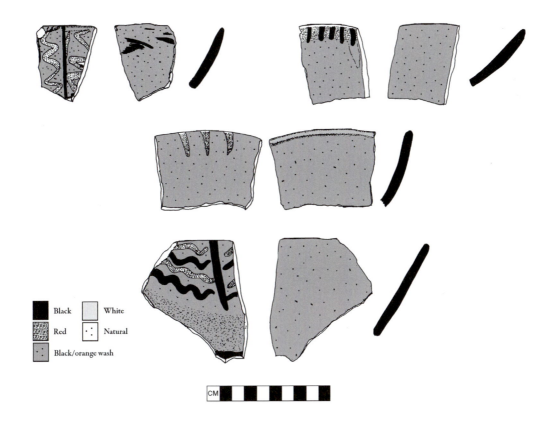

Black White

Red Natural

Black/orange wash

CM

FIGURE A8.4. Chanka Phase bowls. These decorations are reminiscent of earlier Wari-style pottery.

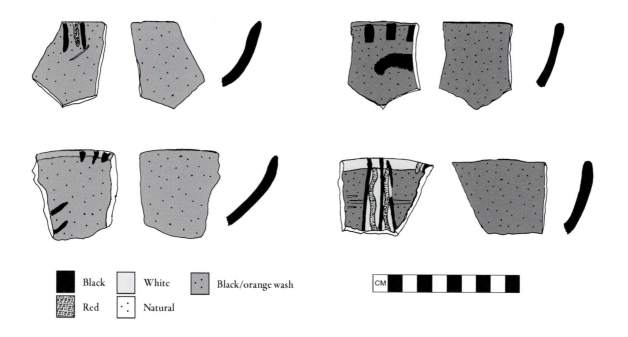

FIGURE A8.5. Chanka Phase bowls. These decorations are reminiscent of earlier Wari-style pottery.

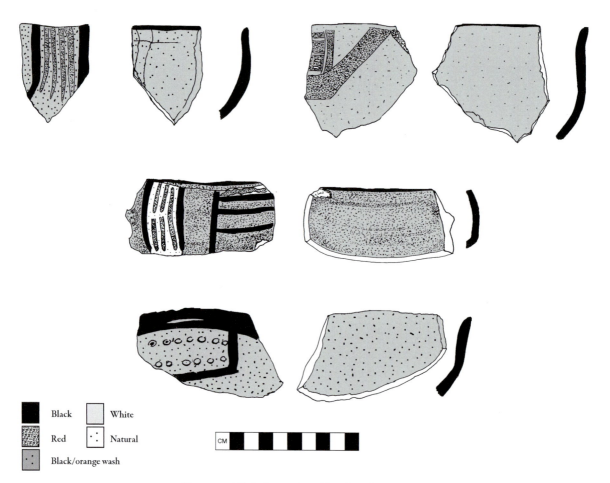

FIGURE A8.6. Incurving Chanka Phase bowls.

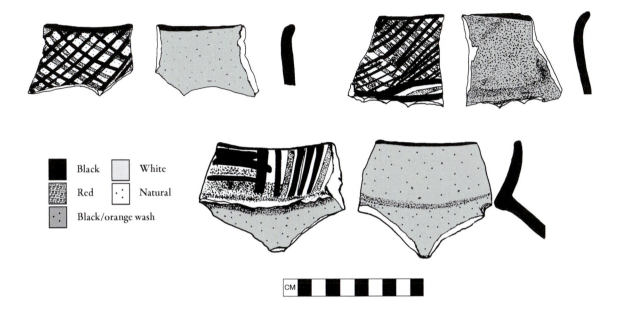

Black   White
Red   Natural
Black/orange wash

FIGURE A8.7. Chanka Phase jars and storage vessels.

Small Jars

The only necked vessels identified in our surface collections of Chanka pottery constitute a class of small jars. The necks on these jars are approximately 30–50 mm in length and slightly thicker (4–7 mm) than the lower vessel body (< 5 mm). The jars consistently have very short (< 10 mm wide) flaring rims with rounded lips.

These small Chanka jars exhibit great uniformity in decoration, with exterior necks painted with black and red cross-hatching lines upon a cream slip. Below these cross-hatching lines is a series of horizontal black or red lines which frame the upper design. Jar interiors are undecorated, except for a light orange or black wash (Figure A8.7: *top*). Occasionally, the vessel lip may be painted with a thin (< 7.5 mm) black line.

Some of the necked jars also bear appliqué faces along the neck. These raised faces show well-defined projecting eyes, noses, and mouths (Figures A8.8–A8.9).

Storage Vessels

The storage jars from Chanka Phase sites are globular and were produced in various sizes and with variable rim forms (Figure A8.7: *bottom*). Most are neckless, while some can exhibit short, straight necks. Rims forms include flat, rounded, and flaring. Wall thicknesses range from 5 to 10 mm. The storage jars, like all other forms of Chanka pottery, are frequently covered with an orange and/or a black wash. Occasionally, the rim may have the black wash, while the vessel body has the orange wash. On the wide rims, decoration can have vertical, parallel red or black lines, which are painted on a white background. Decoration can closely mimic that of the shallow bowls.

Drinking Cups

The small drinking cups of the Chanka Period commonly have very short (5–7.5 mm wide), slightly flaring rims with rounded or slightly tapering lips. Wall thicknesses of these small cups do not exceed 7 mm, and recovered samples suggest a vessel depth between 60 and 90 mm. They generally display a dark orange wash, which completely covers the vessel exterior while often only extending down the cup interior between 20 and 40 mm. A dark red or black line is frequently painted on the vessel rim as well. Decoration on

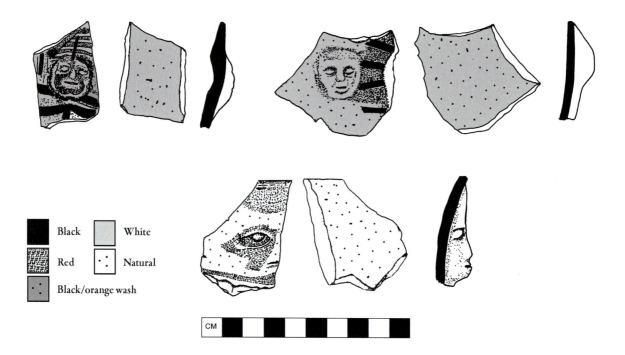

FIGURE A8.8. Face-necked Chanka Phase jars.

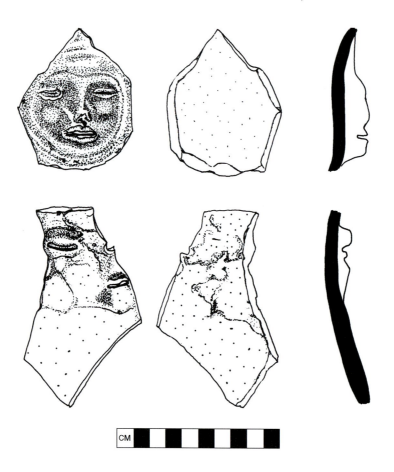

FIGURE A8.9. Face-necked Chanka Phase jars.

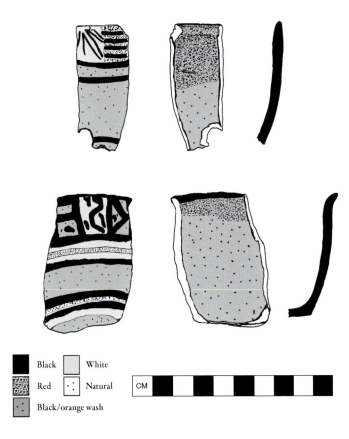

Black		White	
Red		Natural	
Black/orange wash			

FIGURE A8.10. Chanka Phase drinking cups.

the cup exterior consists of a series of horizontal and vertical black or red lines, which may frame other black geometric line designs, such as rectangles, triangles, dots, and parallel or wavy lines (Figure A8.10).

BIBLIOGRAPHY

ARCHIVAL SOURCES

Archivo Departamental del Cuzco

ADC   Corregimiento de Andahuaylas, Leg. 1
(1626–1672).
Padrón de Indios tributarios de los Indios de
Andahuaylas (1684).

ADC   Corregimiento de Andahuaylas, Leg. 2
(1680–1699).
Visita de 1684.

ADC   Corregimiento de Andahuaylas, Leg. 2
(1680–1699).
Sobra las demandas hecha por Dona Juana
Caruapoco contra Juan Fernández (deterio-
rated).

ADC   Corregimiento de Andahuaylas, Leg. 2
(1680–1699).
Padrón de Indios tributarios de los Indios de
Andahuaylas (1684). (Second half of the
document. The first half of the document is
found in ADC, Corregimiento de Andahuaylas, Leg. 4 [1730–1744]).

ADC   Corregimiento de Andahuaylas, Leg. 2
(1680–1699).
Autos seguidos por Diego Checmullo (1686).

ADC   Corregimiento de Andahuaylas, Leg. 3
(1701–1729).
Fragmento de escritura de censo, que otor-
gada por Sebastián Velásquez de una tierras
que están debajo del Tambo de Cochacaxas
nombradas Churucana y Vilcabamba, que
estad en términos de Guancarama.

ADC   Corregimiento de Andahuaylas, Leg. 4
(1730–1744).
Padrón de los indios de las parcialidades de
Hanansaya y Hurinsaya de Andahuaylas (1684).

ADC   Corregimiento de Andahuaylas, Leg. 5
(1745–1749).
Autos ordinarios que sigue Francisco Soto
contra los herederos de Miguel de Ayala y
Claudula de su testamento, en que no siendo
suyas las tierras aquí contenidas nombradas
Chuspiguacho las declaro por sus bienes y se
vendieron.

ADC   Corregimiento de Andahuaylas, Leg. 6
(1750–1763).
Causa seguida por Don Thomas Intusca
mandón del pueblo de Talavera . . . sobre
despojo de varios pedazos de tierras que por
repartimiento son de ellos y hoy poseen
varios españoles . . . (1753).

ADC   Caja de Censos. Leg. 1, Cuaderno 2. Petición de los indios de Andahuaylas. 18 de febrero de 1659.

ADC   Notariales de Andahuaylas del siglo XVI. Escritura publica de Antonio Sánchez. Testamento de Don Diego Condorguacho Cacique del pueblo de Andahuaylas hijo natural de Don Diego Guasco Señor y Cacique Principal de la provincia de Andahuaylas repartimiento de la encomienda del Capitán Diego Maldonado vecino de esta gran ciudad del Cuzco (1568).

ADC   Notariales de Andahuaylas del siglo XVII. Escritura publica de Pedro Julio de Ojeda (1659–1663). Testamento del Capitán Álvaro Gil de Aragón hijo legitimo de Álvaro Gil de Aragón y de Luisa Días, naturales de la gran ciudad del Cuzco (1659).

ADC   Notariales de Andahuaylas del siglo XVIII. Leg. 3 (1700–1820). Escritura publica de José Gabriel Pacheco (1786–1796). Testamento de Juliana Rojas natural de este pueblo de San Pedro de Andahuaylas la Grande hija legítima de legítima matrimonio de Don Antonio Royas y de Doña Bernarda Quino también natural de este pueblo (1796).

ADC   Notariales de Andahuaylas del siglo XVIII. Leg. 3 (1700–1820). Escritura publica de José Gabriel Pacheco (1786–1796). Venta de tierras entre Manuel Medina y José Altamirano (Aymarespata).

ADC   Notarial de Andahuaylas del siglo XVIII, Leg. 3 (1700–1820). Escritura publica de Gregorio Antonio Pacheco (1786–1795). El teniente Coronel Don José Carrillo vecino de este partido y arrendatario de la Hacienda Cañaveral de Chacabamba sita en la Doctrina de Ongoy.

ADC   Notarial de Andahuaylas del siglo XVIII, Leg. 3 (1700–1820). Escritura publica de Pedro Julio Ojedo (1660). Venta de Tierras entre Francios Arenas y Juan de Alarcón y Valenzuela.

ADC   Notarial de Andahuaylas del siglo XVIII, Protocolo 1. Escritura publica de Joseph Antonio Castro (1742–1744). Venta de Tierras entre Bentura Basques de Puga y María Barma viuda de Miguel Ayala. (1742).

ADC   Notarial de Andahuaylas del siglo XIX, Protocolo 4. Escritura publica de Laurencio Menacho. Venta de la Hacienda Acccopaccha (1868).

Archivo General de Indias (Sevilla)

AGI   Patronato 93, No. 11, Ramo 2. Información de los méritos y servicios de Diego Maldonado (1561).

Archivo General de la Nación (Lima)

AGN   Derecho Indigena, Leg. 3, Cuaderno 17. Autos que el visitador Juan de Palomares sequío de oficio en nombre y voz de la Justicia Real contra Juan Arias Maldonado, vecino de la ciudad del Cuzco y heredero del Capitán Diego Maldonado (1568–1573).

AGN   Derecho Indígena, Leg. 3, Cuaderno 50. Autos que promovió Agustín Arce de Quiroz, juez y escribano que fue de la revisita de los yndios de la Provincia de Andaguaylas la Grande encomienda de la Corona, sobre que se le abonasen el salario y derechos que devengo durante el tiempo de la visita. . . .

AGN   Real Audiencia Causas Criminales, Leg. 154, Cuaderno 579. Autos seguidos por Diego Checmullo y su heredero para que sean exentos de mita de Huancavelica.

AGN   Superior Gobierno, Leg. 10, Cuaderno 210. Expediente seguido por Don José Mendieta Corregidor de la Provincia de Andahuaylas en Abancay sobre que de la Caja del Cuzco se le pagase 707 pesos por razón de su salario (1754).

Biblioteca Nacional (Lima)

BN   Ms. B28. Relación de la visita practicada al repartimiento de los Indio Chancas de Andahuaylas (1606–1607). (Loose sheets; the document has been damaged by fire and water).

BN   Ms. B405. Testimonio del expediente sobre la composición de tierras y estancias efectuadas con el Oidor Licenciado Alonso Maldonado de Torres en nombre de su majestad, Miguel Moreno de Lezana (1669/1596).

PUBLISHED SOURCES

Abbott, Mark B., Mark W. Binford, Mark Brenner, and Kerry R. Kelts
   1997 A 3500^{14}C yr. high resolution record of water-level changes in Lake Titicaca. *Quaternary Research* 47: 169–180.

Abbott, Mark B., Brent B. Wolfe, Ramon Aravena,
Alexander P. Wolfe, and Geoffrey O. Seltzer
  2000 Holocene hydrological reconstructions from
        stable isotopes and paleolimnology,
        Cordillera Real, Bolivia. *Quaternary Science
        Reviews* 19: 1801–1820.

Acosta, José de
  2002 *Natural and Moral History of the Indies* [1590].
        Edited by Jane E. Mangan, with an introduc-
        tion and commentary by Walter D. Mignolo.
        Translated by Frances López–Morillas.
        Durham, NC: Duke University Press.

Albornoz, Cristóbal de
  1984 Instrucción para descubrir todas las guacas
        del Pirú y sus camayos y haziendas [ca.
        1582]. In "Albornoz y el espacio ritual andi-
        no prehispánico," edited by Pierre Duviols.
        Revista Andina 2 (1): 169–222.

Amorín Garibay, José
  1998 Arquitectura y patrón de enterramiento Inka
        en Sondor. Tesis de Licenciado, Universidad
        Nacional de San Cristóbal de Huamanga,
        Facultad de Ciencias Sociales, Escuela de
        Arqueología e Historia.

Amorín Garibay, José, and Edgar Alarcón Gutiérrez
  1999 Exploración arqueológica en Curamba y su
        relación con Sondor. *El XII Congreso Peruano
        del hombre y la cultura andina* 2, edited by
        Ismael Pérez C., Walter Aguilar S., and
        Medardo Purizaga V., 2: pp. 287–294. Ayacu-
        cho: Universidad Nacional de San Cristóbal
        de Huamanga.

Angrand, Léonce
  1972 *Imagen del Perú en el siglo XIX [1847].* Lima:
        Editorial Carlos Milla Batres.

Anonymous Description of Peru
  1972 Anonymous description of Peru (ca. 1610).
        In *Colonial Travelers in Latin America*, edited
        by Irving A. Leodard, pp. 97–117. New York:
        Knopf.

Arca Parró, Alberto
  1923 Dónde vivían los Chankas? *Inka* (Lima) 1
        (4): 970–974.

Arkush, Elizabeth N.
  2006 Collapse, conflict, conquest: The transfor-
        mation of warfare in the Late Prehispanic
        Andean highlands. In *The Archaeology of War-
        fare: Prehistories of Raiding and Conquest*, edit-
        ed by Elizabeth N. Arkush and Mark W.
        Allen, pp. 286–335. Gainesville: University
        Press of Florida.
  2008 War, chronology and causality in the Titi-
        caca Basin. *Latin American Antiquity* 19 (4):
        339–373.

Arkush, Elizabeth N., and Charles Stanish
  2005 Interpreting conflict in the Ancient Andes:
        Implications for the archaeology of warfare.
        Current Anthropology 46 (1): 3–28.

Arriaga, Pablo José de
  1968 *The Extirpation of Idolatry in Peru* [1621].
        Translated and edited by L. Clark Keating.
        Lexington: University of Kentucky Press.
  1999 *La extirpación de la idolatría en el Pirú* [1621].
        Edited by Enrique Urbano. Cuzco: Centro
        de Estudios Regionales Andinos, "Bartolomé
        de las Casas."

Bandera, Damián de la
  1965 Relación general de la disposición y calidad
        de la provincia de Guamanga [1557]. In
        Relaciones geográficas de Indias, edited by Mar-
        cos Jiménez de la España. Biblioteca de
        autores españoles 183: 176–180. Madrid:
        Ediciones Atlas.

Barreda Murillo, Luis
  1991 Historia y arqueología del Qosqo pre-Inka.
        Revista Municipal del Qosqo 1 (2): 20–36.
  1995 *Cuzco: Historia y arqueología pre-Inka*. Institu-
        to de Arqueología Andina Machupiqchu.
        Cuzco: Perú.

Barrio Contreras, Juan
  1975 *Antahuaylla en la ruta de los libertadores*. Lima:
        Editorial Santa Isabel.

Bauer, Brian S.
  1987 Sistemas andinos de organización rural antes
        del establecimiento de reducciones: El ejem-
        plo de Pacariqtambo (Perú). *Revista Andina* 9
        (1): 197–210.
  1991 Pacariqtambo and the mythical origins of
        the Inca. *Latin American Antiquity* 2 (1): 7–26.
  1992 *The Development of the Inca State*. Austin:
        University of Texas Press.
  1996 The legitimization of the Inca state in myth
        and ritual. *American Anthropologist* 98 (2):
        327–337.
  1998 *The Sacred Landscape of the Inca: The Cuzco
        Ceque System*. Austin: University of Texas Press.
  1999 *The Early Ceramics of the Inca Heartland*. Fiel-
        diana Anthropology, New Series 31. Chica-
        go: Field Museum of Natural History.
  2002 *Las antiguas tradiciones alfarerías de la región
        del Cuzco*. Cuzco: Centro de Estudios Regio-
        nales Andinos, "Bartolomé de Las Casas."
  2004 *Ancient Cuzco: Heartland of the Inca*. Austin:
        University of Texas Press.
  2006 Suspension bridges of the Inca Empire. In
        Andean Archaeology, Vol. 3, edited by Helaine
        Silverman and William H. Isbell, pp.
        468–493. New York: Kluwer Academic Press.

2008   *Cuzco antiguo: Tierra natal de los Incas*. Cuzco: Centro de Estudios Regionales Andinos, "Bartolomé de Las Casas."

Bauer, Brian S. (editor)
2007   *Kasapata and the Archaic Period in the Cuzco Valley*. Los Angeles: Cotsen Institute of Archaeology, University of California.

Bauer, Brian S., Miriam Aráoz Silva, and Lucas C. Kellett
2002   Resultados del trabajo del campo, 2002 (Proyecto Arqueológico Andahuaylas). Report submitted to the National Institute of Culture, Lima, Peru.
2004   Resultados del trabajo del campo, 2004 (Proyecto Arqueológico Andahuaylas). Report submitted to the National Institute of Culture, Lima, Peru.

Bauer, Brian S., and R. Alan Covey
2002   Processes of state formation in the Inca heartland (Cuzco, Peru). *American Anthropologist* 10 (3): 846–864.

Bauer, Brian S., and David S. P. Dearborn
1995   *Astronomy and Empire in the Ancient Andes*. Austin: University of Texas Press.

Bauer, Brian S., and Bradford Jones
2003   *The Early Intermediate and Middle Horizon Ceramic Styles of the Cuzco Valley*. Fieldiana Anthropology, New Series 34. Chicago: Field Museum of Natural History.

Bauer, Brian S., and Lucas C. Kellett
2010   Cultural transformations of the Chanka heartland (Andahuaylas, Peru) during the Late Intermediate Period (AD 1000–1400). *Latin American Antiquity*.

Bauer, Brian S., and Charles Stanish
1990   Killke and Killke-related pottery from Cuzco, Peru, in the Field Museum of Natural History. *Fieldiana Anthropology*, New Series 15. Chicago: Field Museum of Natural History.
2001   *Ritual and Pilgrimage in the Ancient Andes: The Islands of the Sun and the Moon*. Austin: University of Texas Press.

Beck, Robin A.
2003   Consolidation and hierarchy: Chiefdom variability in the Mississippian Southeast. *American Antiquity* 68 (4): 641–661.
2006   Persuasive politics and domination at Cahokia and Moundville. In *Leadership and Polity in Mississippian Society*, edited by Brian M. Butler and Paul D. Welch, pp, 19–42. Occasional Paper No. 33, Center for Archaeological Investigations. Carbondale, IL.

Benavides, Mario
1976   *Yacimientos arqueológicos en Ayacucho*. Ayacucho, Perú: Universidad Nacional San Cristóbal de Huamanga.

Berg, Ronald H.
1987   Sendero Luminoso and the peasantry of Andahuaylas. *Journal of Interamerican Studies and World Affairs* 28 (4): 165–196.
1992   Peasant responses to Shining Path in Andahuaylas. In *The Shining Path of Peru*, edited by David Scott Palmer, pp. 83–104. New York: St. Martin's Press.

Betanzos, Juan de
1987   *Suma y narración de los Incas* [1557]. Edited by Carmen Martín Rubio. Madrid: Ediciones Atlas.
1996   *Narrative of the Incas* [1557]. Translated and edited by Roland Hamilton and Dana Buchanan from the Palma de Mallorca manuscript. Austin: University of Texas Press.

Billman, Brian R.
1999   Reconstructing prehistoric political economies and cycles of political power in the Moche Valley, Peru. In *Settlement Pattern Studies in the Americas: Fifty Years since Virú*, edited by Brian R. Billman and Gary M. Feinman, pp. 131–159. Washington, DC: Smithsonian Institution Press.

Binford, Michael, Mark Brenner, and Barbara Leyden
1996   Paleoecology and Tiwanaku ecosystems. In *Tiwanaku and Its Hinterland. Archaeology and Paleoecology of an Andean Civilization*, edited by Alan Kolata, Vol. 1, pp. 89–108. Washington, DC: Smithsonian Institution Press.

Binford, Michael, Alan L. Kolata, Mark Brenner, John W. Janusek, Matthew Seddon, Mark Abbott, and Jason Curtis
1997   Climate variation and the rise and fall of an Andean civilization. *Quaternary Research* 47: 235–248.

Blanchard, Peter (editor)
1991   *Markham in Peru: The Travels of Clements R. Markham, 1852–1853*. Austin: University of Texas Press.

Borgstade, Greg, and James R. Mathieu
2007   Defensibility and settlement patterns in the Guatemalan Maya highlands. *Latin American Antiquity* 18 (2): 191–211.

Browman, David L.
1987   Agro-pastoral risk management in the Andes. *Research in Economic Anthropology* 8: 171–200.

Brundage, Burr C.
1963   *Empire of the Inca*. Norman: University of Oklahoma Press.

Brush, Stephen B., and David W. Guillet
1985   Small-scale agro-pastoral production in the central Andes. *Mountain Research and Development* 5 (1): 19–30.

Burger, Richard
  1992 *Chavin and the Origins of Andean Civilization.* London: Thames and Hudson.
Burger, Richard, and Frank Asaro
  1979 Análisis de rasgo significativos en la obsidiana de los Andes centrales. *Revista del Museo Nacional* 43: 281–325.
Burger, Richard L., Karen L. Chávez, and Sergio J. Chávez
  2000 Through the glass darkly: Prehispanic obsidian procurement and exchange in Southern Peru and Northern Bolivia. *Journal of World Prehistory* 14 (3): 267–362.
Burger, Richard L., Fidel A. Fajardo Ríos, and Michael D. Glascock
  2006 Potreropampa and Lisahuacho obsidian sources: Geological origins of Andahuaylas A and B type obsidians in the Province of Aymaraes, Department of Apurimac, Peru. *Ñawpa Pacha* 28: 109–127.
Busto Duthurburu, José Antonio de
  1963 Maldonado, el Rico, Señor de los Andahuaylas. *Revista Histórica* (Lima) 26: 113–145.
Cabello de Balboa, Miguel
  1951 *Miscelánea antártica, una historia del Perú antiguo* [1586]. Edited by L. E. Valcárcel. Lima: Universidad Nacional Mayor de San Marcos, Instituto de Etnología de Cuzco, Perú.
Callapiña, Supno, and other Quipucamayocs
  1974 *Relación de la descendencia, gobierno y conquista de los Incas* [1542/1608]. Edited by Juan José Vega. Lima: Ediciones de la Biblioteca Universitaria.
Carabajal, Pedro de
  1974 Relación de la ciudad de Guamanga y sus términos [1586]. *Huamanga. Una larga historia: Homenaje al sesquicentenario de la Batalla de Ayacucho.* Edited by Pedro de Rivera and Antonio de Chávez y de Guevara, pp. 149–182. Lima: Consejo Nacional de la Universidad Peruana.
Cerrón-Palomino, Rodolfo
  2006 Tucuyricoc. *Boletín del Academia Peruana de la Lengua* 42: 209–226. (Lima, Peru).
Chávez, Karen Mohr
  1980 The archaeology of Marcavalle, an Early Horizon site in the Valley of Cuzco, Peru: Part I. *Baessler-Archiv*, neue Folge, 28 (2): 203–329.
  1981a The archaeology of Marcavalle, an Early Horizon site in the Valley of Cuzco, Peru: Part II. *Baessler-Archiv*, neue Folge, 29 (1): 107–205.
  1981b The archaeology of Marcavalle, an Early Horizon site in the Valley of Cuzco, Peru: Part III. *Baessler-Archiv*, neue Folge, 29 (1): 241–386.

  1982 Resumen de los trabajos en Marcavalle. In *Arqueología de Cuzco*, compiled by Italo Oberti Rodríguez, pp. 1–8. Cuzco: Instituto Nacional de Cultura.
Chepstow-Lusty, Alex, Michael R. Frogley, Brian S. Bauer, Mark B. Bush, and Alfredo Tupayachi Herrera
  2003 A Late Holocene record of El Niño/arid events from the Cuzco region, Peru. *The Journal of Quaternary Science* 18 (6): 491–502.
Cieza de León, Pedro de
  1976 *The Incas of Pedro Cieza de León* [Part 1, 1553, and Part 2, 1554]. Translated by Harriet de Onís and edited by Victor W. von Hagen. Norman: University of Oklahoma Press.
  1995 *Crónica del Perú: Primera parte* [1553]. Introduction by Franklin Pease G. Y. and notes by Miguel Maticorena. Lima: Academia Nacional de la Historia, Pontificia Universidad Católica del Perú.
  1996 *Crónica del Perú: Segunda parte* [1554]. Introduction by Franklin Pease G. Y. and notes by Miguel Maticorena. Lima: Academia Nacional de la Historia, Pontificia Universidad Católica del Perú.
  1997 *Crónica del Perú: Tercera parte* [1554]. Introduction by Francesca Cantú. Lima: Academia Nacional de la Historia, Pontificia Universidad Católica del Perú.
  1998 *The Discovery and Conquest of Peru* [1554]. Edited and translated by Alexandra Parma Cook and Noble David Cook. Durham, NC: Duke University Press.
Cipolla, Lisa M.
  2005 Preceramic Period settlement patterns in the Huancane-Putina River Valley, Northern Titicaca Basin, Peru. In *Advances in Titicaca Basin Archaeology* 1, edited by Charles Stanish, Amanda B. Cohen, and Mark S. Aldenderfer, pp. 55–64. Los Angeles: Cotsen Institute of Archaeology, University of California.
Cobo, Bernabé
  1964 *Historia del Nuevo Mundo* [1653]. In *Obras del P. Bernabé Cobo de la Compañía de Jesús*, edited by P. Francisco Mateos. Biblioteca de autores españoles (continuación), vols. 91 and 92. Madrid: Ediciones Atlas.
  1979 *History of the Inca Empire: An Account of the Indians' Customs and Their Origin Together with a Treatise on Inca Legends, History, and Social Institutions* [1653]. Translated and edited by Roland Hamilton. Austin: University of Texas Press.
  1990 *Inca Religion and Customs* [1653]. Translated and edited by Roland Hamilton. Austin: University of Texas Press.

Cook, Noble David
1981 *Demographic Collapse, Indian Peru, 1520–1620.* Cambridge: Cambridge University Press.
1998 *Born to Die: Disease and New World Conquest, 1492–1650.* Cambridge: Cambridge University Press.

Covey, R. Alan
2006 *How the Incas Built Their Heartland. State Formation and the Innovation of Imperial Strategies in the Sacred Valley, Peru.* Ann Arbor, MI.: University of Michigan Press.
2008 Multiregional perspectives on the archaeology of the Andes during the Late Intermediate Period (ca. AD 1000–1400). *Journal of Archaeological Research* 16 (3): 287–338.

Dean, Carolyn S.
1999 *Inka Bodies and the Body of Christ: Corpus Christi in Colonial Cuzco, Peru.* Durham, NC: Duke University Press.

D'Altroy, Terence
1992 *Provincial Power in the Inka Empire.* Washington, DC: Smithsonian Institution Press.
2002 *The Incas.* Oxford: Blackwell Press.

D'Altroy, Terence, and Christine A. Hastorf (editors)
2001 *Empire and Domestic Economy.* New York: Plenum.

Degregori, Carlos Iván, and Jaime Urrutia Balutansky
1980 Apuntes sobre el desarrollo del capitalismo y la destrucción del área cultural Pokra-Chanka. In *El Hombre y la cultura andina, III Congreso Peruano* (Tomo 1), edited by Ramiro Matos Mendieta, pp. 480–491. Lima: Editorial Lasontay.

DeMarrais, Elizabeth
2001 The architecture and organization of Xauxa settlements. In *Empire and Domestic Economy,* edited by Terence N. D'Altroy and Christine A. Hastorf, pp. 115–153. New York: Plenum.

Diez de San Miguel, Garci
1964 *Visita hecha a la provincia de Chucuito por Garci Diez de San Miguel en el año 1567.* Lima: Casa de la Cultura.

Dillehay, Tom D., Duccio Bonavia, and Peter Kaulicke
2004 The first settlers. In *Andean Archaeology,* edited by Helaine Silverman, pp. 16–34. Oxford: Blackwell Press.

Dillehay, Tom (editor)
1997 *Monte Verde,* Vol. 2: *The Archaeological Context and Interpretation.* Washington, DC: Smithsonian Institution Press.

Discurso de la sucesión y gobierno de los yngas (Anonymous)
1906 Discurso de la sucesión y gobierno de los yngas [ca. 1570]. In *Juicio de límites entre el Perú y Bolivia: Prueba peruana presentada al gobierno de la República Argentina,* Vol. 8, edited by Victor M. Maúrtua, pp. 149–165. Madrid: Tipografía de los Hijos de M. G. Hernández.

Duviols, Pierre
1973 Huari y Llacuaz: Agricultores y pastores. Un dualismo prehispánico de oposición y complementaridad. *Revista del Museo Nacional* (Lima) 39: 153–191.
1983 El contra idolatriam de Luis de Teruel y una versión primeriza del mito de Pachacámac-Vichama. *Revista andina* 1 (2): 385–392.

Dwyer, Edward Bridgman
1972 A Chanapata figurine from Cuzco, Peru. *Ñawpa Pacha* 9: 33–40.

Earle, Timothy K., Terence N. D'Altroy, Christine A. Hastorf, Caterina Scott, Cathy L. Costin, Glenn S. Russell, and Elsie Sandefur
1988 *Investigations of Inka Expansion and Exchange.* Monograph 28. Los Angeles: Institute of Archaeology, University of California.

Fernández, Diego ("El Palentino")
1963 *Primera y segunda parte de la historia del Perú* [1571]. In *Crónicas del Perú,* edited by Juan Pérez de Tudela Bueso. Biblioteca de autores españoles (continuación), Vols. 164 and 165. Madrid: Ediciones Atlas.

Frye, Kirk L., and Edmundo de la Vega
2005 The Altiplano Period in the Titicaca Basin. In *Advances in Titicaca Basin Archaeology* 1, edited by Charles Stanish, Amanda B. Cohen, and Mark S. Aldenderfer, pp. 173–184. Los Angeles: Cotsen Institute of Archaeology, University of California.

Gade, Daniel W., and Mario Escobar M.
1982 Village settlement and the colonial legacy in southern Peru. *Geographical Review* 72 (4): 430–449.

Garcilaso de la Vega, Inca
1960 *Comentarios reales de los Incas* [1609]. In *Obras completas del Inca Garcilaso de la Vega.* Biblioteca de autores españoles (continuación), Vols. 132–135. Madrid: Ediciones Atlas.
1966 *Royal Commentaries of the Incas and General History of Peru, Parts 1 and 2* [1609]. Translated by H. V. Livermore. Austin: University of Texas Press.

Gasparini, Graziano, and Luise Margolies
1980 *Inca Architecture.* Translated by P. J. Lyon. Bloomington: Indiana University Press.

Gibbon, Lardner
1854 *Explorations of the Valley of the Amazon Made under the Direction of the Navy Department (Part 2).* Washington, DC: Robert Armstrong.

Glowacki, Mary

1996 *The Wari Occupation of the Southern Highlands of Peru: A Ceramic Perspective from the Site of Pikillacta*. Ph.D. dissertation, Department of Anthropology, Brandeis University. Ann Arbor, MI: University Microfilms.

2002 The Huaro archaeological site complex: Rethinking the Huari occupation of Cuzco. In *Andean Archaeology 1: Variations of Sociopolitical Organization*, edited by William H. Isbell and Helaine Silverman, pp. 267–285. New York: Kluwer Academic Press.

2005 Pottery from Pikillacta. In *Pikillacta: The Wari Empire in Cuzco*, edited by Gordon F. McEwan. Iowa City: University of Iowa Press.

González Carré, Enrique

1967 Periodo Intermedio Temprano, arqueología de Ayacucho. *Wamani* (Ayacucho, Perú) 2: 196–108.

1972 Exploraciones en Ñawinpukio, Ayacucho. *Arqueología y Sociedad* 7–8: 30–46. Lima: Museo de la Universidad Nacional Mayor de San Marcos.

1979 El estudio de los Chankas. *Investigaciones* 2 (2): 55–76. Ayacucho, Perú: Universidad Nacional San Cristóbal de Huamanga.

1982 *Historia prehispánica de Ayacucho*. Ayacucho, Perú: Universidad Nacional San Cristóbal de Huamanga.

1992a *Los Señoríos Chankas*. Ayacucho, Perú: Universidad Nacional de San Cristóbal de Huamanga, Instituto Andino de Estudios Arqueológicos.

1992b *Historia prehispánica de Ayacucho*. Ayacucho, Perú: Universidad Nacional de San Cristóbal de Huamanga.

González Carré, Enrique, and Augusto Cruzatt Añaños

1966 Arqueología en el Departamento de Ayacucho. *Wamani* (Ayacucho, Perú) 1 (1): 76–86.

González Carré, Enrique, and Fermín Rivera Pideda

1988 Reflexiones acerca de los mitos de origen de los señoríos Chankas. In *Antiguos dioses y nuevos conflictos andinos*, edited by E. González Carré and Enrique y Rivera Pideda, pp. 89–105. Ayacucho, Perú: Universidad Nacional de San Cristóbal de Huamanga.

González Carré, Enrique, and Denise Pozzi-Escot

2002 Arqueología y etnohistoria en Vilcashuamán. In *Boletín de Arqueología PUCP 6, Identidad y transformación en el Tawantinsuyu y en los Andes coloniales. Perspectivas arqueológicas y etnohistóricas (Primera parte)*, edited by Peter Kaulicke, Gary Urton, and Ian Farrington, pp. 79–105. Lima: Pontificia Universidad Católica del Perú.

González Carré, Enrique, Denisse Pozzi-Escot, Muriel Pozzi-Escot, and Cirilio Vivanco Pomancanchari

1987 *Los Chankas: Cultura material*. Ayacucho, Perú: Laboratorio de Arqueología de la Universidad Nacional San Cristóbal de Huamanga.

González Carré, Enrique, Denise Pozzi-Escot, and Cirilio Vivanco Pomancanchari

1988 *El Área Histórica Chanka*. Ayacucho, Perú: Laboratorio de Arqueología de la Universidad Nacional San Cristóbal de Huamanga.

González Carré, Enrique, and José Gálvez Pérez

1987 Molinuyoq: Terrazas y reservorios en un pueblo prehispánico de Ayacucho. *Boletín de Lima* 53: 19–24.

González Holguín, Diego

1989 *Vocabulario de la lengua general de todo el Perú llamada lengua Qquichua o del Inca* [1608]. Edited by Ramiro Matos Mendieta. Lima: Universidad Nacional Mayor de San Marcos, Editorial de la Universidad.

Graffam, Gray

1992 Beyond state collapse: Rural history, raised fields, and pastoralism in the south Andes. *American Anthropologist* 94 (4): 882–904.

Grossman, Joel

1972a Early ceramic cultures of Andahuaylas, Apurimac, Peru. Unpublished Ph.D. dissertation, Department of Anthropology, University of California, Berkeley.

1972b An ancient gold worker's tool kit: The earliest metal technology in Peru. *Archaeology* 25: 270–275.

1983 Demographic changes and economic transformations in the south-central highlands of pre-Huari Peru. *Ñawpa Pacha* 21: 45–126.

Guaman Poma de Ayala, Felipe

1980 *El primer nueva corónica y buen gobierno* [1615]. Edited by John V. Murra and Rolena Adorno. Translated by Jorge I. Urioste. 3 vols. Mexico City: Siglo Veintiuno.

Guillén, Lizardo

1946 Algunos aspectos de la historia y arqueología de la cultura Chanka. Tesis de Bachiller. Lima: Universidad Nacional Mayor de San Marcos.

Gutiérrez Velasco, Arturo

1999 *Cronohistoria y patrimonio Chanka*. Lima: Propaceb.

Haas, Jonathan, and Winifred Creamer

2006 Crucible of Andean civilization: The Peruvian coast from 300 to 1800 BC. *Current Anthropology* 47 (5): 745–775.

Hastorf, Christine A.

1993 *Agriculture and the Onset of Political Inequality before the Inka*. Cambridge: Cambridge University Press.

Hastorf, Christine A., and Terence N. D'Altroy
   2001 The domestic economy, households, and imperial transformation. In *Empire and Domestic Economy*, by Christine A. Hastorf and Terence N. D'Altroy, pp. 3–21. New York: Plenum.

Hemming, John
   1970 *The Conquest of the Incas*. New York: Harcourt Brace Jovanovich Press.

Hostnig, Raimer
   1988 Caza de camélidos en el arte rupestre del Departamento de Apurimac. In *Llaichos y paqocheros. Pastores de llamas y alpacas*, edited by Jorge Flores Ochoa, pp. 67–76. Cuzco: Centro de Estudios Andinos, CEAC.
   1990 Una nueva localidad de arte rupestre en Apurimac-Perú: Lamayocc. Anexo: Inventario de sitios de arte rupestre en Apurimac-Perú. *Boletín de la Sociedad de Investigación del Arte Rupestre de Bolivia* 1990: 46–51.
   2003 *Arte rupestre del Perú: Inventario nacional*. Lima: CONCYTEC.

Huaypar, Yezena, Luise Vetter, and Jorge Bravo
   2007 The metallurgic furnaces at the Curamba Inca site (Peru): A study by Mossbauer spectroscopy and X-ray diffractometry. In *LACAME 2006: Proceedings of the 10th Latin American Conference on the Applications of the Mössbauer Effect (LACAME 2006) Held in Rio de Janeiro City, Brazil, 5–9 November 2006*, edited by C. Larica, R. C. Mercader, C. Partiti, and J. R. Gancedo, pp. 15–21. Springer.

Hyland, Sabine
   2002a Los Chachapoyanos en San Jerónimo. *Milenio* (Lima, Peru) 14: 8.
   2002b La lucha por Uranmarca. *Milenio* (Lima, Perú) 16: 7.
   2007 *The Quito Manuscript: An Inca History Preserved by Fernando de Montesinos*. New Haven, CT: Yale University Publications in Anthropology.

Hyland, Sabine, and Donato Amado González
   n.d. The Chankas: Power, kinship and religion during two centuries of Spanish rule. Manuscript.

Hyslop, John
   1976 *An Archaeological Investigation of the Lupaca Kingdom and Its Origins*. Ph.D. dissertation, Department of Anthropology, Columbia University. Ann Arbor: University Microfilms.
   1984 *The Inca Road System*. New York: Academic Press.

Isbell, William H.
   1997 *Mummies and Mortuary Monuments*. Austin: University of Texas Press.

Isbell, William H., and Gordon F. McEwan (editors)
   1991 *Huari Administrative Structure: Prehistoric Monumental Architecture and State Government*. Washington, DC: Dumbarton Oaks Research Library and Collection.

Isbell, William H., and Katharina J. Schreiber
   1978 Was Huari a state? *American Antiquity* 43: 372–389.

Jennings, Justin
   2006 Understanding Middle Horizon Peru: Hermeneutic spirals, interpretative traditions, and Wari administrative centers. *Latin American Antiquity* 17 (3): 265–286.

Jennings, Justin, and Nathan Craig
   2001 Polity wide analysis and imperial political economy: The relationship between Valley political complexity and administrative centers in the Wari Empire of the Central Andes. *Journal of Anthropological Archaeology* 20 (4): 479–502.

Jennings, Justin, and Willy Yépez Álvarez
   2003 Architecture, local elites, and imperial entanglements: The impact of the Wari Empire on the Cotahuasi Valley of Peru. *Journal of Field Archaeology* 28 (1/2): 143–159.

Julien, Catherine
   2002 Diego Maldonado y los Chancas. *Revista Andina* 34: 183–197.

Kellett, Lucas C.
   2006 Public archaeology in an Andean community. *SAA Archaeological Record* 6 (2): 8–11.
   2008 High altitude settlement-subsistence dynamics of the Chanka heartland (Andahuaylas, Peru). 73rd Annual Meeting of the Society for American Archaeology, Vancouver, Canada.
   2010 Chanka settlement ecology: Hilltop sites, land use and warfare in Late Prehispanic Andahuaylas, Peru. Ph.D. dissertation, University of New Mexico, Albuquerque.

Klink, Cynthia J.
   2005 Archaic Period research in the Rio Huenque Valley, Peru. In *Advances in Titicaca Basin Archaeology* 1, edited by Charles Stanish, Amanda B. Cohen, and Mark S. Aldenderfer, pp. 13–24. Los Angeles: Cotsen Institute of Archaeology, University of California.

Klink, Cynthia J., and Mark Aldenderfer
   2005 A projectile point chronology for the south-central Andean highlands. In *Advances in Titicaca Basin Archaeology* 1, edited by Charles Stanish, Amanda B. Cohen, and Mark S. Aldenderfer, pp. 25–54. Los Angeles: Cotsen Institute of Archaeology, University of California.

Knobloch, Patricia J.
   1991 Stylistic date of ceramics from the Huari centers. In *Huari Administrative Structure:*

Prehistoric Monumental Architecture and State Government, edited by William H. Isbell and Gordon F. McEwan, pp. 247–258. Washington, DC: Dumbarton Oaks Research Library and Collection.

n.d. An Early Intermediate Period deposit of Huarpa style ceramics from the site of Huari, Department of Ayacucho, Peru. (http://wwwrohan.sdsu.edu/~bharley/HuarpaNPms4Web. html).

Kowalewski, Stephen
2008 Regional settlement pattern studies. *Journal of Archaeological Research* 16: 225–285.

Lagos Aedo, Gladis
1999 *Historia y arqueología de Abancay*. Cuzco: G. Lagos Sedo.

La Lone, Mary Burkheimer
1985 *Indian Land Tenure in Southern Cuzco, Peru: From Inca to Colonial Patterns, Peru*. Ph.D. dissertation, University of California, Los Angles. Ann Arbor, MI: University Microfilms.

Lavallée, Danièle Michèle
1983 *Asto. curacazgo prehispánico de los Andes centrales*. Lima: Instituto de Estudios Peruanos.

LeBlanc, Catherine J.
1981 *Late Prehispanic Huanca Settlement Patterns in the Yanamarca Valley, Peru*. Ph.D. dissertation, University of California, Los Angles. Ann Arbor: University Microfilms.

LeBlanc, Steven A.
1999 *Prehistoric Warfare in the American Southwest*. Salt Lake City: University of Utah Press.

Lechtman, Heather
1976 A metallurgical site survey in the Peruvian Andes. *Journal of Field Archaeology* 3: 1–42.

Leoni, Juan B.
2006 Ritual and society in Early Intermediate Period Ayacucho: A view from the site of Nawinpukyo. In *Andean Archaeology III (North and South)*, edited by William H. Isbell and Helaine Silverman, pp. 279–306. New York: Kluwer Academic Press.

Levillier, Roberto
1940 *Don Francisco de Toledo, supremo organizador del Perú*. Vol. 2, *Sus informaciones sobre los Incas (1570–1572)*. Buenos Aires: Espasa-Calpe.

Lockhart, James
1968 *Spanish Peru 1532–1560*. Madison, WI: University of Wisconsin Press.
1972 *The Men of Cajamarca: A Social and Biographical Study of the First Conquerors of Peru*. Austin: University of Texas Press.

Lumbreras, Luis G.
1959 Sobre los Chankas. In *Actas y trabajos del II Congreso Nacional de Historia del Perú* 1, pp. 211–242. Lima: Centro de Estudios Histórico Militares del Perú.
1974a *The Peoples and Cultures of Ancient Peru*. Translated by Betty J. Meggers. Washington, DC: Smithsonian Institution Press.
1974b *Las fundaciones de Huamanga. Hacia una prehistoria de Ayacucho* Lima: Editorial "Nueva Educación."
1978 Acerca de la Aparición del Estado Inka. In *El Hombre y la cultura andina, III Congreso Peruano* (Tomo 1), edited by Ramiro Matos Mendieta, pp. 101–109. Lima: Editorial Lasontay.
1999 Andean urbanism and statecraft (C.E. 550–1450). In *The Cambridge History of the Native Peoples of the Americas*, Vol. III, *South America*, Part 1, edited by Frank Salomon and Stuart B. Schwartz, pp. 518–576. Cambridge: Cambridge University Press.

Lynch, Thomas F.
1980 *Guitarrero Cave: Early Man in the Andes*. New York: Academic Press.
1999 The earliest South American lifeways. In *The Cambridge History of the Native Peoples of the Americas*, Vol. III, *South America*, Part 1, edited by Frank Salomon and Stuart B. Schwartz, pp. 188–263. Cambridge: Cambridge University.

Malpass, Michael A. (editor)
1993 *Provincial Inca: Archaeological and Ethnohistorical Assessment of the Impact of the Inca State*. Iowa City: University of Iowa Press.

Marcus, Joyce
2008 The archaeological evidence for social evolution. *Annual Review of Anthropology* 37: 251–266.

Marcoy, Paul
1875 *Travels in South America: From the Pacific Ocean to the Atlantic Ocean*. London: Blackie and Son.

Markham, Clements R.
1871 On the geographical position of the tribes which formed the Empire of the Incas. *Journal of the Royal Geographical Society* (London) 41: 281–338.
1923 Las posesiones geográficas de las tribus que formaban el imperio de los Incas. *Colección de libros y documentos referentes a la historia del Perú*, Series II, Vol. VII. Lima: Imprenta y librería Sanmarti y Co.

MacNeish, Richard S., Robert K. Vierra, Antoinette Nelken-Terner, R. Lurine, and Angel Garcia Cook
1980 *The Prehistory of the Ayacucho Basin, Peru*. Ann Arbor: University of Michigan Press.

McCormac, F. G., A. G. Hogg, P. G. Blackwell, C. E. Buck, T. F. G. Higham, and P. J. Reimer
2004 SHCal04 Southern Hemisphere Calibration 0–1000 cal BP. *Radiocarbon* 46: 1087–1092.

Meddens, Frank M.
1985 The Chicha/Soras Valley during the Middle Horizon: Provincial aspects of Huari. Ph.D. dissertation, University of London.
1991 A provincial perspective of Huari Organization viewed from the Chica/Soras Valley. In *Huari Administrative Structure: Prehistoric Monumental Architecture and State Government*, edited by William H. Isbell and Gordon F. McEwan, pp. 215–231. Washington, DC: Dumbarton Oaks Research Library and Collection.
2001 La Secuencia cultural en la cuenca de Chicha-Soras. In *XII Congreso Peruano, "Luis Lumberas,"* edited by Ismael Pérez C., Walter Aguilar S. and Medardo Purizaga V., Vol. 2, pp. 200–210. Ayacucho, Perú: Universidad Nacional de San Cristóbal de Huamanga.
2006 Rocks in the landscape: Managing the Inka agricultural cycle. *The Antiquaries Journal* 86: 36–65.

Meddens, Frank M., and C. Vivanco Pomacanchari
2005 The Chanca Confederation: Political myth and archaeological reality. In *Xama* 15–18 (51st International Congress of Americanists–Symposium Tawantinsuyu 2003: Avances Recientes en Arqueología y Etnohistoria), pp. 73–99. Mendoza, Argentina.

Menzel, Dorothy
1964 Style and time in the Middle Horizon. *Ñawpa Pacha* 2: 1–106.

Middendorf, Ernest
1895 *Peru. Beobachtungen und Studien über das Land und seine Bewohner*. 3 vols. Berlin.
1974 *Perú; Observaciones y estudios del país y sus habitantes durante una permanencia de 25 años* [1895]. Translation by Ernesto More. 3 vols. Lima: Dirección Universitaria de Biblioteca, Universidad Nacional Mayor de San Marcos.

Millones, Luis (editor)
1990 *El retorno de las huacas: Estudios y documentos sobre el Taki Onqoy siglo XVI*. Lima: Instituto de Estudios Peruanos.

Molina, Cristóbal de
1989 Relación de las fábulas i ritos de los Ingas [ca. 1575]. In *Fábulas y mitos de los Incas*, edited by Henrique Urbano and Pierre Duviols, pp. 47–134. Crónicas de América 48. Madrid: Historia 16.

Montesinos, Fernando de
1920 *Memorias antiguas historiales del Perú* [ca. 1644]. Translated and edited by Philip Ainsworth Means. Introduction by Clements R. Markham. The Hakluyt Society Publications, 2nd ser., Vol. 48. London: The Hakluyt Society.

Monzón, Luis de
1965 Descripción de la tierra del repartimiento de Atunsora, encomendado en Hernando Palomino, jurisdicción de la ciudad de Guamanga, año de 1586. In *Relación geográficas de Indias (Peru)*, edited by Marcos Jimenez de la Espada, pp. 220–225. Biblioteca de autores españoles 183. Madrid: Atlas.

Moore, Jerry M.
1995 The archaeology of dual organization in Andean South America: A theoretical review and case study. *Latin American Antiquity* 6 (2): 165–181.

Murúa, Martín de
1946 *Historia del origen y genealogía real de los reyes Incas del Perú* [1590]. Introduction and notes by Constantino Bayle. Biblioteca "Missionalia Hispánica," Vol. 2. Madrid: Instituto Santo Toribio de Mogrovejo.

Morales Chocano, Daniel
1998 Importancia de la Salinas de San Blas durante el Periodo Formativo en la sierra central del Perú. In *Boletín de Arqueología PUCP 2, Perspectivas regionales del Periodo Formativo en el Perú*, pp. 273–288. Lima: Pontificia Universidad Católica del Perú.

Navarro del Águila, Víctor
1937 Las tribus de Ankcu Hualloke: Primitivos pobladores de Andahuaylas, Ayacuho i Huancavelica. *Revista del Instituto Arqueológico* (Cuzco, Perú) 3: 42–46.
1939 *Las Tribus de Ancku Walloke*. Cuzco: Imprenta H. C. Rozas.

Niles, Susan A.
1999 *The Shape of Inca History: Narrative and Architecture in an Andean Empire*. Iowa City: University of Iowa Press.

Oberti Rodríguez, Italo
1997 Investigaciones preliminares en Usno-Moq'o Abancay. *Tawantinsuyu* 3: 15–19.

Ochatoma Paravicino, José
1992 Acera del Formativo en Ayacucho. In *Estudios de arqueología peruana*, edited by D. Bonavia, pp. 193–214. Lima: FOMENCIAS.
1998 El Periodo Formativo en Ayacucho: Balance y perspectivas. In *Boletín de Arqueología PUCP 2, Perspectivas regionales del Periodo Formativo en el Perú*, pp. 289–302. Lima: Pontificia Universidad Católica del Perú.

Olaechea, Teodorico
1901 Apuntes sobre el castillo y fundición de Curamba. *Anales de la Escuela de Ingenieros de C. C. de Minas e Industrias del Perú* 1: 1–21. Lima: Escuela de Ingenieros.

Owen, Bruce
  2007 Rural Wari far from the heartland: Hua-
         manga ceramics from Beringa, Majes Valley,
         Peru. *Andean Past* 8: 287–373.
Pardo, Luis A.
  1969 *La guerra de los Quechuas con los Chancas.*
         Lima: Socio Correspondiente del Centro de
         Estudios Histórico-Militares del Perú.
Parsons, Jeffrey R., and Charles M. Hastings
  1988 The Late Intermediate Period. In *Peruvian
         Prehistory*, edited by Richard W. Keatinge,
         pp. 190–229. Cambridge: Cambridge Uni-
         versity Press.
Parsons, Jeffrey R., Charles M. Hastings, and Ramiro
Matos Mendieta
  1997 Rebuilding the state in highland Peru:
         Herder-cultivator interaction during the
         Late Intermediate Period in the Tarama-
         Chinchayacocha region. *Latin American
         Antiquity* 8 (4): 317–341.
  2000a *Prehispanic Settlement Patterns in the Upper
         Mantaro and Tarma Drainages, Junín Peru*,
         Vol. 1, Part 1, *The Tarama-Chinchaycocha
         Region.* Ann Arbor: Museum of Anthropol-
         ogy, University of Michigan.
  2000b *Prehispanic Settlement Patterns in the Upper
         Mantaro and Tarma Drainages, Junín Peru*,
         Vol. 1, Part 2, *The Tarama-Chinchaycocha
         Region.* Ann Arbor: Museum of Anthropol-
         ogy, University of Michigan.
Pärssinen, Martti
  1992 *Tawantinsuyu, the Inca State and Its Political
         Organization.* Helsinki: SHS.
Pérez, Ismael, Cirilo Vivanco, and José Amorín
  2003 Sondor, establecimiento inca en Pacucha,
         Andahuaylas. *Boletín de arqueología PUCP* 7,
         *Identidad y transformación en el Tawantinsuyu y
         en los Andes coloniales. Perspectivas arqueológicas
         y etnohistóricas (Segunda parte)*, edited by
         Peter Kaulicke, Gary Urton, and Ian
         Farrington, pp. 365–385. Lima: Pontificia
         Universidad Católica del Perú.
Pesce, Hugo
  1942 Relación somera de algunas ruinas pre-
         colombinas en la provincia Chanca de
         Andahuaylas. *Waman Poma* (Cuzco) 2: 9–10.
Pizarro, Pedro
  1921 *Relation of the Discovery and Conquest of the
         Kingdoms of Peru* [1571]. Translated and edit-
         ed by Philip Ainsworth Means. New York:
         The Cortés Society.
  1986 *Relación del descubrimiento y conquista de los
         reinos del Perú* [1571]. Lima: Pontificia Uni-
         versidad Católica del Perú.

Polo de Ondegardo, Juan
  1990 Notables daños de no guardar a los indios
         sus fueros [1571]. In *El mundo de los Incas*,
         edited by Laura González and Alicia Alonso,
         pp. 33–113. Crónicas de América 58.
         Madrid: Historia 16 .
Puente Brunke, José de la
  1992 *Encomienda y encomenderos en el Perú: Estudio
         social y político de una institución colonial.* Sevi-
         lla: Excma. Diputación Provincial de Sevi-
         lla.
Quintana, Gerardo
  1967 *Andahuaylas: Prehistoria y historia.* Lima:
         Viloch.
Quintanilla, Lino
  1981 *Andahuaylas: La lucha por la tierra. Testimonio
         de un militante.* Lima: Mosca Azul Ediciones.
Quito Manuscript (anonymous)
  2007 The Quito Manuscript [ca. 1644]. Appendix in
         *The Quito Manuscript: An Inca History Preserved
         by Fernando de Montesinos*, pp. 105–155. Edited
         by Sabine Hyland. Yale University Publica-
         tions in Anthropology. New Haven, CT.
         (Formerly attributed to Fernando de Mon-
         tesinos).
Raimondi, Antonio
  1876 *El Perú: Historia de la geografía del Perú*
         (Tomo I). Lima: Imprenta del Estado.
Ramos Gavilán, Alonso
  1988 *Historia del Nuestra Señora de Copacabana*
         [1621]. Academia Boliviana de la Historia.
         Las Paz: Cámara Nacional de Comercio,
         Cámara Nacional de Industrias.
Rick, John W.
  1980 *Prehistoric Hunters of the High Andes.* New
         York: Academic Press.
  1988 The character and context of highland pre-
         ceramic society. In *Peruvian Prehistory*, edited
         by Richard W. Keatinge, pp. 3–40. Cam-
         bridge: Cambridge University Press.
Romero, Carlos
  1940 *Los orígenes del periodismo en el Perú: De la
         relación al diario, 1594–1790.* Lima: Libreria
         e Imprenta Gil.
Rostworowski de Diez Canseco, María
  1953 *Pachacutec Inca Yupanqui.* Lima: Editorial
         Mejía Baca.
  1978 Una hipótesis sobre el surgimiento del esta-
         do Inca. In *El Hombre y la Cultura Andina, III
         Congreso Peruano* (Tomo 1), edited by Ramiro
         Matos Mendieta, pp. 89–100. Lima: Editora
         Lasontay.
  1988 *Historia del Tahuantinsuyu.* Lima: Instituto de
         Estudios Peruanos.

Rowe, John H.
1944   An introduction to the archaeology of
       Cuzco. In *Papers of the Peabody Museum of
       American Archaeology and Ethnology*, Vol. 27,
       No. 2. Cambridge, MA: Harvard University.
1946   Inca culture at the time of the Spanish Con-
       quest. In *Handbook of South American Indians*,
       Vol. 2, *The Andean Civilizations*, edited by
       Julian Steward, pp. 183–330. Bureau of
       American Ethnology Bulletin, No. 143.
       Washington, DC: U.S. Government Printing
       Office.
1956   Archaeological explorations in southern
       Peru, 1954–1955. *American Antiquity* 22 (2):
       135–150.
Sahlins, Marshall
1983   Other times, other customs: The anthropol-
       ogy of history. *American Anthropologist* 85:
       517–544.
1985   *Islands of History*. Chicago: University of
       Chicago Press.
Salazar, Antonio
1867   De vireyes y gobernadores del Perú [1596].
       In *Colección de documentos inéditos, relativos al
       descubrimiento, conquista y organización de las
       antiguas posesiones españolas*, 8: 212–293.
       Transcribed by Luis Torres de Mendoza.
       Madrid: Imprenta de Frías y Compañía.
       (Formerly attributed to Tristán Sánchez.)
Sancho de la Hoz, Pedro
1898   *Relación de la conquista del Perú* [1534]. Edited
       by Joaquín Garcia Icazbaslceta. Biblioteca de
       autores mexicanos 8, pp. 309–423. Mexico
       City: Imprenta de V. Agueros.
1917   *An Account of the Conquest of Peru* [1534].
       Translated by Philip A. Means. Documents
       and Narratives Concerning the Discovery
       and Conquest of Latin American, No. 2.
       New York: The Cortés Society.
Santa Cruz Pachacuti Yamqui Salcamayhua, Juan de
1950   Relación de antigüedades deste reyno del
       Perú [ca. 1613]. In *Tres relaciones de antigüe-
       dades peruanas*, edited by Marcos Jiménez de
       la Espada, pp. 207–281. Asunción, Paraguay:
       Editorial Guaranía.
Santillán, Hernando de
1950   Relación del origen, descendencia política y
       gobierno de los Incas. . . . [1564]. In *Tres
       relaciones de antigüedades peruanas*, edited by
       M. Jiménez de la Espada, pp. 33–131. Asun-
       ción Paraguay: Editorial Guaranía.
Sarmiento de Gamboa, Pedro
1906   *Segunda parte de la historia general llamada
       Indica . . .* [1572]. In *Geschichte des Inkareiches
       von Pedro Sarmiento de Gamboa*, edited by
       Richard Pietschmann. Abhandlungen der
       Königlichen Gesellschaft der Wissenschaften
       zu Göttingen, Philologisch-Historische
       Klasse, neue Folge, Vol. 6, No. 4. Berlin:
       Weidmannsche Buchhandlung.
2007   *The History of the Incas* [1572]. Translated and
       edited by Brian S. Bauer and Vania Smith.
       Introduction by Brian S. Bauer and Jean
       Jacque Decoster. Austin: University of Texas
       Press.
Schaedel, Richard P.
1978   Early state of the Incas. In *The Early State*,
       edited by H. J. M. Claessen and P. Skalnik,
       pp. 289–320. The Hague: Mouton.
Schjellerup, Inge
1997   *Incas and Spaniards in the Conquest of the
       Chachapoyas: Archaeological and Ethnohistorical
       Research in the North-eastern Andes of Peru*.
       Göteborg, Denmark: Göteborg Universi-
       ty/National Museum of Denmark.
Schreiber, Katharina J.
1987   Conquest and consolidation: A comparison
       of the Wari and Inka occupation of a high-
       land Peruvian valley. *American Antiquity* 52
       (2): 266–284.
1991   Jincamocco: A Huari administrative center in
       the south central highlands of Peru. In *Huari
       Administrative Structure: Prehistoric Monumental
       Architecture and State Government*, edited by
       William H. Isbell and Gordon F. McEwan, pp.
       199–214. Washington, DC: Dumbarton Oaks
       Research Library and Collection.
1992   *Wari Imperialism in Middle Horizon Peru*.
       Anthropological Papers, Museum of Anthro-
       pology, University of Michigan No. 87. Ann
       Arbor: Museum of Anthropology, University
       of Michigan.
1993   The Inca occupation of the Province of
       Andamarca Lucanas, Peru. In *Provincial Inca:
       Archaeological and Ethnohistorical Assessment of
       the Impact of the Inca State*, edited by Michael
       A. Malpass, pp. 77–116. Iowa City: Universi-
       ty of Iowa Press.
1999   Regional approaches to the study of prehis-
       toric empires: Examples from Ayacucho and
       Nasca, Peru. In *Settlement Pattern Studies in
       the Americas: Fifty Years since Virú*, edited by
       Brian R. Billman and Gary M. Feinman, pp.
       160–171. Washington, DC: Smithsonian
       Institution Press.
2004   Sacred landscape and imperial ideologies: The
       Wari Empire in Sondor, Peru. In *Foundations
       of Power in the Prehistoric Andes*, edited by
       Kevin J. Vaughn, Dennis Ogburn, and Christi-
       na A. Conlee, pp. 131–150. Archaeological
       Papers of the American Anthropological Asso-
       ciation, No. 14. Montpelier, VT: Capital Press.

Seltzer, Geoffrey O., and Christine A. Hastorf
  1990 Climatic change and its effect on prehispanic agriculture in the central Peruvian Andes. *Journal of Field Archaeology* 17 (4): 397–414.
Skar, Harald O.
  1981 *The Warm Valley People: Duality and Land Reform among the Quechua Indians of Highland Peru*. Oslo: Universitetsforlaget.
Shea, Daniel E.
  1969 Wari Willka: A Central Andean oracle site. Unpublished Ph.D. dissertation, Department of Anthropology, University of Wisconsin.
Socualaya Dávila, Carlo
  2005 Uranmarca: Prehistoria. Tesis de Licenciado en arqueología, Universidad Nacional San Antonio Abad del Cuzco.
Squier, Ephraim George
  1877 *Peru: Incidents of Travel and Exploration in the Land of Incas*. New York: Harper and Brothers Publishers.
Stanish, Charles
  1997 Nonmarket imperialism in a prehispanic context: The Inca occupation of the Titicaca Basin. *Latin American Antiquity* 8 (3): 195–216.
  2003 *Ancient Titicaca*. Los Angles: University of California Press.
Stanish, Charles, and Brian S. Bauer (editors)
  2004 *Archaeological Research on the Islands of the Sun and the Moon, Lake Titicaca, Bolivia: Final Results from the Proyecto Tiksi Kjarka*. Monograph 52. Los Angeles: Cotsen Institute of Archaeology, University of California.
Stanish, Charles, Edmundo de la Vega M., Lee Steadman, Cecilia Chávez Justo, Kirk Lawrence Frye, Luperio Onofre Mamani, Matthew T. Seddon, and Percy Calisaya Chuquimia
  1997 *Archaeological Survey in the Juli-Desaguadero Region of Lake Titicaca Basin, Southern Peru*. Fieldiana Anthropology, New Series 29. Chicago: Field Museum of Natural History.
Stern, Steve J.
  1982 *Peru's Indian Peoples and the Challenge of Spanish Conquest*. Madison, WI: University of Wisconsin Press.
Stuiver, Minze, and Paula J. Reimer
  1993 Extended ^{14}C database and revised CALIB radiocarbon calibration program. *Radiocarbon* 35: 215–230.
Tello Valdivia, Rómulo
  2001 *Breve historia de Andahuaylas*. Andahuaylas, Perú: Municipalidad Provincial de Andahuaylas.
Thompson, L. G., E. Mosley-Thompson, J. F. Bolzan, and B. R. Koci
  1985 A 1500-year record of tropical precipitation in ice cores from the Quelccaya ice cap, Peru. *Science* 229: 971–973.

Thompson, L. G., E. Mosley-Thompson, W. Dansgaard, and P. Grootes
  1986 The Little Ice Age as recorded in the stratigraphy of the tropical Quelccaya ice cap. *Science* 234: 361–364.
Thompson, L. G., E. Mosley-Thompson, M. E. Davis, P.-N. Lin, K. A. Henderson, J. Cole-Dai, J. F. Bolzan, and K.-B Liu
  1995 Late glacial stage and Holocene tropical ice core records from Huascaran, Peru. *Science* 269: 46–50.
Toledo, Francisco de
  1940 Informaciones que mandó levantar el Virrey Toledo sobre los Incas . . . [1570–1572]. In *Don Francisco de Toledo, supremo organizador del Perú: Su vida, su obra (1515–1582)*. Edited by Roberto Levillier. Buenos Aires: Espasa-Calpe, S.A.
  1975 *Tasa de la visita de Francisco de Toledo* [1570–1575]. Introduction and paleographic version by Noble David Cook, and studies by Alejando Málaga Medina and Thérèse Bouysse Cassagne. Lima: Dirección Universitaria de Biblioteca y Publicaciones, Universidad Nacional Mayor de San Marcos, Seminario de Historia Rural Andina.
Truyenque Caceres, Carlos Fernando
  1995 *Sondor: Posibilidad turística*. Andahuaylas, Perú: Municipalidad Distrital de Pacucha, Centro de Apoyo a la Juventud de Andahuaylas.
Turner, Terence S.
  1984 Dual opposition, hierarchy and value: Moiety structure and symbolic polarity in central Brazil and elsewhere. In *Differences, valeurs, hierarchie: Textes Offerts a Louis Dumont et reunis par Jean-Claude Galey*, edited by Jean-Claude Galey, pp. 335–370. Paris: Éditions de l'École des Hautes Études en Sciences Sociales.
Vaca de Castro, Cristóbal
  1908 *Ordenanzas de Tambos* [1543]. Edited by Antonio Rodríguez Nilla. *Revista Histórica* (Lima) 3 (4): 427–492.
Valdez, Lidio M.
  2002 Y la tradición continua: La alfarería de la época Inka en el valle de Ayacucho, Perú. *Boletín de Arqueología, PUCP 6, Identidad y transformación en el Tawantinsuyu y en los Andes coloniales. Perspectivas arqueológicas y etnohistóricas (Primera parte)*, edited by Peter Kaulicke, Gary Urton, and Ian Farrington, pp. 395–419. Lima: Pontificia Universidad Católica del Perú.
Valdez, Lidio M., and Cirilo Vivanco
  1994 Arqueología de la cuenca del Qaracha, Ayacucho, Peru. *Latin American Antiquity* 5 (2): 144–157.

Valdez, Lidio M., Cirilo Vivanco, and Casimiro Chávez
    1990 Asentamientos Chanka en la cuenca del Pampas Qaracha (Ayacucho). *Gaceta Arqueológica Andina* 17: 17–26.
Van de Guchte, Maarten J.
    1990 *Carving the World: Inca Monumental Sculpture and Landscape*. Ph.D. dissertation, University of Illinois. Ann Arbor, MI: University Microfilms.
Vázquez de Espinosa, Antonio
    1948 *Compendio y descripción de las Indias Occidentales* [1628]. Transcribed from the original by Charles Upson Clark. Smithsonian Miscellaneous Collections, Vol. 108. Washington, DC: Smithsonian Institution.
Vivanco Pomacanchari, Cirilo
    1999 Raqaraqaypata y Ñawpallaqta: Dos poblados de la época Chanka en el área sur de Ayacucho. *El XII Congreso Peruano del hombre y la cultura andina* 2, edited by Ismael Pérez C., Walter Aguilar S. and Medardo Purizaga V., pp. 271–286. Ayacucho: Universidad Nacional de San Cristóbal de Huamanga.
Von Hagen, Victor W. von
    1959 *Highway of the Sun*. New York: Duell, Sloan and Pearce.
Wernke, Stephen
    2006 The politics of community and Inka statecraft in the Colca Valley, Peru. *Latin American Antiquity* 17 (7): 177–208.
    2007 Negotiating community and landscape in the Peruvian Andes: A trans-conquest view. *American Anthropologist* 109 (1): 130–152.
Wiener, Charles
    1993 *Perú y Bolivia. Relato de viaje seguido de estudios arqueológicos y de notas sobre la escritura y los idiomas de las poblaciones indígenas* (1880). Translated by Edgardo Rivera Martí-nez. Lima: Instituto Francés de Estudios Andinos, Universidad Nacional de San Marcos.
Williams, Patrick Ryan
    2001 Cerro Baúl: A Wari center on the Tiwanaku frontier. *Latin American Antiquity* 12 (1): 67–83.
    2002 Rethinking disaster-induced collapse in the demise of the Andean Highland states: Wari and Tiwanaku. *World Archaeology* 33 (3): 361–374.
    2006 Agricultural innovation, intensification, and sociopolitical development: The case of highland irrigation agriculture on the Pacific Andean watersheds. In *Agricultural Strategies*, edited by Joyce Marcus and Charles Stanish, pp. 309–333. Los Angeles: Cotsen Institute of Archaeology, University of California.
Yamamoto, Norio
    1985 The ecological complementarity of agropastoralism: Some comments. In *Andean Ecology and Civilization*, edited by Shozo Masuda, Isumi Shimada, and Craig Morris, pp. 85–100. Tokyo: University of Tokyo Press.
Zapata Rodríguez, Julinho
    1998 Los cerros sagrados: Panorama del Periodo Formativo en la cuenca del Vilcanota, Cuzco. *Boletín de arqueología PUCP 2, Perspectivas regionales del Periodo Formativo en el Perú*, pp. 307–336. Lima: Pontificia Universidad Católica del Perú.
Zárate, Agustín de
    1981 *A Translation of Books I to IV of Agustín Zarate's History.* . . . Translated by J. M. Cohen. London: The Folio Society.
    1995 *Historia del descubrimiento y conquista del Perú* [1555]. Lima: Pontificia Universidad Católica del Perú.

INDEX

195